MRS. LONGFELLOW:

Selected Letters and Journals of
Fanny Appleton Longfellow

By EDWARD WAGENKNECHT

BIOGRAPHICAL: *The Man Charles Dickens* (1929); *Geraldine Farrar, An Authorized Record of Her Career* (1929); *Jenny Lind* (1931); *Mark Twain, The Man and His Work* (1935); *Longfellow: A Full-length Portrait* (1955); *Mrs. Longfellow: Selected Letters and Journals* (1956)

CRITICAL: *Lillian Gish, An Interpretation* (1927); *Values in Literature* (1928); *A Guide to Bernard Shaw* (1929); *Utopia Americana* (1929); *Cavalcade of the English Novel* (1943); *Cavalcade of the American Novel* (1952); *A Preface to Literature* (1954); *The Unknown Longfellow* (1954)

ANTHOLOGICAL: *The College Survey of English Literature* (with others) (1942); *Six Novels of the Supernatural* (1944); *The Fireside Book of Christmas Stories* (1945); *The Story of Jesus in the World's Literature* (1946); *When I Was a Child* (1946); *The Fireside Book of Ghost Stories* (1947); *Abraham Lincoln, His Life, Work, and Character* (1947); *The Fireside Book of Romance* (1948); *Joan of Arc, An Anthology of History and Literature* (1948); *A Fireside Book of Yuletide Tales* (1948); *Murder by Gaslight* (1949); *The Collected Tales of Walter de la Mare* (1950); *An Introduction to Dickens* (1952)

INTRODUCTORY: *The Chimes*, by Charles Dickens (Limited Editions Club, 1931); *Life on the Mississippi*, by Mark Twain (Limited Editions Club, 1944); *A Tale of Two Cities*, by Charles Dickens (Modern Library, 1950); *Great Expectations*, by Charles Dickens (Pocket Books, 1956)

MRS. LONGFELLOW:

Selected Letters and Journals of
FANNY APPLETON LONGFELLOW

(1817–1861)

EDITED BY

EDWARD WAGENKNECHT

LONGMANS, GREEN AND CO.

NEW YORK · LONDON · TORONTO

1956

LONGMANS, GREEN AND CO., INC.
55 FIFTH AVENUE, NEW YORK 3

LONGMANS, GREEN AND CO. LTD.
6 & 7 CLIFFORD STREET, LONDON W 1

LONGMANS, GREEN AND CO.
20 CRANFIELD ROAD, TORONTO 16

MRS. LONGFELLOW

PUBLISHED SIMULTANEOUSLY IN THE DOMINION OF CANADA BY
LONGMANS, GREEN AND CO., TORONTO

FIRST EDITION

LIBRARY OF CONGRESS CATALOG CARD NUMBER 56–12080

Printed in the United States of America

Contents

Contents

Illustrations

Following page 114

Fanny Appleton Longfellow
From a painting by G. P. A. Healy

Mrs. Longfellow's parents
After the paintings by Gilbert Stuart

Fanny Appleton and her sister Mary
From a miniature on ivory by Jean Baptiste Isabey

Fanny Appleton
From a marble bust by Lorenzo Bartolini

Henry Wadsworth Longfellow

105 Brattle Street, Cambridge, Massachusetts

The children of Henry Wadsworth Longfellow and Fanny
Appleton Longfellow
From a painting by Thomas Buchanan Read and a pastel by
Eastman Johnson

Fanny Appleton Longfellow

All the paintings and other works of art shown in this volume are in the Longfellow House, Cambridge, Massachusetts, and are reproduced by permission.
The photographs are from the Longfellow House collection.

Introduction

Born in Boston in 1817, Fanny Appleton was married to Henry Wadsworth Longfellow in 1843, and died in 1861. This volume contains selections from her extensive journals and correspondence.

But what are Mrs. Longfellow's claims upon the attention of posterity? Why should her memorabilia be published?

The most obvious reason, of course, is her connection with one of the representative figures of the nineteenth century, a poet who awakens love as no other poet quite does it. Fanny knew Longfellow as no other human being ever knew him. In her pages we see him and his work as they have never appeared before.

Through Longfellow, moreover, and through her own family connections as well, she knew many other distinguished men and women—New Englanders best of all, of course, yet by no means exclusively. For if, in these pages, we catch vivid glimpses of Emerson, Hawthorne, and Whittier which we should not otherwise possess, there are equally vivid glimpses (to take but a few examples at random), of Fanny Kemble and Kossuth and Carlyle.

The Longfellows were literary people, but literature was not their only interest. They lived through great historic movements. One sees the Civil War creeping up on the nation as one cannot see it in formal histories written after the event. National and local movements and events impinge upon our consciousness as they impinged upon those who were then alive. An important step in the conquest of pain is taken when ether is used in surgery at the Massachusetts General Hospital, and Mrs. Longfellow, feeling herself very much the pioneer, becomes the first woman in America to bear a child under anesthesia. Professor John White Webster kills Dr. George Parkman; in Fanny's pages we see a whole community struggling to adjust itself to the shocked realization that a murderer has been living among them.

But it is not only in its relationship to war and murder and scientific discovery and the publication of new books that a community lives; besides all this, there is the everyday life which continues in very much its own way year after year whatever is being written in the history books. Fanny Appleton was the daughter of a rich man. In her early days she lived the life of what we should now call a "society girl." After her marriage to Longfellow she assumed her rightful place with the intellectual aristocracy of the Boston area. If we would know—and feel—how a great American lady lived a hundred years ago, I know of no place where we are more likely to find the answer than in the pages of this book.

These considerations would abundantly justify the publication of the documents here presented, but there is another reason which far outweighs them all together. This is Mrs. Longfellow's own character—her beauty, her goodness, her charm. To meet such a woman, to know her as intimately as one can know her through her letters and journals, is to enrich one's experience of life and to find rational justification for thinking well of human nature. Longfellow hated to write letters. Mrs. Longfellow loved to write them, and wrote them superlatively well. Her journals are far superior to his. Letters and journals alike are filled with precisely the kind of detail that we cherish in the novel of manners, for she had the keen observation, the delighted relish of everyday life experience that have made women incomparably superior to men in this area of literary production. We all own thankfully that our lives have been blessed by contact with many noble heroines of fiction. Here is a woman as rich and as warm and as winning as any of them. She should not appeal less to us because she really lived.

Omissions are indicated in the usual manner. I have indented at the beginning of each selection for typographical reasons. All additions of my own have been placed within square brackets. I have replaced all ampersands by the word "and." Obvious misspellings have been silently corrected; punctuation has been silently altered only when the reader's convenience seemed to make it advisable. I am not reproducing with fanatical fidelity; neither am I standardizing.

When the name of the correspondent is not given in a heading preceding a letter, the reader is to understand that the person named before the preceding letter is again indicated. The same rule has been employed in giving and omitting the name of the place where the letter was written. In general, salutations, complimentary closes, and signatures have all been omitted. I have annotated as sparingly as possible and only in the interest of general intelligibility.

All the materials written by Mrs. Longfellow contained in this volume are printed by kind permission of the Longfellow trustees. Without their generosity and cooperation, neither this book nor *Longfellow: A Full-Length Portrait* would have been possible. My debt is very great and is gladly acknowledged. The curator of the Longfellow House, Mr. Thomas H. de Valcourt, has put up with me now through two long books, with unfailing kindness and patience. He has also furnished some of the material contained in my annotations, especially those which refer to the Longfellow and Appleton families.

With the exceptions noted below, all the documents are in the Longfellow House, in Cambridge, Massachusetts. As indicated in the footnotes hereinafter, one letter of Mrs. Longfellow's is in the Henry E. Huntington Library, at San Marino, California, to whom I express my thanks for permission to include it. One letter of Mrs. Longfellow's and four letters from C. C. Felton to Charles Sumner, describing the circumstances of her tragic death, are in the Houghton Library. The Harvard College Library also has jurisdiction over the publication rights of the poem to Mrs. Longfellow by James Russell Lowell which constitutes my Appendix (though the manuscript itself is in the Longfellow House). To Harvard College and to Mr. William A. Jackson, Director of the Houghton Library, I make my grateful acknowledgment.

EDWARD WAGENKNECHT

Boston University
March 26, 1956

MRS. LONGFELLOW:

Selected Letters and Journals of
Fanny Appleton Longfellow

CHAPTER I

Girlhood

Frances Elizabeth Appleton (always, after her earliest years, called Fanny), was born at 54 Beacon Street, Boston, on October 6, 1817, and grew up in the handsome residence at Number 39, overlooking the Common, which is now a part of the Women's City Club. (Longfellow always remembered the number by reminding himself of the Thirty-Nine Articles.)

Her father, Nathan Appleton, banker, manufacturer, and politician, was one of the founders of the City of Lowell, and earned a fortune of some $1,800,000 in the textile industry and trade.[1] His intelligent use of water power and the employment of female labor were important factors in his success, but he himself believed that "accident and not effort has made me a rich man." He did not lack public spirit; neither was he indifferent to the working conditions of his employees. In 1830 he was elected to Congress, where he proved himself a friend of the slave, though not an abolitionist, and championed a protective tariff, opposing Henry Clay's compromise tariff of 1833. His Currency and Banking *(1841) is an important document in connection with the controversy over the Bank of the United States. He was active in the affairs of the Boston Athenaeum, the Massachusetts Historical Society, and other organizations.*

In 1806 he married Maria Theresa Gold, daughter of Thomas Gold, a prominent lawyer of Pittsfield, Massachusetts, and his wife, Martha Marsh. Thomas Gold was the son of the Reverend Hezekiah Gold, who married Sarah Sedgwick, thus making Fanny and the rest of Maria Gold Appleton's children distant cousins of Catharine Maria Sedgwick, the novelist.

Unfortunately, though quite naturally, surviving documents give us only glimpses of Fanny Appleton's early years. Her earliest dated

---

[1] This figure has been taken from the records in the Suffolk County courthouse. The article on Nathan Appleton in the *Dictionary of American Biography* erroneously reports his fortune as consisting of $200,000.

1

*letter in the Longfellow House collection was written to her sister
Mary, who was nearly four years older than she was, in the summer
of 1825. The writer still had three months to go before reaching her
eighth birthday. Internal evidence would seem to indicate, however,
that the following undated letter to her brother Tom (born 1812) is
even earlier. (All Fanny's childhood letters are given here exactly as
she wrote them.)*

To Thomas Gold Appleton

Dear Thomas

As I have not written to you yet, I will now try to. But you must
not expect me to write well, as I dont know how to write letters. I
have a little kitten, it is a very pretty little thing, and it is all black;
it has blue eyes, and is named after Mrs Sedgwick's little dog Sable.
Mary, Charles,[2] and myself had a very pleasant ride this morning,
at half past 6 oclock, it was very cool, and we enjoyed it very much.
I now go to Miss Minots school, & like it very much. I study Dictionary, Geography, Grammar, and Arithmetic, and work in the
afternoon. Aunt Eben[3] and her family expect to go to Lowell this
summer. I have left off going to dancing this summer, because it is
so warm, but I sometimes go to see them dance. Mary is teaching
Cousin Louisa[4] and myself French; but I dont expect to learn very
fast, as I dont study much: but I shall some time in my life write you
a letter in French if I can. The people have taken all the water out
of the frogpond[5] and it does not look well now; but I suppose it
will look very pretty soon, as they are building a stone wall round it.
We spent the vacation in Lowell, and I thought the church very
pretty. Aunt Gardiner lives at Lowell and has got a very pretty house
and Aunt Martha[6] is now staying with her. When we were there we
went into the factory and we saw the great wheel on [word
illegible] Father calls it we saw them print and dye calicoes. The
second day we were there we dined with Mrs. Boot and we took a

[2] Fanny's sister and brother.
[3] Mrs. Eben Appleton, Fanny's aunt by marriage to her father's brother.
[4] A distant cousin of Fanny's, Maria Louisa Appleton, born Boston, 1815.
[5] On the Common.
[6] Aunt Gardiner and Aunt Martha Gold were both sisters of Mrs. Appleton.

ride with her about Lowell and we thought it a beautiful place. Charles spent that week at Tewksbury with Mrs Motley and her family and he had a fine time with Edward his cronye. When we were at Lowell we saw a beautiful procession of Free Masons wh wher going to lay the corner stone of a church. As I have no india rubber I hope you will excuse these lines. I hope you will answer this soon.

your affectionate sister
Frances

To Mary Appleton

Pittsfield, Mass., [7] August 3, 1825

My Dear Sister

Mother went to Saratoga last Tuesday week. I am now staying at Aunt Frances.[8] Mr. Perkins Mrs. Perkins and the two Miss Perkins's and Miss Warren were upset in the Stage coming to Pittsfield week before last. Miss Warren bruised her arm. The last time I saw her she had it in a sling. One of the Miss Perkins' received no injury, the other bruised her eye in several places. Mr and Mrs Perkins bruised themselves very much. Aunt Frances sends her love to you all. I now go to Miss Kittredge's school with Charles and Frances Wright. Week before last on thursday, we had a large Wedding party at Grandmothers.[9] I suppose you would like to have been here. Last week I went to see a grand Picture at the Lecture room. First came the Roman Soldiers, Second a Centurian and his family 3d A Ruffian pulling off Jesus robe, which Pilate put on him. Another Ruffian attempting to draw his Attention to a paper on which his title was Written in diferant Languages. 4th Our Saviour crowned with thorns. 5th Pilate setting down distinguisted by a Wreath of laurel on his head 6th The High Priest crying away with him away with him and crucyfy him, while all the multitude cried out release not this man but Barrabbas. Next came an Elder holding out his hands crying Barrabbas Barrabbas. Next came Barrabbas in chaines to a

[7] Where Fanny was visiting her Sedgwick relatives.
[8] Another sister of Fanny's mother.
[9] Mrs. Thomas Gold's.

block—behind him were these two thieves in chaines, next Joseph of Arithmea, next Peter weeping for having denied his Lord, next came the Women, the wife of Cleophas, and Martha and Mary the Sisters of Lazarus. Mary Magdalen was kneeling prostrated on the Cross. John the beloved disciple was supporting the Mother [of] Jesus. There was the executioner telling three boys the story, with a hammer in his hand, and a nail, shewing them how he was going to drive the nails, into Jesus hands and feet. Uncle and Aunt William went to Ballstown with Mother. We expect them home this week. Doct. & Mrs Handy are here they dined with Father when they were in Boston. I now bid you good bye, because I am tired of writing—hoping you will write me soon—good bye Frances E Appleton

By 1827 Fanny had made considerable progress in the epistolary art.

To Thomas Gold Appleton

Boston, February 20, 1827

Dear Thomas,

I suppose, you think it rather strange, that I have not written you a letter this term;[10] but I have not had much time, and when I have, I always forget it, therefore I will now try to, but I think *you* ought to write oftener. The baby [11] is very well, and grows very fast; I believe it weight's 8 pounds. I now go to Miss Peabody's [12] school; and I like Her very well, though I have to walk in the cold, a great way, as it is in Franklin Place. Mary and Charles are very well, and I suppose if they were here, they would give their love to you. I suppose you have heard of the death of Grandfather,[13] which grieves us all very much. Mother is pretty well, and I suppose, would write to you, if she had time enough. I go to dancing school, and like it very much. Miss Mallet who is the school mistress, told me that she heard, that you were going to be a poet, and she told

[10] Tom was a pupil at the Round Hill School, at Northampton, Massachusetts.
[11] Fanny's brother, George William Appleton, who lived only seven months.
[12] Elizabeth Peabody, later Hawthorne's sister-in-law.
[13] Thomas Gold.

me to tell you, "that you must not be a poet because if you were, you would be poor," she said, "that poets always turn out poor," therefore I think that you had better not, if that is the case. . . .

13

To Maria Gold Appleton

Milton, Mass., August 20, 1830

I was extremely obliged to you My dear Mother, for your very kind letter, which I received since I have been here, and I will endeavor to fulfil your wishes, as much as I can, which you desired in it. You amused me very much, when you thought that I was at Nahant, when all the time I was here, enjoying the cool mountain breeze, instead of the refreshing sea breeze which you mentioned. I have a most delightful time, and what makes it still more pleasant is, that Father and Mary come to see me every week; therefore I do not seem entirely away from my friends. Mrs. Bryant also comes out to see Elizabeth, every week, and we thus have communication with Boston, for whatever we want. I will now inform you how we spend our time. In the morning we get up about sunrise, dress ourselves, and go down to breakfast. After breakfast we go to walk until it grows too warm, and then come home and study. We generally translate French, and cipher. We read, work, or draw, in the afternoon, and we go to walk again about sundown. In the evening we generally read, but I assure you that I do not go to bed so late here, as at home. There are most delightful walks in the woods, and so many different ones that we go a new walk almost every day. There are a great many berries of all kinds, and when the grapes are ripe, we shall have a very great abundance of them. Also, Milton produces a great variety of wild flowers, many of which we have pressed. There is a most beautiful wood, belonging to the church that we often walk in. One part of which, it is said (being so beautiful) Mr Guild the minister, often writes his sermons in. But I will now tell you, what I know will please my dear Mother, more than any thing I have already said; which is, that I have grown so fat. and rosy, that you would hardly know me. I was quite pale when I first came out here, but I have now recovered my natural color. And

I hope that you, and I, will both go home, so much improved that we shall astonish every body. We have most delicious milk here, and we almost subsist upon it, which added to the exercise we take, and the strengthening air, is enough to make anybody healthy. . . .

The following letters were sent by Fanny to her father while he was in Washington. They mark the beginning of her interest in public affairs.

To Nathan Appleton

Boston, January 21, 1832

Snow, snow, snow, oh dismal! what a change from the four or five enchanting days we have had when one could hardly believe that it was not Spring, so bright was the Sun, and so mild the air! The Common was about putting on its green mantle, quite gaily, except a few patches of the old one of snow, which peeped through here and there; but now alas! such flattering prospects are entirely dispersed. . . .

We had some hope that this warm weather would have thawed Dr. Channing's [14] cold, for he has not favored us with a sermon for a great while, and tomorrow I have got one to write for composition, and shall be in despair if he does not preach. Mother also will regret this return of winter, for she has been able for one or two days to breathe the mild air, as she walked on our sunny street.

I belong to a sewing circle . . . which always meets at Mr. W. Sullivan's, for the benefit of poor Irish or any children, to procure for them thick garments of flannel, cotton, etc., composed of a number of agreeable young ladies who make it extremely pleasant. . . .

March 1, 1832

The bearer of this letter is a young Cherokee chief, who, together with Mr. Bodenot (Mother's cousin) have been sent as deputies by their nation to plead their rights. He is an extremely interesting

[14] Fanny's pastor, William Ellery Channing (1780–1842), the great Unitarian preacher.

youth, very well instructed in everything, and a perfect wonder as to civilization. He dined with us the other day, and was vastly agreeable, and sung us several real Indian songs, etc. We were all very much pleased with him. Last night we went to our Church to hear them speak, where we were surrounded by an enormous audience—the very aisles were filled. Mr. A. Everett began, and spoke very well on the rights of the Indians, etc. and was succeeded by Mr. Bodenot, who received a great deal of applause. He spoke extremely well and brought out several curious facts. . . . Then arose our friend, who by the way is very good looking, and he was truly fine—the true eloquence of the heart. . . . He said, "I do not wish by showing these inconsistencies to tarnish the fame of this nation—far from it. We are confident we have many friends—friends in New England—and some of the greatest statesmen of these United States are ready to plead our cause in the sacred halls of justice at Washington. We know we have there an Everett! a Webster! and an *Appleton! !*" . . .

I forgot to tell you his name—Mr. Ridge. He told us a most poetical one (his Indian name) which translated means "He that walks on the mountain tops," and therefore he has been called Ridge for shortness.

In the spring Fanny herself made a trip to Washington; in her journal she recorded one vivid moment of her seeing from the point of view of a somewhat superior young Bostonian. This note is sounded again in a letter to a young friend, written after her return to Beacon Street.

Mr. Clay is a most fascinating speaker. His voice is full, clear and melodious, his manner animated, and his words seem to come straight from his heart—he has no tortuous channels. Good, honorable patriot, my wishes are for thee! What an odd mixture of splendor and meanness in the President's house. A stupid, countryfied servant ushered us to the luxurious drawing rooms, where the spermaceti of the last levee was still adorning the elegantly cut chandeliers and a broom stood at the side of the marble fireplace. The President [15] is courteous and polite enough but not very polished in his manners.

[15] Andrew Jackson.

To Susan Benjamin

Boston, June 11, 1832

Being at last fairly ensconced at home, dear Sue, and having become somewhat accustomed to the sober routine of this quakerlike place, after the bustle and constant occupation I have of late been subjected to, I sit down with delight to write to you, with the hope of again receiving such a sweet letter as I seized with eagerness at Washington, when I was afraid I was almost forgotten by my friends, so "long and far between" were their communications. Yes, this journey is indeed over, and here am I returned at last to Boston and Beacon Street. Never did I enjoy travelling more, or appreciate the beauties of the Common and its muddy frogpond so well as now! But when we first arrived it seemed here like some town in the midst of the country, or a deserted city, so quiet and orderly did everything appear. No carts, no dandies, and (last but not least) no *pigs* which had so continually greeted our vision in every place we had visited, not excepting the neat Philadelphia, which I prefer above all places but Boston.

. . . The commencement of our travels was not quite so propitious as it might have been, but nothing in the line of adventure occured afterward, worthy of note, except one misfortune which grieved me especially. I had a sketch-book, in which I had drawn several views, besides divers caricatures and likenesses of the party, and as I was seated on a wood-box, on board the steamboat to New York, just having finished a very flattering likeness of Mr. Brigham, who was humming at my elbow . . . well, as I was thus gazing about me, I felt a something lightly touch my feet, and on looking down, lo! my book was in the water, floating off in grand style. I was in despair, and told Mr. B. he should have *jumped overboard* after it, which he did not seem much inclined to do, I must say.

Alas! poor book! no doubt in some future day, some romantic fisherman will find it in his net, whence will follow a long tale, full of mysteries and romance!

In December, 1832, we get the first reference in Fanny's journal to her mother's final illness. The end came two months later. This was the first great sorrow of Fanny's life, and it seems to have exercised an important maturing effect upon her.

(JOURNAL)

February 7, 1833

Mother continues very ill, the doctor has been afraid that she would not survive the night. Feet and hands much swollen. She sang a hymn last night in her sleep, in a clear, sweet voice, although she had great difficulty in speaking. . . .

February 8, 1833

. . . She is obliged, for the first time, to keep her bed entirely; is lifted for a few moments upon another bed in the same room. Makes not the slightest complaint. This evening she called all her children to her bedside, and by an incredible exertion of moral fortitude and principle, with the agony of speaking, addressed to them a most touching exhortation to walk in the way in which she had trained them up, to adhere to that religion which was her Rock of trust in that hour of death, to make that their only guide and support, to fulfil all their duties and realize all her wishes and hopes in regard to them, ending by asking them never to forget her but to let her memory be sweet and consoling to them.

February 9, 1833

She continues today much the same, with great difficulty of breathing. In the evening she called in the servants and addressed them each separately an exhortation to do their duty and to follow the precepts of religion. . . .

February 10, 1833

She passed a quiet night and appeared calm this morning. She noticed the rising sun and appeared to look on it with interest as the last she should witness. . . . At about 2 o'clock we were called to her bedside when we found her apparently dying. After Dr. W. had rubbed her she appeared to revive a little but was for a long time unable to swallow anything and suffered great distress for want of breath. Yet even at that hour of agony she was never for a moment unmindful of others. She asked us once if we were not going to church and requested Thomas to leave the chamber lest he should take cold from the open windows. She kept her eyes anxiously fixed on the clock, either to see how the time of suffering passed or to watch for the hour of my father's arrival,[16] whom she expected to see until the last moment. But he came not! She continued in this state until nearly four having the position of the pillows constantly changed, when she experienced a violent struggle for breath, her countenance changed, and she exclaimed, "I am dying," and then "raise me!" She was raised on the pillow, when she said "Amen" and with a slight convulsion of the features, followed by an expression of calm serenity, her spirit took its everlasting flight from its wreck of clay. Truly, "blessed are the dead who die in the Lord."

In June, Fanny made a trip to West Point, Niagara, and Canada, of which we may permit ourselves a few glimpses as preserved in her journals for the light they shed on the maturing girl.

June 20, 1833

Left for Niagara. . . . The road runs the whole way near the river Niagara and we were astonished at the immense number of islands succeeding each other continually. . . . We did not cross the river at Blackrock but continued on the American side the whole way. It rains fast, and alas! there is no window-sash, and we are to be drenched as usual! The road now turns into a thick wood and the black mud slippery with the rain makes these deep holes quite dangerous. . . . An immense log of wood coolly inserted itself between the spokes of the wheel thereby threatening us with an overturn. . . . At the distance of eight miles we fancied we heard the dull roar of the cataract but I could only hear the pattering of the rain and the rustling of the leaves. As we proceeded the rapids commenced and became very fine, the whole appearance of the river resembling much the ocean. The distant mist at last became apparent, but as yet we saw no other indication of the falls.

[16] From Washington.

We arrived at the village and the hotel, large and commodious but most provokingly situated, only overlooking plenty of mills of all descriptions and factories and houses, but no falls were to be seen, and we were woefully disappointed, expecting certainly to behold this grand object of our search from the piazza. We were conducted off to a most ancient and dilapidated wing of the mansion, fast falling to ruin and already nearly a foot apart from the main house, an immense crack intervening. Here, in a forlorn, carpetless room, we mourned over our disappointments and regretted beyond measure that we had not crossed to the British side. . . .

After dining in a dismal dark room with red curtains we begin to equip ourselves for a walk. The sun has made his appearance and we have a lovely afternoon for our first view.

A few steps from the house we reached a long wooden bridge curiously constructed and with great difficulty, being directly over the violent rapids which are here extremely beautiful and larger than any I ever saw. The water foams and whirls in all directions and appears still more like a disturbed ocean. We rested here a long time to admire them, and Emmeline's [17] romance was sadly provoked by the appearance of mills and artificial water-works. Factories at Niagara! what profanation, what sacrilege!

This bridge extends across the river to Goat Island, the most lovely spot in creation. We stopped for a few moments at a shop, where were some very good Indian things—moccasins, etc.—but abominably dear. We wandered through the shady walks and rural paths of Goat Island, anxiously gazing forth to catch the slightest glimpse of the river, and an opening in the trees at last unfolded to us the whole wondrous scene. We saw, indeed, that exquisite combination of perfect loveliness, that emerald green, that snowy foam and wreathing mist, that mixture of sublimity and beauty, of grandeur and picturesque loveliness. We saw it all, and heroines as we certainly are, we did not faint or scream or tremble like the sensitive Mrs. Trollope,[18] but we *looked* in silent admiration and wondered too that

[17] Emmeline Austin (later Mrs. Wadsworth), a Beacon Street neighbor, Fanny's closest girlhood friend and lifelong correspondent.
[18] Probably a reference to Mrs. Trollope's account of her visit to Niagara toward the close of her *Domestic Manners of the Americans* (1832), which is not, however, nearly so hysterical in tone as Fanny's words would indicate.

anyone, however unromantic or however quiet and matter-of-fact a disposition, could ever be disappointed with a scene like this.

The whole appears at first a perfect fairy scene, the water being of such an exquisite shade of green, a shade peculiar to itself; the gradual change from green to white, and the whole enveloped in the ethereal veil of mist and spray, renders the first appearance very striking. . . .

We afterwards descended to the platform directly over the grand fall, and here the view is perfectly appalling. This seems a perfect work of man's daring, these few planks extended over a bottomless abyss, and trembling with the mighty rush of waters, especially one point stretched out to the farthest verge of safety and too terribly near to be enjoyed. We were much disappointed at the house that the noise was not louder, and it is here and at Table Rock only that one hears the deep moaning roar like ceaseless thunders above even the crashing sound of the water. The sublimity of the whole scene now becomes more apparent, such a mass of water, a falling ocean! . . .

After tea we seated ourselves in the parlor and were quite alarmed by the appearance of a green-eyed, morose-looking man with a most sinister aspect who seated himself directly opposite Emmeline and never turned his eyes from her face, joining in the conversation and staring most outrageously. . . .

We retired to our dismal apartment but not to sleep. The confused sound of the water rushing over Niagara and carrying us with it, horrible apprehensions of crazy men with spectacles peering in at the keyhole, and more real fears that the house would every moment fall down, having seen divers ominous cracks in the wall and ceiling, the light going out and no matches to be procured, no wonder Morpheus fled terrified at the accumulation of so many horrors!

June 21, 1833

A lovely day! . . . Walked out to the American fall, along a pretty path by the side of the river. Obtained an entirely new view of all the falls and a very splendid one. The morning was so delightful that we determined to cross over to the British side and make our visit there, and we therefore descended the long staircase from which the view is very fine. Half way down we walked along the rocks and came directly upon the fall and too near to enjoy it. It is terrific when within a few yards of it, and the deafening noise and overwhelming rush of the water are bewildering. It seemed to us like a myriad of comets and meteors rushing after each other in an endless succession. We found crossing in the boat much more agreeable than we had anticipated, and though a little alarmed at first, the skill of the boatmen is such that we soon learned to consider it perfectly safe and most delightful. . . .

Having safely arrived on the British side and in his Majesty's dominions, we had leisure to admire the falls all together, and at a distance. . . . We *crawled* up the long and steep ascent to the summit of the bank and after gazing our fill at the noble view of the river which is of a most exquisite green hue, we got into a stage and drove to Forsyth's a mile or so on, over a bad road. There we were received by a flourishing landlord and were charmed with the civility and English look of the servant-boys and chambermaid. This hotel is splendidly situated, overlooking the fall and the view from the piazza is very fine but not so good for a first one as on the other side. . . .

This midsummer letter from Newport is interesting for Fanny's first, rather guarded approach to the great English actress, Fanny Kemble, whom she afterward loved so much both as an artist and a friend. Fanny Kemble married the American, Pierce Butler, in 1834 and divorced him in 1848. See Margaret Armstrong, Fanny Kemble, A Passionate Victorian, *(Macmillan, 1938). The "book of travels" hereinafter referred to was published in 1835 as* Journal of a Residence in America.

To Susan Benjamin

Newport, R.I., August 19, 1834

. . . Here we are in this land of fog and windmills undergoing all the horrors of a dry northeaster, i.e. freezing to death in this dreary, carpetless mansion, with a canopy of murky clouds overhead eclipsing every hope of a renovating sunbeam. We have been in these regions nearly a fortnight and begin to weary of the stupid dissipation of the place. We are in the center of gaiety and fashion and yet have little very desirable of either. I must say I was disappointed both in the society and accommodations of Newport. The latter are somewhat forlorn. We have the most ludicrous scrambling at meals to get anything to satisfy the enormous appetite which this bracing air produces—when succeeding, some purloin the provender and retire with it to their apartment, to munch *à loisir!* . . .

Mrs. Pierce Butler is here and her pretty sister-in-law, Ella Mims that was. She is so engaged in writing her book of travels that she only appears in the evening, when she is very gay, waltzing and gallopading most gracefully. Her manners have become much more affable, and I must say she is capable of being truly fascinating. I have got very well acquainted with her and feel myself bound by the spell which attracts every one to her. She has taken a great fancy to Mary and sends for her constantly to come and chat with her. She allowed me to dress her hair the other day but was quite distressed because Pierce thought it becomed her. She clubs hers round in such a plain fashion from a *principle* that the form of the head should not be disfigured. Her flashing glances are still beautiful though she is frightfully coarse to examine. By exposure to the sun she is burned to a bright mahogany color and yet wears every evening a white muslin with bare neck and gloveless arms! She dresses in shocking taste. The other afternoon I met her walking on the rocks with a muslin dress over yellow silk and a transparent blond hat in a piercing wind that made me wrap up in my blankety shawl and boa! . . .

In the fall we glimpse Fanny briefly as quite the perfect Boston "society girl."

To Susan Benjamin

Boston, October 20, 1834

Many thanks, dear Sue, for thinking of me on the sixth, though I suppose you were unconscious of the important era in my life which it commemorated. "Sweet seventeen" is, as you know, generally quite

an interesting period to young damsels, though, for my part, I am
very indifferent to particular "times and seasons," inasmuch as they
usually mark but the progress of Time upon the outward faculty and
are not always welcome monitors. But I learned to moralize before I
was seventeen, and therefore begin to think it wiser to abjure now all
such tottering theories and try to recover a little of the freshness and
"happy ignorance" of younger days. You see how foolish I have already become, "exposing" myself to you, who deservedly detest such
nonsense. On the strength of my being somewhere in the neighborhood of seventeen, I have been dragged *nolens volens* lately into
"considerable much" dissipation and am now "resting on my oars" a
little for a fresh "tug." The Tremont has been receiving and turning
away its thousands, as usual, this autumn, and consequently gaiety
has flowed along in an unbroken stream. I think these little parties
at this season are charming, so easy and sociable, and then such a
relief to see so many new physiognomies and quaint costumes and
droll peculiarities. There has been a constant succession of strangers
from all quarters of the globe, and some very agreeable. I like so
much to extend your acquaintance a little out of your own narrow
sphere—it seems to give you an interest in distant places, which you
might never otherwise have felt, and also to extend your own importance, it being pleasant to reflect that you are known somewhere
beyond Boston Common.

I am so sorry that you have not been here to enjoy some of this.
However we will have some good fun together this winter, to make
amends. I "calculate" on a very merry season for divers reasons.
There are to be innumerable weddings, which must bring many
parties in their train; then, such unusual attraction[s] at the theater,
and to us by no means least, the arrival of my brother, who will give
us all a new life. Sheridan Knowles is acting here now, and pray
hasten home if you have any curiosity to see a plump, jolly Irishman,
with a fine, rich brogue, a most merry phiz, and a hearty good
nature about him which breathes of his own Emerald Isle, its
potatoes and whisky! I saw him in *The Hunchback*, and of course
took a double interest in his acting though I must say it destroyed
much of the romance associated with both the character and author.
He is very natural and earnest in his acting and I should think might

succeed better in comedy. . . . I have just finished Mrs. Siddons' life, and have been much entertained by it. I have always had the greatest curiosity to know her history, and had no idea before of her high moral character. What a royal creature she must have been! . . .

(JOURNAL)

July 4, 1835

Was awoke by the ringing of bells and roaring of cannon. Had a sort of nightmare of guns and bells which seemed spun out through a century. A good hint for Dante's Inferno! The weather too hot for comfort. . . . In the P.M. sat at the window and read a horrible French book—amused with one eye by the concourse of people collected on the Common to see the balloon. One mass of bright colors —a painted pallette—how it did sicken one of all tints and hues and finery! The balloon went up finely, notwithstanding a shower— laughed to see the people scatter in every direction, the women with their handkerchiefs over their bonnets to save their "best" from a sprinkling, very like a turning kaleidoscope! Fanny Inglis came in and we rushed on the top of the house to see the balloon's fate. It poured—I tied a handkerchief over my head—Mr. Wolcott held an umbrella over me—an interesting group to be relieved against the sky, with thousands of spectators below and around! . . . It contined to rain, thereby defrauding the public of the grand fireworks for which the Common's verdure had been immolated. . . .

July 7, 1835

Packed all the morning—then shopped. When I came home found a great commotion because the key of my trunk had vanished. Speedily transferred all the things into another and as soon as I had finished the trunk key was found! . . . I liked the railroad extremely. It was a delicious afternoon, and we slid along as on wheels of glass. The country rolled off like a dream at the touch of our invisible feet. This fiery dragon with his asthmatic lungs takes the place of the winged griffins that bore off fair damsels in days of eld. The chief drawback to the pleasure of this unearthly speed is the sacrifice of one's eyes in consequence of the constantly falling ashes which, sifting through veils even, have given us all most flaming orbs. . . . Near Worcester the road goes through the rocks for some distance, whose rough and jagged edges stand ready to grasp you if you protrude a finger. What an invasion of Nature's secret palaces —what a surprise to the insects who have lodged within a mountain for centuries to see one day an enormous monster with a hundred people riding on his back come puffing and roaring through their solitude!

Friendship and social interests continued into the summer, and in July Fanny went to Pittsfield, Massachusetts, to stay with her mother's family, the Golds. It seems to have been an interesting summer.

July 13, 1835

. . . After dinner "Crazy Sue" made us a visit to my delight, for I was crazy to see her. She was not so frantically demented as I expected, but rambled on, a thousand thoughts pushing away others half formed, with now and then an amazingly shrewd "hit" at matters and things. Religion is her main topic, which she seems to view more rationally than many sounder heads. Tom tried to sketch her, but you might as well take hold of a streak of lightning. She was in tolerably fanciful garb with roses stuck through a hole in her antique bonnet, one whole shoe, and another strapped round her foot all manner of ways, which she called her "cloven foot." She sung us an old ballad, of a youth crazed for love, pretty much her own story as I supposed, though she gives a much more rational and less romantic cause for her madness, namely that it runs in the family. She must have been beautiful once, for weatherbeaten as she is, she is very fine looking, and her straight nose and black bright eyes bear evidence of better days. I was infinitely amused with her odd comparisons and quick retorts. Mary gave her a dollar to buy a pair of shoes and she strode off for them at a most majestic pace. . . .

July 14, 1835

While we were at prayers, this morning, Crazy Sue suddenly appeared at the door in an attitude of phophecy, with her hands raised over her head and her eyes glaring mildly enough. She joined us, listening most intently and occasionally interrupting with a groan in the Methodist style. She is amazingly active and strides about constantly all over the country though she is over sixty. She thinks a good deal of her immortalization by Miss Sedgwick as "Crazy Bet." [19]

On August 3 she records having met the formidable English writer, Harriet Martineau, whom she found somewhat good-looking, partly because she had been told she was "particularly hideous."

. . . The face, however, wants the intelligence that I expected to see—it is very commonplace. The features are bad and her eyes entirely void of expression or intellect. But I was very much charmed with her easy unaffected manners and extreme good nature and affability, allowing anyone to pour out their cup full of ideas into her tube which she plays with as carelessly as a child with cup and ball. It is very long and flexible with a small ivory orifice at one end which she applies to her ear and an ivory cup at the other which you hold under your lip conversing in your natural voice. I did not attempt to expose myself, but Mary talked a great deal with her with great ease. It is amusing to see her conversing with two people at the same time. She first tosses it over to one, then back to the other.

To Robert Apthorp

Boston, September 2, 1835

. . . The ride on the railroad was very fatiguing and we were heartily glad to welcome aristocratic Beacon Street and the Common which quite "cut out" even Berskshire verdure. The house loomed on us as a palazzo, and though brooms and pails strewed the entry and confusion reigned in every room, it looked magnificent indeed after our rustic habitations, where mountain, rock, and tree furnish forth palaces more glorious than brick and mortar dream of. The dear "green room," loved for its beauty and almost sacred in my eyes for a thousand associations of happy hours passed in it, is

[19] In *A New England Tale* (1822).

lost to us forever, as Father has converted it into a chamber. Strange that local attachments can be so strong. I wept bitterly to see it so desecrated. . . .

(JOURNAL) *18*

September 7, 1835

Went with Aunt Sam,[20] Tom, and Sue to see some of Healy's pictures—a Sybil at Dr. Keats', which is very beautiful, and a Venus at Mr. Preston's, which is altogether in Paradise costume and would have made a Harriet Byron [21] faint. He is a great genius *sans doute*, and there is a possibility that in some future day we shall be revered for being patrons and acquaintances of great man.[22]

Another letter to Robert Apthorp, written early in September, is lighthearted and gay—and especially interesting to us in view of who it was that Fanny finally married.

September 7, 1835

. . . As to my "intended," I shall not be satisfied with even your high praises, for *par parenthese*, I am by no means flattered that you find so many worthy of my smiles. You seem eager to shift off the responsibility of *chooser* very soon: know that I am the most fastidious person in the world and shall not be satisfied with mere everyday excellences. You have a thankless office after all, for there is no uncertain probability that I should fancy *ever* one *selected* for me by my best friend even, either from obstinacy or unwillingness to have my free impulses swayed by a hint. Indeed, I have often felt a sort of presentiment that I should marry somebody disapproved of by all my friends, for I have universally found that those I was inclined to like best showed always the least and perhaps most unattractive portion of their character to common observers. I feel always pleased in making discoveries of characters veiled from the

[20] Mrs. Samuel Appleton, wife of Nathan Appleton's brother.
[21] The prudish heroine of Richardson's *Sir Charles Grandison*.
[22] George Peter Alexander Healy (1818–1894), distinguished portrait-painter. He painted a picture of Fanny reproduced in this book and other Appleton and Longfellow portraits.

many, in sounding unknown seas whose pearls have not sought the hand of every careless diver. . . .

Matrimonial chaffing and kindred frivolities were all forgotten in October, when Charles Appleton died. Like Fanny's account of her mother's death—and Longfellow's record of the passing of his first wife—this picture of a brother's peaceful departure would seem to indicate that the deathbed scenes in nineteenth-century novels were much closer to actual experience than they have often been credited as being.

She is again writing to Apthorp.

October 29, 1835

. . . Though I had been long aware of the certainty that that loved life was fast changing its destiny for a more congenial atmosphere, the conviction entered not into the immediate present, and I owe it to your friendship to confess that the "few days" of your letter sent a pang to my heart which almost unnerved me for the declaration which I had long felt to be my duty to make, which your words only confirmed. That afternoon I read to him those last life-fraught breathings of our divine Master in St. John beginning "Let not your heart be troubled," and, as I read on, he seemed pleased and listened most intently, and whenever I ceased, to gain strength and composure for the task, he exclaimed, "Is that all!" with such a longing thirst for the peace and hope which they offered that I felt his mind was in a right state to receive that which is thought to be a shock by those to whom this world's hollow comforts are all-sufficient. I knelt at his feet and talked of the love which, in its last agonies, had breathed forth such promises to those whose hearts were troubled and anxious with doubts, and he thanked me with smiles in which the nearly transformed spirit shone forth, but before I could summon words which would snap forever the tenure which mortality while mortal ever clings to, the love of life which our earthly frame claims as its reward, we were interrupted by company and the opportunity was lost. . . . Sunday, being a cool, invigorating air, he seemed quite as well if not better than for some days previous and intended going to take a drive as usual, but the doctor's late visit prevented him and he determined to defer it till the afternoon. He talked occasionally and his face beamed with the peace which earth knows not of. Feeling death's shadows weighing upon him, he walked with father's assistance into the bathing room for a change of air (about one o'clock), and suffered much from want of breath, having the windows open, etc. I shall never forget the strange look of wonder, almost pity, which he gave me as I was chafing his hands, as he saw the tears which I could not restrain streaming from my eyes. It was a silent rebuke that I could mourn for what opened to him happiness ineffable. He requested to be carried about, and he was conveyed in a sort of cradle of straw all over the house as he desired, suffering apparently very little except from difficulty in breathing, but even this did not disturb the serenity of his countenance for a moment. He at last put his hand to his eyes and exclaimed, "I can hardly see." These were his last words, and like a happy child he "went to sleep," to wake to those joys which are imperishable and eternal. . . .

I have written so much, dear Robert, that I have hardly given myself room for a determination which I know will amaze you and which is so sudden that I do not undertake to realize or comprehend it but feel as if still wandering in the land-of-Dreams. We are now so desolate, with nothing to anticipate, and one loss making the few left more anxious for each other than ever, that father has actually sent to New York to engage our passage to sail for Europe in a fortnight! The slightest thought of it staggers and bewilders me so that I dare not yield to the excitement and the indifference with which it now is viewed—would have seemed last year incredible. Come to us, dear Robert, if you can, to Godspeed us, at least; perhaps you will accompany us? Farewell in haste.

CHAPTER II

First Trip to Europe
and
Meeting with Longfellow

At ten o'clock on the morning of November 16, 1835, the Apple-
ton party set off to join their steamer in New York harbor, attended,
as Fanny says, by as numerous a company of relatives and friends
as if they had been General Jackson setting out on his tour. Of the
voyage and the long sojourn abroad—they did not return to America
until the summer of 1837—Fanny made a very elaborate record, both
in her letters and in her journals. From the wealth of material avail-
able, I have tried to choose that which is not only interesting in
itself but which bears importantly upon the writer's development
and sheds light on her character and personality.

To Robert Apthorp

Atlantic Ocean. On board ship *Francis de Pau*, December 3, 1835
16 days out. Lat 47.40. Lon 15.

Here we are, dashing bravely along at ten knots or thereabouts,
with a fine northwester roaring behind us and an enormous "head-
sea" breaking from our bows in silvery showers and casting its spray
far over our deck! . . . After a day's anchorage in New York harbor
on account of adverse winds, we set sail with a gentle breeze, a calm
sea, and mild weather, which lasted us nearly a week, which we
passed delightfully, amusing ourselves on the sunny deck with all
the strange sights and sounds about us, getting accustomed to our
Lilliputian accommodations, and concluding the sea was a very nice,
quiet place after all. But since then, for nearly ten days, we have
had nothing but a succession of hailly, squally tempestuous weather,

the wind blowing most furiously from the northwest and a very heavy sea bearing down upon us from the northeast. . . . The waves have been truly mountain high and crested with foamy white caps, flashing with rainbows when breaking, but I will not rhapsodize about the sea, for it is beyond words. Our passengers are rather quiet, well-meaning sort of folks, but on the whole quite agreeable, and we have conjured up a vast deal of fun on divers occasions. . . . But you have no idea how agreeably disappointed we are in the captain. He is, to be sure, sufficiently severe with the sailors (but so stupid as they are!) and gives them threats of the rope's end now and then, but with us he is gentlemanly, full of fun, and well informed on every subject you can propose. He has been most zealous for our accommodation, and is more active and beauish than any of the juveniles aboard, sings us sailor songs and seems to take real pleasure in giving us information about the ship and explaining all the sea-phrases, in which he thinks us wondrous apt pupils. . . . Today we surmise is Thanksgiving in New England, and we are going to celebrate it on venison and plum-pudding! I wonder what the folks are about in old Boston? . . .

Friday evening. I have just come down from a very interesting scene—the first sounding! Ninety fathoms brought us up sand— French earth! One of the shells attached I preserve as a relic of a world seldom visited—the bottom of the sea! We expect to arrive now in three or four days, and I shall finish my letter in Havre, perhaps to go by the packet of the eighth, for thereby hangs a bet of the captain's. . . .

December 7. I had hoped to finish this, dear Robert, on *terra firma*, but here we are provokingly becalmed in La Manche, about forty miles from Havre, and with little prospect of reaching our port till tomorrow night! And the packet of the eighth will pass us tomorrow; so we dispatch all our letters by it. You must imagine us arrived! But as we took our pilot yesterday, we call our passage nineteen days. This is doing so well we can't complain much of present delay. . . .

Havre! December 9. This letter seems destined never to end but I only open it to say we are arrived at last, have eaten and enjoyed fully a French dinner and are half bewildered with the variety of novelties in every direction. We came up the harbor today in a freezing rain which successfully rivals even Boston east winds and have been shuddering ever since over the stone floors, enormous fire places with their bits of wood, which disappear like magic before our Yankee ideas of warmth. The picturesqueness of the entrance, houses, men, women, everything is so strange that it seemed like a panorama on a picture. Right-heartily rejoiced are we to welcome Mother Earth once more though old Neptune has been tolerably civil too! Day after tomorrow we go to Rouen, thence Paris! How much I have scribbled! Addio.

At Rouen, on December 12, she first felt the full power of Gothic archcitecture. Here, too, she saw the spot "where perished the heroic Jeanne d' Arc—the heroine of the world!" The memory of Rouen spoiled Notre Dame for her, when she got to Paris and found it whitewashed!

Fanny arrived in Paris on December 15, 1835. Wretched weather seriously handicapped sightseeing at the beginning, but fortunately there were indoor pleasures. On December 17, she heard Giulia Grisi for the first time. (We savor this and other pleasures through journal entries.)

. . . I cannot attempt to describe the effect of that voice! It is forever ringing in my ears, and the whole floats through my memory as a vision filled with melody not of this earth. And her beauty and grace and tragic power! The play is very touchingly pathetic, and the heroine (Norma) is a grand dramatic character independent of the music. She acted it with great energy, flinging forth her trumpet notes like a meteor—a blaze of song! A duet with her rival beginning "*Si, fin all' ore estreme*" was like the play of silver lightning and was called for thrice. . . .

But Fanny did not confine herself to the opera. Instead, she explored the Parisian theaters in numerous aspects.

December 22, 1835

Went to Mr. Le Comte's *Théâtre des Enfans* and were excessively amused with performance. It is of a Lilliputian size and filled with children and their bonnes, who munch sugar plums and oranges by way of *entremet* to the feast of the eyes. There is quite a good orchestra and very respectable scenery, and these pretty little vaudevilles were charmingly acted by *enfans* of all sizes from six to nineteen. They grow up in the course of the evening, and in the last play they were in appearance men and women. I suppose the little ones would get too sleepy to act with spirit so late. *Byron at School* was quite an interesting piece, and the hero was acted by a fine-looking youth resembling very strikingly the little lord. He made it really pathetic and was as inspired with fine speeches as if he had already written *Childe Harold*. Some of the very juvenile actors were excellent, performing with great spirit and ease. . . .

December 24, 1835

. . . Went to the *Théâtre Français* and saw a splendid drama called *Don Juan d'Autriche*. The heroine . . . was lovely with a delicious voice and in some scenes thrillingly heroic. There were a great many fine dramatic effects, and the simplicity of the most energetic parts, the rich costume never breaking the illusion, and the perfect ease of excellence of every actor made a new era of my stage enjoyment. The historical truth of the whole story made it very interesting, and the sad end rather "did me up" for the time. . . . The cool, venomous dispatch of the king was admirable. . . .

On the last day of the year she heard Grisi again, this time in Semiramide:

. . . The music is splendid but it is a most dreary, solemn subject, and even Grisi hardly redeemed it from being very stupid. She is too young for the part (Pasta's grand one), but is often very majestic and is an excellent scold, flinging forth her arms with great energy, flashing her beautiful eyes with a lightning expression of scorn, and pouring out a perfect rush and Niagara of sound which might annihilate brazen walls. The opera is too full of Rossini's pet machinery —unnatural quirks and trills and labyrinths—and the bang-bang of cymbals and drums was deafening. It is all glitter and noise without one clear exquisite air to haunt the memory. . . .

January 11, 1836

. . . In the evening went to the Porte St. Martin to see the Bedouins—listened patiently through a five-act revolutionary piece which
was, however, very good and tolerably interesting, and were well
repaid at last by the Bedouins for any trial of patience. They are
"most wonderful, wonderful, and still wonderful beyond all whoop-
ing"! About a dozen objects dressed in white come tumbling in, like
so many porpoises, turning somersets with the rapidity of lightning
and of immense height, pirouetting in a style to make Taglioni die
of envy, whirling over and over in the air without support and with
swords ready to enter their eyes or throats if they slip an instant,
leaping over scarfs or comrades and firing guns and pistols in their
progress and finally building themselves up into a human pyramid,
one sturdy chief supporting one on his head, one on his shoulder,
and a child above those!! Their agility and grace are inconceivable,
and each one seems a man of india rubber who can double himself
up at pleasure and bound with an elasticity that does not belong to
bone and muscle. There was one youth particularly, graceful as a
stag, who leaped over a solid mass of drawn swords held up by his
companions, whirling again as he touched the ground. . . .

*Fanny had a more intimate contact with the world of Parisian
art next day, when she and her sister sat to the famous miniaturist,
Jean Baptiste Isabey, for the exquisite dual portrait which still hangs
in the Longfellow House.*

January 12, 1836

Had our first sitting at Isabey's. He is the most fascinating old
man! His wife is very agreeable and talks a good deal to us that he
may paint to advantage when we are laughing over her speeches!
He showed us a cabinet filled with snuff boxes and curiosities given
him by distinguished persons. He has one of Napoleon with a very
curious agate in the shape of a dog's head and with some of the
Emperor's snuff still reposing inside. Also one on the lid of which he
painted Napoleon and another of Josephine with a small miniature
of her lord round her neck which with a microscope appears a fine

likeness! She is beautiful and the finish is beyond belief. He has a miniature he has taken of Talleyrand, Marie Louise, etc. etc. His wife showed us one he took of Napoleon when First Consul which is very striking and spirited.

19

January 14, 1836

. . . In the evening went to the Cirque Olympique (Franconi's) and saw the most ludicrous play that was ever invented by human brains. It was one of the Arabian Nights stories dramatized and improved upon and was very prettily got up. It is the tale of the three young princes in search of the greatest wonders to gain a fair princess. One goes to the King of Chess, where the stage is covered with a carpet of enormous checks and a king and queen, knights, pawns (almost Tom Thumbs) and castles, which walk round and stand in proper order, one count arrayed entirely in white, the other in black. Another arrives in a balloon into the Kingdom of Dominoes and plays a game with the Queen before a palace of domino-architecture (quite pretty), using men who, when called, notch themselves on to their companions, to all appearance nothing but gigantic dominoes, the actor being completely incased. The effect was very droll. The third goes to the Card Kingdom, fights a horrible *diable*, dressed like a dandy with flame-colored pants and tail and releases all the Queens of Cards he had shut up in a tower. They each present him with their rose (à l'Allemagne), which finally cures the princess the heroes were striving for. One plays cards with his brother *with the Count*, which was very amusing. Their dresses were so painted and connected with the pasteboard card behind them as to look precisely like a real pack and even the backs were finished in the common style. They shuffled themselves and cut and when tapped on hopped round to display their number. The whole was like a nightmare. Such taste as the French have for such things. The name of this play was *Zazezizozu.* . . .

The next day it was the opera again—this time Robert the Devil:

. . . It was magnificent and terrific and diabolical and enchanting and everything else fine. The music and the show and the dancing!

The famous witch's dance, in the freezing moonlight in the ruined abbey, was as impressive as I expected, though there was no Tagli-oni to lead the troop. They drop in like flakes of snow and are cer-tainly very charming witches with their jaunty Parisian figures and most refined pirouettes! . . . The diabolical music and the dead rising from their tombs and the terrible darkness and the strange dance unite to form a stage effect almost unrivalled. The whole cathedral visible at the end with the organ and worshippers was very grand.

January 17, 1836

We were invited to meet a few Americans at Mrs. Sidgreaves' (sister of Mr. William Lyman), but were so fatigued with the pack-ing that we, with little reluctance, sent a refusal and went instead to the Théâtre Français to see Mademoiselle Mars! [1] We were in the *balcon*, in the first row and next the stage, yet did she appear no more than thirty-six in the first play and in the last still younger and this only from difference of dress! Fifty-nine years she will agree to, but being called ten more in the papers was justly indignant. It is a miracle! Her figure, her manners, her voice are all so youthful, so graceful, so fresh. Her voice particularly is very plaintive and musi-cal and beautifully modulated and treads with dainty feet over the awkward rhymes. Though so near the stage it was delightful to in-spect the costumes—they are so rich and beautiful. There is no putting some mean thing to look like something fine; all is real and true to the age; and somehow or other the actors always resemble in feature the sort of characters they enact. Mademoiselle Mars was brilliant with diamonds. She dresses *fait à ravir*! The audience ap-plauded her as a favorite and at any beautifully modulated sentence we heard many a *"Oh quelle est charmante!"* from our neighbors.

On the same day she records having seen a celebrated diorama.

We saw at last the diorama Madame Jany has been so long extoll-ing. It is most beautiful. There are three pictures: one, the valley of

---

[1] One of the most distingushed French actresses of her time, Anne Françoise Hippolyte Mars (1779–1847) was equally good in comedy and tragedy, in clas-sical and modern plays. She retired from the stage in 1841.

the Goldau, *riante* with summer verdure, surrounded by fine mountains and with two lakes. Gradually darkness falls over it and distant
flashes of heat-lightning appear in the horizon. At last it becomes
quite dark, then a beautiful moonlight beams over it and shows the
scene changed into its present state—the mountain fallen across one
of the lakes and a billowy mass of rocks and earth, people lifting up
their hands with horror in the road which was before empty, etc.
The effect is wonderful, and equally beautiful is the relighting of the
scene till it shines in full day and freshness. Then there is a view of
the Church of St. Etienne (Madame Jany's favorite). It goes through
the same metamorphosis. Twilight darkens to a mysterious dimness
the aisles and galleries; gradually a stream of light bursts from
behind the altar, spreads over the massive columns, and over the
heads of a crowd of worshippers, as if creating them from chaos;
faint tones of the organ are heard, and meanwhile the cold moonlight shines along the upper columns in fine contrast with the light
of the tapers. It is very impressive, and the wondrous changes are
incomprehensible.

January 17, 1836

Our last week in Paris was a very active and bustling one. Every
morning we went to our séance at Isabey's for two hours, which,
though always a tedious operation, was very much enlivened by his
anecdotes and droll remarks. . . . He has nearly finished the heads
and the likenesses are satisfactory and excellent. I sent him locks of
our hair to copy the color. This and the costumes he finishes after
we are gone: we hardly know what they will be but trust everything
to his preeminent taste. Josephine, having remarkably beautiful
shoulders, wished to be painted with her back turned, but as it
would never do to immortalize an empress in that manner, he happily has placed her before a Psyche mirror, where her fine figure is
reflected.

*Through France and Italy, Fanny carried the sensitive eyes and
heart—and the indefatigable pen—of the romantic nineteenth-century traveler. In Rome she deliberately avoided a daylight view of*

the Colosseum, being determined to see it first by moonlight: "Some-
how I cannot feel on what ground I am treading—my mind wants
tutoring by breathing longer the atmosphere of ruins to make the
Past the yesterday of the Present. I am unworthy of Rome and feel
ashamed to come so unprepared on all its wonders." But sound New
England standards of judgment were not forgotten: "I am immensely
disappointed in the modern people of Rome. . . . The women are
hideous and there is a little too much dirt even for picturesqueness."

She did see the Colosseum by moonlight, but it was spoiled for
her by what she considered the frivolity of some of the other mem-
bers of the party.

March 3, 1836

. . . I must say with as much charity as I can muster their pygmy
voices sounded as would apes' in a cathedral. To me it was *desecra-*
tion even here. I can never forget glimpses of wild beauty as the
torches flashed along the huge arches like the glare of fiends beside
the pale, celestial flooding of the clear moonlight, which spiritualized
the big skeleton into an awful majesty, but I did not undertake to
feel where I was, or to enjoy anything I saw. I was all wearied and
disgusted and what might have been an inexhaustible delight became a heavy nightmare. What is there creditable in insulting and
mocking the most solemn sermon ever preached to man? Why are
people ashamed of feeling strongly and deeply? Instead of ridiculing
those that can, how pitiable is the lot of those that are wholly of
"earth earthy." Thank God, I can peep through the clay at times.
Not as the Pharisee say I this, but in sorrow for them, gratitude that
I am endowed with the "folly of feeling."

In May at Florence she sat to Lorenzo Bartolini (1777–1850) for
the marble bust still in the Longfellow House.

May 24, 1836

This morning I took my first séance at Bartolini's. I sit in a high
chair of state while he punches in eyes, nose, and mouth upon a
clay globe—the first rough sketch is already thought quite a likeness.

He is a nice old man, short and broad, with an intelligent, good-natured face and a smile that is full of drollery. He converses delightfully. Got upon Napoleon with the air of a man who has found his hobby. Said he was his sculptor at Elba and elsewhere. Lauded with the greatest enthusiasm his goodness of heart and was certainly original in his notions of his character. . . . Upon Byron his enthusiasm is equally great. . . .

May 28, 1836

. . . Bartolini talked much about Nature and Ideality. Says the former is the only guide—all artists have failed when attempting to portray the latter. "Nature is never ugly. People ask me if they will make a good bust. Everyone will make a good bust, for it is Nature. I wish young artists would never take the antique for models—they are not Nature. Greenough [2] was doing himself much harm by this till I talked it out of him. I hope none of your sculptors will come abroad. Let them copy Nature at home and form a national style!" I could not but laugh. What nature would they take! Indian-nature? Told him the strict notions of the people utterly opposed such things, much afraid sculpture would never flourish with us. . . . He abused all the antique statues in one fell swoop—the Apollo, the Laocoön, the Niobe, etc.—strange notions for a sculptor. Am rather sceptical if he follows Nature so strictly while his exquisite "Nymph of the Arno" and "Nymph extracting a thorn" repose in snowy majesty behind me. . . .

June 1, 1836

Bartolini gave us very amusing anecdotes today of some of the great people whose busts he has made. Madame de Staël, whose vanity (he says), was beyond all rhyme or reason. Her bust was requested for some school in America, so explained that she cheerfully sat thinking it ordered by Government!—also Lady Morgan, whose book we have been reading and can't help screaming over her witty descriptions, though slightly profane at times. Bartolini grasps eagerly every hour I will give but promises this afternoon shall wind up the affair.

[2] Horatio Greenough (1805–1852), American sculptor.

Made our *adieux* to Bartolini with some sadness. He is a nice man and a feeling, and if he does have ugly days and makes me look solemn in clay, why he means well and talks well into the bargain. So I was sorry to look my last on the old red chair and the sweet nymphs and the pale lads hammering eternally for another's fame and all that goodly company of smirking lords and ladies, turned to clay before their time.

. . . a cordial good bye shake of the hand with Mr. Wilde who came to see us off—a farewell "not loud but deep" to our gilt Cupids and Arno-overlooking windows and away we dash over the quaint old shop-excrescenced bridge through the grey swarms of fete-loving people, all staring with open mouth that on such a day there could be mortals leaving Florence. A wave of a white hat in the air and a profound bow fixed my eye gliding over the mass, and Bartolini's kind face beamed in view, looking all regret and good wishes. Swallowed my tears till I reached the hill, where the whole valley with its towers, villas, and vineyards first entrances the eye coming hitherward. . . .

At Thun, in Switzerland, on July 20, Fanny found herself approaching the greatest experience of her life, though she did not know that as yet.

Prof. Longfellow sends up his card to Father. Hope the venerable gentleman won't pop in on us, though I did like his *Outre-Mer*.

She met Longfellow at Interlaken on July 31—"a young man after all," she notes, "or else the son of the poet." The next day she walked and drove with him along Lake Brientz: it was "quiet and lovely." August 2 at Unterseen finds him talking to her about Shelley, Nathaniel Parker Willis, and other poets.

. . . Quoted some poetical conceits of W's; agree that he has many such, but whether inborn flashes or well-polished prettinesses?

If one could separate the man's personal character, so false, so flimsy, from his poetry might admire much more. His best thoughts now seem but affectations, mimicries of other people's best, garnished out his own way.

. . . Have a nice walk in the P.M. with Mr. L to the old bridge, sketch the cloister-spires from a wall, then, on the other side of the river, a dark, picturesque cottage. A nice talk—delicious twilight. Replied to the courteous *"Guten Abend"* of the little children we met; my first German phrase.

On August 3, a sultry dogday, in the "pretty steamer" to Thun: "Mr. L gave us a lesson in German—pretty ballads of Uhland: 'Der Jung König und der Schäferin' and 'Das Schloss am Meer'—simple and touching." This continued through the fourth and fifth, when the party reached Lucerne, and on the sixth she found "Mr. L very inquisitive." Were there strained relations at this point, and is that why Longfellow stayed behind with Fanny's invalid cousin, William Appleton, already within days of his end, when the rest set out on horseback on August 7 for the ascension of the Rigi, or could he not quite brace himself for such exertion even when he was falling in love? In any event they are together on the eighth, when they reach Arth, and all seems well again, though Fanny finds herself "Horribly depressed," which she explains as "a reaction for this morning's delight. Get thinking of the puzzling 'wolf-dens and charnel-houses' in human condition and forget how few hours ago the world was under my feet." They translated "Das Schloss am Meer" together, but found the Muse "very coy. Could find no English word for 'neiderniegen,' which I think so beautiful, conveying to me the graceful motion of a swan's neck." At Zurich, on August 10, she rowed up the lake with Longfellow, William, and her brother Tom.

. . . Glaring sun and sultry atmosphere. John Neal [3] discussed and praised. Feel wilted and weary. Dip hand in water and should like to sink into its depths profound for three days at least to see if that cool blue color would mingle with my exhausted spirit,

[3] (1793–1875), Maine novelist and journalist.

strengthen and cleanse it. How pleasant to be dragged by a boy's kite through cold water "bobbing our noses through the brine" with that lurly, lurly at our throat a boat has! Poor William looks as if he could relish such strengthening processes even better. How can I think of myself while he is growing so feeble daily, so patiently relinquishing the active habits he delights in and breaking our hearts with his self-forgetting thoughtfulness of all about him.

On August 11, at the Corbeau Inn, Longfellow "wrote in the traveller's book these true and jocose admonitions to future victims of this vile inn,

> Beware of the Raven of Zurich!
> 'Tis a bird of omen ill,
> A noisy and an unclean bird,
> With a very, very long bill."

In the carriage between Zurich and Schaffhausen, they read and discussed Hazlitt "on fear of Death." [4] The next day Fanny and Longfellow walked through Schaffhausen together "to hunt up some books to amuse the poor invalid, slippers, etc." Then they "wandered up to a public walk under trees," where they "sat down and had a long talk about Boston, the Liebers, society, and such dull topics." On the fourteenth they both sat with William all morning, and Longfellow read "two beautiful sermons of Dewey's." [5] The same day she listened to Longfellow discussing education and the German universities with Mr. Ticknor, which she found "Quite interesting." Next day they are walking again.

. . . The wind was sweeping through the long avenue of trees in the twilight stillness—the rushing of the river mingled is like a dirge—altogether very sad and autumnal-like, the few leaves already falling. Talked about autumn, which my companion prefers to the rest of the year. So do I for the matter of thinking and the thrilling

---

[4] "On the Fear of Death" is Essay XXXIII in Hazlitt's *Table-Talk*.

[5] Probably Orville Dewey (1794–1882), Unitarian clergyman and writer, of Sheffiield, Massachusetts.

exhiliration of an Autumnal mind, but I know it is not good for me. My mind is too morbid, and I dread delivering myself up to such influences. . . .

August 16, 1836

. . . I sallied forth with Mr. L, walked through the town, saw the same ducks gabbling (scandal perhaps) under their Rialto, crossed the Rhine on an old bridge and sat down on a wall to sketch a Castle-like fortification with the old houses and staircase roofs, the gate with its clock, and the clear, deep blue river sweeping below. Followed a rural road near the river, through mud and mire—a walk is cheering, however, at any time—feel like wet paper or those gelatinous seafish! Mr. L read aloud walking behind me The *Excursion*. Decided it was too ponderous and prosaic a style for all moods, a dose to read much of at a time, like *Paradise Lost*. Got caught in the rain. Stop under a gateway and enter into a discussion on the unpoeticalness of the present and to be state of the world, begun by me, never imagining to be so opposed. He seemed never to have thought of it before. We determined to discuss it fully when our wits were brighter: came home well draggled. . . .

On July 17 this first stage in Appleton-Longfellow relations came to an end, when Longfellow received a letter from Clara Crowninshield "which decides him to leave us immediately as she is out of patience awaiting an escort to America." She had come abroad with Longfellow and his first wife, Mary Potter Longfellow, in April 1835; Mary's death at Rotterdam, on November 29, had left Clara in Longfellow's care; she was, therefore, well within her rights when she sent him this message. Fanny recognized this, but she was "quite sorry to have him go; he has been so kind to William and helped to keep up our spirits. William felt the parting too, knowing it was a final one."

August 18, 1836

Took a walk with Mary round about and up to that lovely promenade, light flickering between the leaves, a delicious air but a freshness Autumnal. Talked about my firm disbelief in a long life and all my feeling thereon (which perhaps it is kinder to keep to myself), and of the happy state of childhood, innocence and ignorance, before the down is rubbed off and the skeleton in all things revealed, and that fiend Doubt become our fireside companion. Experience can best be compared to that dungeon narrowing daily, clipping far-bounding hopes, far-soaring trusts, all Faith almost, and all Joy, till our orbit contracts to a mere squirrel cage and our senses are our only vouchers of truth. Is this to make us relish the more the final, glorious liberty from all cages, that the remembrances that haunt our childhood of better things are thus smirched out for a time? God knows.

August 19, 1836

Miss Mr. L considerably.

On August 24, still at Schaffhausen, William died, and six days later, at Strasburg, Fanny saw Longfellow again, with Clara Crowninshield and the wife and daughter of William Cullen Bryant, for the last time, apparently, before the poet returned to America to assume his duties as Smith Professor of Modern Languages at Harvard.

The first anniversary of their sailing found the Appleton party again in Paris, where they settled down for the winter.

There was less sightseeing now than on the first visit; most of that, as Fanny says, had been "happily 'killed' last winter," but the Parisian theater had not yet palled, and there was a court presentation besides.

November 27, 1836

. . . Saw Taglioni the other night for the first time. It is well that I have seen so much dancing before hers or it would be impossible to appreciate how truly she alone is the goddess of the art. With all others it is effort, well subdued but still effort; with her it seems the breath of life, as if she were born to dance. She floats over the earth like a creature of a rarer element, and you fear, as you gaze at the weaving elasticity of her motion, that she will vanish away like a vapor and ascend to make the clouds her ballroom. All the operatic tricks of pirouetting, etc. she throws in like one of Rossini's flourishes, mere adornments, but the wonderful grace and ease of every motion are her supremacy: she seems indifferent, too, to applause and does not have that horrible plastered smile of all opera dancers. The ballet was beautiful: *La Fille du Danube* and got up with all the splendor and magic of le grand Opera. . . .

January 19, 1837

Notwithstanding our fatigue could not resist the temptation of going tonight to the grand opera to see Taglioni in the *Dieu et la Bayadère*. . . . It is an exquisite opera: the music very pretty and oriental—the scenery the vale of Cashmir, and the story touching. Taglioni was truly supernatural in some parts of her dancing, an inspiration, as Rubini's falsetto in *I Puritani*. She has a trial of skill with her supposed rival, and the first bound brought down a roar of applause. At times she appears to enlarge to a colossal height, her long, thin arms flashing like light, and no marked outline to her figure—rapid and evanescent are attitudes each worthy of being immortalized in marble. Then the unbroken harmony of continued grace in her exquisite walk and pantomimic action; as she flitted round the couch (in the darkness) of her divine lover, she seemed a sudden embodying of the gentle guardian-spirit we fancy watching over us by night. . . .

Some time in January she saw the Countess Guiccioli at a reception.

The Guiccioli is the very personification of all Byron disliked, having the fair complexion of the pallid North he despised and being unquestionably a "dumpy woman"! Light blue eyes, shaded by auburn ringlets, and plump white shoulders worthy of England's blondest maiden. She looks younger than I expected but neither sentimental nor intellectual. Rather sad, however, and care-worn. I could not take my gaze away—so incredible did her vision seem.

February 5, 1837

. . . I thought I had enjoyed the extent of Taglioni's powers in
the *Bayadère* but in that she still clung to earth. As a sylph [in *Les
Sylphides*] she is truly the Ariel Shakespeare conjured. There was
a very pretty contrast between the many Scotch reels and Highland
flings which were danced admirably and her spirit-like motion as
she mingles in their dance, now vanishing up a chimney or through
the wall and ever floating with noiseless feet along. The Sylphide
regions were as lovely nearly in their way as the scenes below the
Danube, the snowy mists rolling over the hoar trunks and the fleecy
sprites sporting in the air (held up, I hope, by very substantial
ropes), rocking in the breezes. Taglioni dances in this a great deal,
many wonderful evolutions. She seems at home in the character.
. . . The death of the Sylphide was very touching; entrapped at last
by the magical scarf, her pretty Psyche wings fall off; she betrays
just enough mortality to confess they were an aid, and drops gently
into the arms of her companions as a flower broken on its stalk and
is then borne aloft by them to be buried in some favorite spot. These
ballets are the best poems the French compose. . . .

*Holland seems to have made no favorable impressions of any kind
on Fanny Appleton. Leaving the country, she sums up (May 1, 1837)
in imitation of Voltaire's alliteration:* "Ducks, dabbling in ditches,
dribbling damps and dikes, dank dirty domiciles, dusty dams, disgusting dreary dullness, and dolefully drowsy drouthy drinking dolts
of Dutchmen!"

If the "dirty domiciles" might be questioned be it known Dutch
cleanliness is all on the outside of the platter! They expend all their
time in scrubbling the frontispiece, like the Pharisees. . . . Napkins
at breakfast never given! Pipes as common as windmills. "Schnapps"
muddy their brain to the consistency of their canals, and living
almost in a sty how could they exist if their humanity was not utterly
merged into a swinish condition, without some show of the water in
useful purposes in which they are nearly drowned? Truly, however,
there is "water water everywhere and not a drop to drink," for Eau

de Seltz is a necessary substitute for their thick, deleterious water. Everything around them goes by wind or water, "slaves of the lamp," and they themselves go amphibiously—one foot on land, one on sea—human steamboats, with a pipe for a chimney and as lumbering in form. No more abuse.

Whatever failure of sympathy may have prevailed here, the situation was quite different when she reached London.

May 4, 1837

. . . Sat all the morning at the window, amused with the constant panorama of passing objects. Curious cabs, with the driver boxed up at one side; splendid equipages with every shade of livery—such neatness in their attire and such sleek glossy steeds; quaint vehicles, like trunks on wheels; ambulating *affiches*—blue-coat boys and "London cues"—all from my childhood's picture books; Punches and wandering minstrels beyond number; an old lady in a genteel barouche buying cauliflowers at a grocery opposite; a damsel sauntering up and down in anxious expectation—"hi! ho! for somebody"—a romantic conjecture amuses me. "Somebody" comes! after a hope deferred a half hour—a nice dapper youth. Ah! she smiles! she has his arm! and off they go "happy as griggs." Now a dashing chariot drives up, the rattat-tat of the brass knocker on the green door bespeaking a visitor. Such beautiful horses! but such toilettes of the visitors! They enter, and in the doorway the spruce footman stands flirting with the buxom chambermaid. What scandal of mistress and master they are exchanging! The soldiers with their neat white pants and scarlet coats enliven the streets much. There goes a fair lady with a flamingo fellow at her heels carrying her purchases. What is the use of those formidable batons the footmen lean on the carriage roof? Dined so *à l'Americaine*—goose and apple sauce and gooseberry tart—that we thought ourselves at Aunt Sam's! How completely everything is changed from the Continent to the smallest minutiae of everyday life. But it comes naturally to us, as native customs. Took a stroll with Tom through St. James Square and along the striking arcades of the Quadrant and the noble sidewalk of Regent Street.

But when she attended an exhibition at the British Gallery, English elegance did not appeal to her.

May 5, 1837

. . . *Quel spectacle* of horrible toilettes! No bad orchestra could jar my nerves with a more painful sensation of discord than such an array of monstrosities in the way of costume. Colors wedded together as inimical as vinegar and honey—all rules of "the unities" disregarded—artificial flowers more fantastically garnishing these plain commonplace visages than Ophelia's mad garlands, and such ill-fitted, ill-made, tastelessly-designed robes! Alas for eyes fresh from Parisian elegance! What are splendid mansions and wealth if such taste masks fair forms and deforms all hidden fascination. . . .

May 8, 1837

. . . Very much amused in the evening at Madame Vestris' charming little theater. . . . The inimitable Liston acted with infinite drollery in two pieces—*A Peculiar Position* and *The Two Figaros*—both very amusing and very well supported by very nice actresses, but not worthy of his powers. He is a fleshy, cumbersome man, with a broad gelatinous phiz which mirrors every expression with astonishing ease. A quiet, straightforward simplicity of humor marks his acting, which could only be appreciated by near inspection, if at all in his droll leers, which electrify the audience into laughter before he opens his mouth. Charles Mathews is rather clever. It seemed very strange to hear English again on the stage, more pleasing at this theater, as it is very much in the French style, each part well supported. Madame Vestris, its "fat, fair, and sixty?" manager, acted very charmingly in the last piece—nothing else than *The Rape of the Lock*, dramatized out of half its poetry and more of its amiability. However, it is beautifully got up and sylphides float in the air with as much grace, if not in such numbers as at the Grand Opera. The dresses are very rich and much spice of wit. The fair Belinda, with her two immortal locks as long as a Bashaw's "two tails" was made merely a fine lady—spiteful and malicious as the gnomes of the spleen could wish, whose court was here a most unpoetical reality. A dozen steel-cold imps, yclept our friends "the blue devils," looking like certain blue beetles, kept in very unearthly attitudes, while as many gnomes carried off a store of lachrymals, pouting vials, etc. to bestow on fair womenkind. Pasteboard clouds, rather too near earth or one's eyes, but on the whole a pretty spectacle. . . .

Fanny Kemble was in London at this time, and inevitably became an important part of Fanny's visit there.

May 11, 1837

. . . In the evening to a very delightful party at her father's house in Park Place. . . . On one ottoman reposed the superannuated limbs, supporting the benign face crowned with a halo of snowy locks, of that "nice old man" (as all the ladies designated him), Rogers the poet, whose own *Pleasures of Hope* must be merged in *Pleasures of Memory,* for his days are nearly run apparently. In a crimson velvet dress and hat, under which protruded an ominous black beaver like a domino, sat Lady Morgan, whose eyes require this blinder, rather becomingly shading her full Irish cheeks. In a fauteuil by the fire lolled a beautiful girl, Miss Macdonald, with the Norman blackness of hair picturesquely adjusted, whose dark eyes sought her shoestring 'neath the piercing gaze of the ferocious Corsair Trelawney at her side. He is a ruffian-looking man, with wild mustache, shaggy eyebrows, and orbs beneath them that have the gimlet property beyond any I ever encountered. It was droll we should meet him here. I was somewhat disappointed in the beauty of Mrs. Lister, who entered late on her husband's arm—a tall man, a very pale, finely-chiselled countenance, haggard with dissipation or ill health. She was dressed cumbersomely, fantastically, but not in good taste—small, agreeable features but no beauty. The treat of the evening, beside gazing at "lions," was the delicious singing of Miss Kemble,[6] whose voice has more music in it than almost any amateur singer's I remember. She sings with great ease and spirit, and her intelligent face lights up into fine expressions, quite inspired. Mrs.

[6] Fanny Kemble's sister Adelaide, known after her marriage as Adelaide Sartoris.

Butler's rich bass voice ascends, as second, delightfully. A fine picture hung over my head of Mrs. Siddons [7] and Mrs. Butler together, and a noble head opposite of Mr. Kemble,[8] who is a very handsome man, I think, with very gentlemanly manners. . . . Old Rogers made up to me, mistaking me for an acquaintance.

May 24, 1837

The birthday of the heiress of the British Throne, the fair Victoria. A future Queen Bess mayhap, of unlovely memory. Incredible that such a people as this could ere have been ruled by a woman's hand. . . . Their Majesties are both so ill there is no knowing how soon "Long live Queen Victoria" may resound in these sooty regions.[9] Hers is "a most interesting situation" say all the Tabbies. Health and happiness to the English Rose Bud!

May 25, 1837

In the evening Mrs. Butler's weekly soirée; another amusing chat with Trelawney, who persecutes me with drawing analogies between Mrs. Butler and my poor self. . . . Mr. Kemble entertained us with reading several scenes from *Hamlet,* which was a treat indeed. He gave the character a plaintive charm I shall never forget, and rendered several hackneyed passages in an original way. *Par exemple,* Hamlet's adjuration to the Ghost—"I will call thee Hamlet" (naturally), "King" (with majesty and respect), "Father" (with touching pathos)—then a pause making this of course the climax, though it is generally read as if "royal Dane," which commences the next sentence, finaled this. Much pleased also with the inexpressible sorrow in his tone when speaking of his mother's marriage, instead of the scorn and irony usually intermingled, so derogatory to the gentleness and feeling of his disposition. The ghost's part was exquisitely read, in a faint, weak, unimpassioned tone, fading away at the "remember me" like the vanishing of a vapor, so much truer than the tone so awful, meaning to freeze everybody's blood as well as Hamlet's with which he is made to groan forth his dismal tale.

[7] Sarah Siddons (1755–1831), the most famous English actress, Fanny Kemble's aunt.

[8] Perhaps Fanny Kemble's uncle, the actor Charles Kemble (1775–1854).

[9] It followed in less than a month.

May 26, 1837

Had an amusing goose chase in the evening after the mansion of
Lady Morgan, thereby growing more modest as to my bump of
locality. Her one small salon and smaller bedroom were filled with
a variety of curious people, several "great" and mostly foreign. She
lamented we were so late as the diplomats had all gone. She herself
ran about like the fairy Cricri in her hat and plumes and dress of a
nuance as "deeply, darkly, beautifully blue" as her inner clothing,
laying on her flattery in Rubens colors sufficiently as a bait to exact
the *golden rule* evidently adjuring the Sybil to be a lady of ton,
malgré her dumpy figure. Irish physiognomy and most anglicized
French. . . . Mrs. Butler picturesque in a gold turban. She and her
sister sing with great effect that hundredth-told tale, "The Leaf and
the Fountain." The "fountain answered no" with an awful solemnity
which admitted of no further parleying.

May 30, 1837

. . . Westminster Abbey surpassed all my dreams: they have been
of the most imaginative texture. . . . It is a noble, old picturesque
pile, full of quaint nooks and corners and a middle-aged spirit. . . .
The long-drawn aisles soar up with a loftiness unsurpassed by any
Gothic temple I have seen, and the fretted lacework of the roof is of
a beauty "all its own." . . .

As a fine feudal effect I much admired this array of antique banners yet waving over the seats of their lords in Henry VII's chapel,
each with its arms and device, a fragile memorial of all their greatness. . . . These tombs are too crowded, particularly Mary and
Elizabeth's, each reposing, one in her beauty (though with very few
fingers left!), the other in her ugliness, carrying her emblems of rule
and coarse vanity even to the tomb. Vile are these wax-mockeries
visitors are shown, unbefitting a church, and a horror anywhere. . . .

*Fanny's interest in the Princess Victoria has already been referred
to. But when she saw her, on June 1, with her mother, the Duchess
of Kent, she was greatly disappointed.*

. . . The Duchess a fine-looking woman towering in plumes, but
alas! for England's future queen, whatever else, beauty is not her

dower—a short, thick, commonplace, stupid-looking girl, dressed simply in white with a wreath of roses, without even a good complexion! Perhaps it is a royal distinction to be plain where there is so much loveliness; natheless I was grievously disappointed.

A week later London was left behind for the native stamping grounds of the Appletons in West Suffolk.

June 8, 1837

Turned our horses' heads early to the Waldingfields great and small. Little did I once think that to these spots of childish reverence I should ever live to make a pilgrimage! About three miles from Sudbury we passed a scattered village and arrested our course at the very walls of the picturesque little church of Great Waldingfield. Around this we perambulated, till a shrill-voiced old woman unlocked the door. We reverently entered, beneath our feet the ashes of the most ancient heads of the illustrious family of the Appletons! Small and neat within but no record or monument left. . . .

From hence we drove over to the most satisfactory place of the two, Little Waldingfield, a more flourishing village, and the church that cuts such a dignified figure in our library. . . .

Here we found the veritable rustic sexton, or "church warden," as he dignifies himself, who assisted Uncle E in all his researches and remembered him perfectly. The family concerns seemed quite at his tongue's end, and he showed us . . . the quaint old chest hooped with iron, containing, he says, all the wills of the Appletons, and opposite it, suspended high from the wall, a trophy which stirred up more interest than I ever yet took pains to cherish for the worthy pilgrims. This is a musty helmet covered with a leathern jerkin, of most antique mustiness, surmounted by something very like a coronet and this by three pine apples which I am inclined to believe are the proper arms of the family. These belonged to Sir Isaac Appleton. How strange a history, thought I, that such a space should rear itself between their graves and those of their children, and that we should come as Strangers to gaze upon these relics, sole links to our original domain. If fate had not driven them into exile where and how might we be living now? Here in this rural quiet? A fine proof here how long good deeds survive all of the giver but his name perchance. On fresh tablets here is yet inscribed the charitable donations of some former Appletons, "to be continued forever!" What an earthly immortality in such an injunction! . . .

The twelfth of June found Fanny at Oxford.

Much pleased with the quaint, musty antiquity of the famous Bodleian Library, with its low, curiously-carved roof, old volumes convenient, paled in recesses, like pens for seclusion and study. Quaint old portraits but of these an especially good array in the picture gallery attached. A particularly pathetic one of Charles I, with very melancholy eyes, as if his destiny was therein writ. Charles II wild haired as usual. A spirited full-length of Charles XII. But the gem here is a most exquisite portrait of Mary Queen of Scots, softly painted and satisfying all one's wishes of the winning loveliness of her who wore the crown of beauty and sorrow, as full of thorns as the diadem of her rival. Infinite sweetness in the small mouth and dove-like eyes, and nothing can be more perfect than the chiselled oval of the face. The cap and puffed chemisette evidently fresh in taste from a French artiste. . . .

Two days later she set down her impressions of a Stratford-on-Avon catering to the tourist trade much less efficiently than it does today!

A worse than Italian breakfast. Amazed to find Shakespeare's house one of this mean, dirty street, so wedged in it would be unseen were it not for a large, swinging sign, "This is the birthplace of the immortal Shakespeare," staring one full in the face. The butcher's board and steel hooks for meat hanging from the ceiling of his ancestors and even successors gave me a more startling evidence than I ever before thought of how genius entering into a man like a separate spirit ennobles and liberates him from lowness of condition, ignorance (that is of things that men teach), and all the vulgarity of tastes in mind and body which his own kin may have possessed for generations and whose blood may resume its common proper ties in his successors, unbiased by this meteor flash of greatness in its current. In him, being greater than other men, this seems more miraculous, as if God willed that at such a time such an oracle should appear on earth and chose, as in the case of His beloved son, an humble peasant's body for the tenement of this spark of heavenly fire. Shakespeare shows such an unearthly sense of all refinement and all character that his condition had no influence upon the texture of his mind; he was beyond all such influences. This brings me to what I often think of—whether lack of education and the weight of a low and miserable position ever encases, like the diamond in its rock, genius, so that it never sees the light. If it was given only to unfold its wings in heaven, and thus wasted on earth? This is meddling with the riddles of the sphinxes, an unprofitable and reprehensible business. . . .

Charmed with the church and its sweet neighborhood—a pretty green bower leading thereto and the modest graveyard overlooking peaceful meadows, and the silver Avon winding gracefully along. The country about is charming and reconciled me to the town. . . .

The party continued to Warwick Castle, Kenilworth, Birmingham, Lichfield, and other points of interest. On June 20 she recorded the pleasure she took in Hardwicke Hall because of its association with Mary Queen of Scots.

. . . It stands with its lantern-like frontispiece of windows in the Elizabethan quaintness in a stiff garden, the box cut in mammoth letters "E.S.," Elizabeth of Salisbury being its patroness. In the hall admired a lovely statue of Mary Stuart, this being one of her many prisons, by Westmacott. Fancied to see her gliding about the musty apartments in that graceful dress, but she was confined in an adjoining building, now an ivy-weathered ruin.

She also found

. . . Many shocking portraits of Mary here. One in black, the pale, haggard face full of suffering. How unlike the sweet, joyous treasure of Oxford, when love was young and Darnley kind.

The Byron country came next. "No wonder Byron inhaled misanthropic notions, bred in such a dreary vicinity" (June 21). In the Wordsworth country (June 28), Fanny showed such a discriminating sense of the poet's greatness and influence that it is hard to remember that she is writing during his lifetime.

. . . Passed the entrance to Wordsworth's eyrie without entering as he is far away. Long afterwards, as his fame is waxing daily greater, and when he is dead, it will be one of the pilgrimages all will feel bound to make. However, all this vicinity is the mirror of his mind and all linked with him in love; he is the gentle interpreter which stamps these sweet lakes with fame eternal.

The next day she met Southey.

A call after breakfast from Southey and his daughter. He a tall spare man in grey checked pants, with rather a stiff manner and a fine halo of grey hair. Features strong and striking. She quiet and somewhat old maidish. Walked to their villa, prettily buried in trees, overlooking the valley, bridge, and strip of lake, with a very unpicturesque foreground of white houses. Had a very pleasant chat in the library. Talked of his poem on the Indians he is yet writing. . . .

At Abbotsford, on June 30, it was, alas, too late to meet Scott but nobody can deny that Fanny communed with him in spirit.

June 30, 1837

Through Teviotdale, wide and rural, then the broad, placid Tweed. Suddenly descend from the road through newly-planted shrubbery and emerge at once upon all the turrets and towers of modern Abbotsford, hid in trees from the road, and so scant in park that our expectancies were taken aback by its sudden appearance. Well designed and finely executed without though too new in color. A statue of the Magician's-fidus-Acaetes-Meda guards the portal of this mimic castle. How truly filled with the spirit of Him is the noble entrance hall, a medley of chivalric glory in the picturesquely-grouped, choicely-selected armor, an iron tapestry to the walls of oak, and hearty national pride in the array of national emblems, like his own mind, as some one has well said, "a romance bound in stone and mortar"! A fine, ample fireplace here, carved about with the designs from Melrose Abbey, so graceful and various, etc. etc. In a little closet hard by, the great Magician was summoned before our senses with a magical reality. Here hung the clothes he daily wore, with the last mortal stains upon them—the large white hat, the grey, farmer-like coat, gaiters, thick shoes, and the stout cane which has so often supported his manly steps or propped his chin in meditation. Interesting relics full of his presence, more sacred than the gilded armor of kings. The reverence and gratitude all must feel here not only for the happiness he has conferred, the brightening of many a weary hour, the realities he has made of the gorgeous or barbarous pageants of the past, the living phantoms he has raised of female and heroic excellence which will remain forever like the high watermarks of Shakespeare are proofs, notwithstanding the efforts of his undervaluers to disenchant his magic influence over men's hearts, that his fame will outlive his century. . . . The library is perhaps the most interesting room in the house: here is the source of that ever-bubbling fountain whose sparkling, rainbow-illuminated waters, have refreshed so many pilgrims, have run to the remotest corners of the earth, shining with the golden sands of one of the most fertile and perfect imaginations which ever stole Promethean fire and created anew humanity. Upon this green baize table were written all the novels; here worked that mighty loom; here were completed those immortal fabrics like the tapestries of old moving with the shadowy forms of gigantic heroes, shrouding the ghosts of past centuries, the fair gliding spectres that once drew breath with pain.

The bust by Chantrey is very inspired: Sir Walter with his best look, as the old woman-cicerone said, for often his heavily-moulded features gave a dull expression when not speaking. Skull "dome of thoughts" like Shakespeare's, but as St. Peter's to St. Sophia's, narrower and higher. The drawing room is a very handsome room with richly-carved ceiling, deep, castle-like windows, etc. Spirited portrait of Miss Scott in Spanish dress. Thought like me about the eyes. Every nook here is crammed with something curious, a museum of antique, chiefly Scotch relics. Rob Roy's gun and purse, *par exemple*, etc. In the dining room pretty landscapes by Turner in water colors, a shocking portrait of Mary Queen of Scots, taken with her head after decapitation, the pallid features just stiffening into death, the flesh starting from the beautiful lips, and the throat all mangled and gory—an awful but impressive *memento mori* of the finale of beauty and highest power. Yet there is a placid resignation on the fast-changing features which tells of blessed repose after prolonged suffering. It is almost less sad to me than the one at Hardwicke, pale with the trials of an unaccomplished destiny. Also a portrait of Nell Gwynn here, and Sir Walter's great grandfather's, who never allowed his beard to be cut after the Pretender's defeat, a sturdy loyalty fast dying from men's hearts. . . .

Some very good caricatures from his family history, illustrating savage border times. One in which the housewife is lifting the dish-cover and displaying under the hungry eyes of the robber-chieftains naught but a pair of well-polished spurs as a gentle hint they must ride for their supper, the last foray's provender being exhausted. Another very ludicrous in which a hapless youth is to choose between a hideously deformed bride with fiery hair and a halter, his indecision and grotesque misery to impale himself on either horn of the dilemma well hit off.[10]

A rich half hour in this modern castle filled with the atmosphere of the past. Took leave of it and the old woman who seemed to love her ci-devant master with regret and drove thence to Melrose town, a small, ill-built hamlet on the Tweed. Hunted up immediately the Abbey.

Disappointed to find it choked up so near other walls, losing, thereby, the beautiful, picturesque setting of English ruins. A very knowing guide . . . showed it off with long-coined eloquence, and pointed out the very stone where Sir Walter usually sat, and where he amused Moore by declaring that though his words "If you would visit fair Melrose aright," etc. had brought every cockney there by

[10] The subject of Browning's poem, "Muckle-Mouth Meg."

moonlight, he himself had never ventured then for fear of rheumatism, but knowing it by heart in daylight could so truly describe how the moon would fall on pavement and wall. It is a small ruin after Fountains but exquisitely finished, the grace and carving of the designs unrivalled, everything in the form of vegetation, as Sir Walter paints with such lovely truth. Saw tomb of Michael Scott and Douglas. Beautiful cloisters, few arches, near gate where William of Deloraine "knocked so long and knocked so late." Ascended tower on broken stairway; fine view from graveyard. Have such an owl-like love of broken arches, shattered columns, shadows of waning moon rather than full, etc. instead of complete finished things. Not very promising taste of my nature, when we are taught to press forward to perfection and despite decaying incompleteness in mind or matter. . . .

On July 1 she is meditating over Mary again, this time at Holy-rood.

"Within the golden circle of a crown Death holds his court And there the hollow antic sits grinning at state," as Shakespeare magnificently says and I badly quote. This is the most melancholy place I ever visited in every way. Rizzio's dying groans still seem to echo through the desolate chambers. From Mary's private chapel we saw the staircase where ascended the murderers, saw too in her antechamber the supposed bloodstains of the unfortunate Italian, her dreary bedchamber with its musty tapestry and hearse-like state bed, the small mirror in which she beheld her charms and where I hoped to catch a shadow of her features, not my own; these associations are so startling but so difficult to seize as realities. There is too an exquisite little miniature of her but it was hard to believe that a creature of such grace, beauty, and rank ever dwelt in these gloomy apartments. . . . In the little closet beyond, where that fatal supper took place, and which we should hardly think roomy enough for a dog kennel, is the armor of Darnley and picture of Rizzio. Recalled that horrible murder, such an outrage before a woman and a queen and felt oppressed with the charnel-like atmosphere and such remembrances.

On the same day the Burns monument inspires this:

. . . On this steep pinnacle of rock stands Burns in marble, well placed to gaze perpetually on the landscapes to which he has given a heart and soul, and well pedestaled for the up-gazing love and respect of his countrymen. From the fields where his ploughshare is rusting he has climbed alone such an Olympus, and there he should rest his labors over above the "carking cares" which fretted away his noble, honest soul, in the clear atmosphere of his *best* thoughts, such as we love to remember, such as were the true inspirations of the Divinity, not promptings of the evil one who struggled hard to possess him wholly. Let the latter die with what of him was of the earth earthy.

Fanny's sojourn in Europe was drawing rapidly to a close. In August she records:

We remained about ten days in London, seeing new sights and old friends. Among the former the *entrée* to the Queen's first "drawing-room." That is, not caring to be presented in this time of *deuil*, we procured tickets for a kind of anteroom gallery through which all the fair ladies passed in their way to the reception-room; so we really saw each one better than if in the midst of the melée. A mournful procession it was, the crape trains and bugles and unrelieved black of the dresses masking the beauty which is usually resplendent with plumes and jewels. So strict was the costume that one poor damsel who ventured upon a white underskirt, though otherwise sufficiently crow-like, was sent back to change her dress before she could be admitted.

They sailed from Portsmouth, on the Quebec, *and enjoyed "a very fair passage of just a month, with little bad weather. Lunar rainbows and most gorgeous sunsets, especially as we neared America." They landed at New York. "Thus ends this glorious dream of two years' travel, but better than a dream, leaving us with minds and hearts enriched for life—a possession time can never destroy!"*

CHAPTER III

Early Womanhood and a Long Courtship

Though Fanny Appleton did not know it at the time, one incident in her European sojourn had determined the course of all the rest of her life. The years 1837–1843 were the last of her maindenhood. They were years of mingled hope and despair for Longfellow, and perhaps for her too, more than the records indicate, and possibly more than she herself realized at the time.

The records for the first year back in America are neither abundant nor significant, and it is fitting that we should take the story up again in the late summer of 1838, when Fanny's letters from the familiar Berkshires show at least that her long visit to Europe had not disqualified her for the enjoyment and appreciation of her native land.

To Emmeline Austin

Lenox, Mass., September 5, 1838

. . . We are sojourning for a week at this quiet little village, having left our kith and kin at Pittsfield to enjoy the society of our friends the Sedgwicks and are now sharing with Mrs. Butler parlor and board—(our beds and dinners could both come under that head)—at a staring brick hotel with Grecian columns in front, looking forth, however, on a noble sweep of hill beyond hill, steeped just now in an Italian mist and clothed in as fresh a green as June. I am enjoying myself excessively, for it is a rare good fortune to be in the constant influence of such rich minds and noble hearts as our friends here are gifted withal. Miss Sedgwick—or my own Aunt Kitty, as she is always called—you know I am enthusiastically fond of. She always seems to me a female St. John, breathing forth, on all who come near her, an atmosphere of goodness and love that is irresistibly winning and heart-warming. All the children great and small run to her ever open arms as to a sanctuary, and there is no human creature she will not bless with some corner of her great heart. Her noble qualities of mind are forgotten beside these divine capacities of heart, and she herself seems to forget them, her extreme simplicity of manner being one of her most striking gifts. More and more does she wind round your heart-strings, adapting herself to the feelings of every age and mood beyond any person I ever saw. You asked me to write about her; it is difficult for one to write or think about anything else when in her neighborhood. Thus go the days: About nine, Mary and I emerge from our straw couch into the breakfast room, where we find Mrs. Butler *en robe de chambre* ready to sit down with us. . . . Then, having performed her maternal duties, [she] arrays herself in her riding costume—white pants (*tout à fait à la mode des messieurs*) and habit, with a black velvet jacket and cap, very picturesque, and when mounted on her own fine steed a picture that puts Miss Sedgwick in raptures. She bends to every motion with such grace and perfect control of a sufficiently fiery quadruped. Either Mary or Kate accompany her, and I usually go walk—yesterday such a one with Aunt Kitty, through sun-chequered woods to a rocky precipice, a wide valley at our feet and pine woods at our back! Then we dine on whatever the charity of our landlord assigns us. . . . Then drives or walks infinite in number and beauty hereabouts lure us out, and the evening usually is passed at Mrs. Sedgwick's, Mrs. Butler always in white muslin, bare arms and neck if it be cold as November, charming us with singing old ballads with a thrilling pathos, and such nervous excitement herself that she often turns cold as marble for a few moments after dancing the *cachucha* with castanets, and great spirit of discoursing on deep topics, with an earnestness and far-reaching intelligence which kindles her face to wonderful shiftings beyond any countenance I ever saw. Her soul seems always boiling at fever-heat, and she reminds me in her various accomplishments and brilliant expressions of some gypsy Fenella.[1] There is surely some southern, un-Saxon blood in her veins. Such a German story she told the other night, that sent us all shuddering home in the moonlight to our

[1] Probably in Scott's *Peveril of the Peak*.

beds. . . . Little Dr. Holmes we met t'other day in Pittsfield, and he was raving about the country here, owning a fine farm near there, on the river too, so he was planning rowing adown it to make me a visit! . . .

A November letter to Fanny's cousin contains some interesting references to the keen contemporary interest in phrenology.

To Isaac Appleton Jewett

Boston, November 15, 1838

. . . What you say about discontent, if spoken truthfully, annihilates your previous argument and all such others about the immortality of the soul—out of your own mouth are you judged—for what is this "restless longing" but a proof that we are worthy of another existence, which you once denied. Go straight to the glass, or feel if the top of your skull is flat and narrow—a deficiency of veneration and hope may explain this idea. No, it was but a hallucination, for your veneration I predict is large . . . and your hope was so in Europe, ever looking more forward than back, but it seems to have sunk down of late, marvelously. . . . Or is there some density in American atmosphere that crushes these aspiring faculties, spreading out so frightfully below acquisitiveness and combativeness. This last has been raging under the elections with a *fiume* worthy of the Middle Ages, in spite of Mr. Combe's complacent theory that the upper tier of the brain is expanding in every successive age, so that future poets will think the "dome of reason" pure prophecy on Byron's part. I am looking at everything now phrenologically, for six hours every week for a month have we been floating in Golgothean theories under Mr. Combe's dry, logical, Scotch teaching.[2] Very entertaining I have found these lectures; nay much more exciting and marvelous thoughts do I owe them about the mental, moral, and physical structure than ever before made my

[2] The reference is to George Combe (1788–1858), Scottish phrenologist. He published his recollections of, and observations on, his American visit in three volumes, *Notes on the United States of North America* (1841).

acquaintance. . . . His last lecture about mental education, betraying the abominable way children are abused and misunderstood should be thundered through New England and written on the wall of every schoolhouse therein. . . .

I have just laid on the shelf Prescott's most interesting history; what a woman and what days! am now in Bishop or Cardinal de Cheverus' [3] saint-like life and looking askance at Franklin's. Shall resume Carlyle [4] now the weather admits of jostling, without suffocation, the "greasy multitude" and an atmosphere of blood and powder. . . .

During the next year, 1839, Fanny's writing was very extensive, and only selections can be given here.

To Isaac Appleton Jewett

April 15, 1839

. . . Mr. Prescott, our historian, is a character you could not find in the old world. A compound of scholar, wit, angel, and child, as full of simplicity, truth, and guilelessness as these last, with an ever-bubbling fountain of playfulness, thought, and fancy, and yet, though looking at all things through half an eye, with the certainty of utter blindness in two years, grasping assiduous subjects, toiling through musty manuscripts, ever writing in a machine, so that for years he has not watched his own handwriting, and always, at home, in the gloomy influence of blue-curtained windows, yet sunny and cheerful and resigned to his fate as if his future were as bright as his handsome face and true soul. . . .

I am glad you like Mrs. Jameson. Has she not a graceful, refined, truly feminine mind? But Corinth[ian], not Doric, and you men don't see that one has often as solid a foundation as the other, but I think it is true, in a measure, that her fancy moulds her thought. I think she has a true, warm, Irish heart, *think*, only, because I have been taught to believe there is so much humbug in the world that

[3] Jean Louis Anne Madeleine Lefebvre de Cheverus (1768–1836), French prelate, who in 1808 became the first Roman Catholic bishop of Boston.
[4] Evidently *The French Revolution*.

outward signs are but will o' the wisps. Is not this a Cain-like office,
this slow poison, doubt, men and women of the world . . . so love
to adminster? . . .

To Matilda Lieber [5]

May 5, 1839

. . . I have launched into the German ocean with Dr. Follen [6] for
pilot, and sorry enough am I that their departure for the country has
cut short our lessons. I shall get on the rocks if I try to steer along
much now, but I keep in pretty safe water, reading simple ballads
and the like. I am charmed with the simplicity of some of the words
and the conciseness of expression in poetry—and the poetical com-
binations—but the terminations of nouns and adjectives appall me. If
I can make some head way in reading, writing and speaking I resign
as a Gordian knot I could neither cut or unravel.

We are just now feasting our eyes and souls with a collection of
nearly all Allston's pictures—the glorious fruit of a great poetic mind,
and nearly everyone who appreciates art marvels that we have such
a one among us in this age of the world. Not even Raphael, I think,
could show a greater diversity of styles, or more perfect power to
handle every subject. And these pictures are not mere bald *truths;*
each one is a poem, writ by a true poet, an artist who has mag-
netized to colors and canvass more ideal beauty, thought, and expression than almost any other I remember even among the mighty
of the past. . . . Allston dined with us some time since, and we
ladies heroically sat through all the cigar smoke till midnight to hear
him tell ghost stories and discuss art. He is a noble old man. . . .

To Emmeline Austin

Stockbridge, Mass., June 19, 1839

. . . Mary (mention it not in Gath) has been deeply studying
Mary Woollstonecraft's *Rights of Women* and I trust is now satisfac-

---

[5] Wife of Francis Lieber (1800–1872), well-known German-American liberal,
historian, and political economist.
[6] Karl Follen (1795–1840), German refugee patriot, professor of German at
Harvard until he was discharged in 1836 for his antislavery agitation, and
Unitarian minister at Lexington.

torily assured what they are. I don't wish to be more discontented with my condition than at present, so rather dread peeping at the bars. What I have read was written with noble eloquence and I should think full of much useful matter for weak, silly women. I don't see as yet why the book should be held in such abomination. Miss Fuller's *Conversations with Goethe* I have also been enlightening myself with, but it is hard to read with so much unwritten poetry about one. . . .

To Isaac Appleton Jewett

July 30, 1839

Most hearty thanks, good coz, first for the welcome literary food you have so bountifully been to market for—good solid Carlylean sirloins and piquante Boz *entremets,* which I hope won't give us mental indigestion after our thin dilutions of newspaper broth, and next for your letters. . . . Carlyle . . . I reserve, not being exactly in the mood for his profundity. . . . Yesterday I skimmed over some of Boz' sketches, reading aloud to Mary in wicked defiance of the brook's more musical voice, thus recalling thoughts of the harsh, sadly-comical parts men act, which good Dame Nature has been teaching me to forget here for my soul's good. . . . I shall beg leave to decline the honor of accepting *Pickwick* if that brobdingnag-display of my Christian name on the blank page implies it is for me, for, frankly, I don't want it, having the English edition at home, sanctified by the fresh laughs impressed, like dried flowers, between every leaf, at the then fresh jokes, read in London and all across the Atlantic. . . .

Longfellow was in love with Fanny Appleton from the time of their meeting in Europe but she did not accept him until 1843. This would not be the place to tell the story of that long wooing, even if it were completely known, which it is not; see the present writer's Longfellow: A Full-Length Portrait *(Longmans, Green, 1955), Chapter XVI. It seems clear, however, that Longfellow played his cards badly, and especially that he offended Fanny by describing her and his affection for her in his novel,* Hyperion, *referred to in the following letter.*

To Emmeline Austin

August 9, 1839

. . . Jewett . . . met the Professor in New York, who civilly sent us a copy of his *Hyperion,* and a rank Swiss cheese! which Mr. Charles S says testifies his admiration, as strong and as disagreeable! There are really some exquisite things in this book, though it is desultory, objectless, a thing of shreds and patches like the author's mind. The type and cool cover are fascinating; then the style is infinitely polished and sparkling with many beautiful poetical *concetti,* for his scholastic lore and vivid imagination create infinite comparisons, very just and well carried out. Some of these tickle my bump of comparison vastly, *par exemple* calling a glacier (its various branches from one center being very like the fingers of a glove) a gauntlet which winter has thrown down and which the sun vainly tries to raise on the point of his glittering lance. The hero is evidently himself, and he sticks ludicrously to certain particulars which will proclaim it sufficiently to annoy him, I should think. The heroine is wooed (like some persons I know have been) by the reading of German ballads in her unwilling ears, and the result is equally natural in both cases! The adventures have not the same zest of novelty to us as to other people, as we have had the misfortune to be behind the scenes, seen the decorations without the advantages of footlights. Many of his old ideas, old lectures, etc. have been fused into these graceful chapters, which is fair enough—a pity they should achieve their destiny solely by enlightening the dull brains of college boys or scornful maidens. . . . The title is cousin *German* to the book, but certainly has no natural relationship. For there are more shadows than sunshine therein—probably given as some of our towns are christened, from the necessity of some name. . . .

(Journal)

Stockbridge, Mass., August 25, 1839

. . . Read aloud the whole of Ecclesiastes and had some new thoughts thereupon. Always felt it before the unhealthy confession of a sated sensualist, sighing for new pleasures and vexed that the old were so rapidly exhausted, but now it seems to me one of the saddest revealings in human nature—a great, wise, far-seeing, far-thinking soul, yearning, Faust-like, after the key of all mysteries, but touching everywhere nothing but the grave and annihilation, sitting down in the dust in utter hopelessness and "vexation of spirit" . . . because . . . all his vast superiority to the herd he teaches, all his innate and imperative longings after immortality are crushed by the black, noisome, impenetrable glooms of the sepulchre, illumined as yet by no star of hope and not one revelation of an eternal future.

September 3, 1839

. . . In P.M. drive to Lenox. . . . Take tea at hotel in Mrs. Butler's salon. . . . On adjourning to Mrs. Sedgwick's find ourselves under a glorious dome of shining light, as of fluted silk, drawn up to one point in mid heaven and as clutched by God's hand, an Aurora Borealis of rare beauty. No portion of chaotic night visible, but this wondrous tent canopied all things, and by and by an exquisite rosy blush, spread here and there, as of dawn through muslin curtains, deepening the contrasting brilliancy of the silvery streaks and kindling the sparkle of the stars, as when we crossed the Atlantic. This struggling of York and Lancaster in the night's serene countenance gave a living beauty to it I never saw before. Now and then the tent parted as if to admit some celestial visitant; the red became nearly purple, and again the shining folds shook out unmarred by a break. In the center of the dome we fancied the white light assumed the form of a dove, with all these rays radiating therefrom, as the glory in Catholic churches, and thought that possibly Constantine's vision of a cross was nothing but this appearance, which might easily take that form and to a superstitious mind work miracles. It approaches nearer our visions of heavenly shows than any other natural phenomenon. How easily one of these rays of strange luminousness might be imagined a Jacob's ladder, fit to be trodden by angel-feet "ascending and descending"; even now as it shifts I can see myriad snowy wings waving round about. This baffles man's comprehension, but I suppose electricity has something to do with it; it is as if now the ends of the earth were drawn upward like hair by this mysterious power and tied together on high, as if a Lilliputian net was weaving over us, to unite us with heaven, a spider's web shining in morning dew. One might multiply similes forever; its changing loveliness suggests so many. Hardly sit patiently in house with such mysteries over our heads but get whelmed in a most interesting discussion of animal magnetism, Tom astounding them with his Parisian experiences and each person having enough of their own to believe tremblingly. An awful, undermining subject, too exciting to think of often. Mrs. Butler explained the magnetizing influence of her husband and friends, and Mr. Charles, skeptical, tried his upon Mary. All wrought up to the highest pitch of nervous excitement by this talk and the phenomena without, we parted at eleven, and we drove home our six miles without moon but enough of this light lingering to show the road. . . . Sat at my window before retiring, it having broke forth anew; amused myself with a million awful conjectures. . . .

September 10, 1839

. . . Had the good fortune to secure at Mrs. Sedgwick's Mrs. Butler's reading of nearly all *The Tempest*. Her richly modulated and flexible voice shifted beautifully from one part to another giving Stephano and Trinculo's humor and Caliban's *sauvagerie* as truly as Miranda's naïveté and Prospero's proud eloquence. What an exquisite poem it is, enfolded in such a truly Southern atmosphere, so simply magnificent. The unities are perfectly kept, of time and place, and yet nothing fatigues the eye, the grouping so admirable—of the coarse, world-knowing sailors and the savage, spirit-knowing Caliban, *par exemple*, and the progression so natural. With what wondrous art are the harshest, rudest human creatures linked by gradual refinings up to the spiritual and unearthly. . . . Drove down with Jewett by cloud and starlight, very late, trusting for the road pretty much to our straightforward steed, visions of that enchanted island floating before me, conjured by as potent a wand as Prospero's, a poet's words read by a good voice. A thousand thanks, good Shakespeare, for this night's pleasure. May you hear the benison that is ever steaming up from human hearts to you wherever you are. That should make a little heaven of itself if you stand in need of such, as doubtless half these Calvinists believe, but *we* say what would Heaven be without you?

Next comes a fascinating description of a visit to the Shaker colony at Lebanon, New Hampshire.

September 15, 1839

. . . Entered with a flock of other "females" the female door and left the gents to seek their kind also, got a good seat in the middle of the side appropriated for "world's people" and awaited the performances as at a theater. Very gradually Shakeress after Shakeress opened noiselessly their side door, glided on tiptoe noiselessly, across the beautiful floor, to their respective pegs, hung thereon their white shawls, fichus, and straw bonnets (which resembled *en masse* huge hornets' nests), then sat down, as jointed dolls do, upon the wall benches, handkerchief straight across lap and hands folded over, turning not an eyelash to the right or left, like so many draped sphinxes or corpses set on end. The little girls copying so well the same rigid repose—so unlike the fidgetiness of youth—is a horrible sight, as if they were under a spell. The men came in later, but visitors flocked in so fast that half their benches were civilly resigned to them by a patriarch elder. After utter repose the men and women staring at each other from their respective benches, rather dangerously if eyes are ammunition to such sanctified shadows of humanity, they all rose, or rather stiffened up their joints like a machine, and putting back the benches began to sing, one of the elders addressing them in unconnected, drawling scraps of morality at one end of the aisle they formed, and then stepping tip-toe to our gay ranks, held forth on the desirableness of proprietous behavior, non-mounting of benches, as it would soil them, etc., pitying us for our poor, lost condition, declaring *them* the favored of Heaven, the "salt of the earth" (rather savorless I should think) and prophesying that one day we should lament we were not Shakers! Confessed there was some virtue in the world, though grossly obscured, but no *faith*—a dim belief in former miracles but utter infidelity about those of the present day, which were vouchsafed much more marvellously. An unhinged, stuttering discourse, as if the petrifaction extended over the man's body was reaching his brain. They then ploughed up and down (for it can't be called dancing), with their backs to us, and sang again very gay airs, terribly shrill under the large sounding board but sometimes sweeping through the gamut with great effect. I could only catch a few words: "Press on, press on to thy happy kingdom," etc. They then filed off into a double circle, one circle going one way, another two or three abreast, "laboring" round this large hall, knees bent, with a sort of galvanized hop, hands paddling like fins and voices chanting these wild airs, with a still smaller circle of elders and children in the center, stationary, giving the pitch of the songs, like so many old witches or enchanters, working over the caldron while the younger ones skipped through the force of their incantations. But no witch's sabbath, no bacchanal procession could be more unearthly, revolting, oppressive, and bewildering. The machinery of their stereotyped steps, plunging on in this way so long without rest, the constrained attitude forward, the spasmodic jumps and twists of the neck, and the ghastly visages of the women in their corpse-like caps, the waving of so many shrill voices, and the rigid expression of their faces combined to form a spectacle as piteous as disgusting, fit only for the dancing hall of the lower regions or the creation of a nightmare. There was one woman whose horrible contortions will haunt me forever. She wrenched her head nearly over her shoulder on one side and the other, and then jerked it nearly to her knee, with a regularity of manner for such an immense time that I thought I should have rushed out for relief, as my eye saw always this dreadful figure. I supposed at first it was St. Vitus dance, or a fit, but she stopped at the end and varied it by spinning like a dervish, twisting her arms round her head like snakes. Shrouded in such a dress, and carried to such a pitch, it was the most frightful human gesticulation ever perpetrated. Doubtless they regard her as a saint, for I saw a faint imitation of it in others. After interminable dancing, varied by changing of feet with great energy, we were relieved of this constant repassing of the same faces, mostly very disagreeable: one head like an idiot or a thief, one full of cunning and self conceit, with thin, *prononcé* features, and a lank of fringe of hair behind I shall never forget, and one youth, evidently wrought upon intensely by a devotional excitation leaping higher than the rest, with painful earnestness of expression; among the women all frightful but one tall girl with a fine profile, who seemed to curl her lip in some scorn at this insane mummery and waved her hands very languidly. There was a fat novice in wordly gear except the cap who presented an amusing contrast to her lank sisters. At one time they all knelt silently, like spectres rising from their graves, as awful a spectacle as the nuns in *Robert le Diable,* then sat waving their hands as if scattering cobwebs from their faces or spirits. The stupefied elder at the end thanked us for our good behavior and right gladly we emerged into fresh air after the close heat and wearisome exhibition we had been forced to endure for so many hours. The concourse of visitors is extraordinary, for surely no mortal could wish to see this twice. I remember as a child being painfully impressed by it, but that was nothing to the shock the maturer judgment receives from such pitiful delusions; however, if this exercise excites in any one of them devotional feeling, doubtless God cares little by what means it is brought to light. . . .

The following, from letters to Isaac Appleton Jewett, are among Fanny's most caustic references to Longfellow during the years of their estrangement.

Boston, November 4, 1839

. . . By the way, don't make me patroness of any of your "thought-children," as you call 'em. I consider myself too juvenile to enact the role of godmother, and have already been hoisted into such a public notoriety by a certain impertinent friend of mine you wot of that I am entirely disgusted with the honor. . . .

December 29, 1839

. . . The Prof has collected all his vagrant poems into a neat little volume christened mournfully *Voices of the Night.* He does not look like a night-bird and is more of a mocking-bird than a nightingale, though he has some sweetly plaintive notes. All the Psalms are fine but the rest *peu de chose.* . . .

*In December, Mary Appleton was married to the son of Sir James
Mackintosh, Robert Mackintosh. Fanny described the wedding at
length in two extant letters—first to Isaac Appleton Jewett, in the
letter of December 29 from which the above extract is taken, and
again in the following letter to Francis Lieber. She had not liked
Mackintosh at first—"a puzzle not Chinese but English," she calls
him in an undated letter sent to Emmeline Austin from Stockbridge
the preceding summer. "He has quite a good face, an awkward
figure, however, laughs spasmodically, is constantly absent when
present, and jerks out his words like a badly-working pump." On
September 28 she recorded in her journal a very spirited argument
with him, in the course of which he declared that Unitarianism was
"worse than Heathenism." "This eternal quizzing wears me out; an
honest opinion deserves a like return, and you never feel sure of
getting that from him. Then he contradicts all your assertions with
a saucy 'oh very like,' implying 'I don't believe a word you say,'
which provokes me like the buzzing of mosquitoes." Before the
wedding she had come to value him much more highly, and she
never thereafter changed her mind. Her separation from her sister
was nevertheless a great wrench.*

To Francis Lieber

January 3, 1840

. . . Yes, Mary is actually married, and certainly no union of life
and soul, except the wedded one, has such oneness as that of two
sisters of nearly the same age, bound to each other from birth. . . .
You can believe, then, what I suffer in my bereaved state, how
undermined has been my peace of mind and hopes of the future,
for if it excites no little jealousy and loneliness to see a stranger
claiming what was once all our own, this sorrow is doubly aggra-
vated when he makes her also a stranger and steals her from her
home and kindred. No one but Death and a lover can thus quietly
bereave hearthsides. I do not wish to make my letter a jeremiad, and
these things are too sacred and heart-hid to be seen on paper even
to a friend, and, thank God, my feelings have attained a less selfish
character. Now that it is over, I actually feel relieved, and live only

in the consciousness of their supreme happiness, which ought to hush all complaints. Yesterday-week she was made a bride, and the joy- and sorrow-fraught name of Mary Appleton ceased to be known on earth!

Neither she or Mackintosh wished any parade, any white satin or orange buds or smirking brides-maids and men, so she was married very quietly in the morning at home, with no one present but the family and Emmeline Austin, and our good Dr. Channing was the important minister of their fate. His solemn prayers were echoed by more aching hearts and streaming eyes than often hallow this most awful ceremony. Mary was dressed simply in white muslin, with no flowers in her hair but a bouquet next her heart (a sprig of myrtle from which I send you), and, they say, never looked more charmingly; her face was radiant with a deep joy and trust which God grant may be eternal!

There was the usual cutting up of cake and spasmodic attempts at hilarity, ending in sighs, and after a lunch the two, by so few magic words made one, drove off to Lexington, where they still are. Dr. and Mrs. Follen being absent, they are very comfortably lodged in their house, and yesterday I went out and dined with them. But so short had been the engagement, and so sudden, that even yet, at times, I think it all a dream on which some gracious dawn will arise. I have told you nothing about my new brother. Not many men could I have ever been induced to think worthy of such a sister, so I can pay no higher compliment to this one than to say I am thoroughly satisfied he should be her husband. I am warmly attached to him for his genuine, upright, manly character, had he no particular claims on my regard. He has all the soundness and purity of religious principle for which his father was so distinguished, with the same *bonhommie* toward mankind, with a true, noble heart and a clear, just head. He is very shy in his manners and keeps back his store of information and acquirement with the modesty of a true soul, but it leaks out *malgré lui*, on intimate acquaintance. He has an infinite fund of humor but never jokes ill-naturedly and has a droll, dry way of telling a story which is irresistible. In fact, the *fond* of his character is so admirable that I feel as confident as any mortal can of the destinies of another that he will secure her a more durable and satisfactory happiness than she has ever yet been blessed with—and I cannot but rejoice, with all my soul, that this change has come upon her. I think as little as possible of *my* future, which now seems a dead blank, but such strange shiftings of our life's kaleidoscope constantly occur that we know not, truly, what a year may bring forth. . . .

I go . . . [with Mary and Mackintosh to Washington] in about a week, and hope to get some amusement out of the strange elements that compose Washington society—mustached diplomats from polished courts and shaggy backwoodsmen from nature's high places. . . .

(JOURNAL)

February 18, 1840

Rainy all day. Kept house and made myself miserable. Wisely lamenting all that is past cure, with faint enough hopes of future amendment. "Let the dead Past bury its dead," but we must wear *demi-deuille* at least. Finished Miss Austen's *Mansfield Park*. Such a sweet gliding style and so true all to life and England.

The trip south was duly made. In this letter, Fanny sums up her impressions of Washington.

To ISAAC APPLETON JEWETT

"The Farm" (near Philadelphia)
February 25, 1840

. . . We went to several very pretty parties, each varying from the other in kaleidoscope fashion, dined agreeably with the President,[7] on spicier dishes than talk, thought him very like Uncle Aaron or Moses, only fatigued with his non-committal manner, pitied him for the bore of being equally gracious to all visitors, even lunatics, who, he says, often come maintaining he usurps their station, went twice to the House *only* and twice that too often. . . . Liked some of our neighbors there but not the society in general; 'tis too like a

[7] Van Buren.

travelling menagerie, a gaping curiosity from group to group and a
constant wish to see the big lions stirred up with a long pole. . . .
Mary wants me very much to accompany her to England,[8] but I
have the virtue to resist, knowing Father never would consent and
that poor Emmeline would be miserable, and I feel myself doing so
little good in the world that a selfish gratification easily yields to the
satisfaction (only less palpably selfish) of conferring my mite of
happiness. . . .

(JOURNAL)

March 3, 1840

A dribbling of visitors and rain drops. A nice long visit from Mr.
Prescott, fresh as a rose. Prof. L[ongfellow] in P.M. and a dripping
walk with Emmeline. . . .

March 8, 1840

A good, zealous sermon from Mr. Gannett [9] on World vs. Church,
making me feel more than think. . . . Read Jeremiah's awful
prophecies. *Great Western* in, bringing news of Queen's marriage. . . .

March 15, 1840

A sermon from Dr. Channing very *à propos* to my recent think-
ings; subject—Trust in God. Such *élans* of divine eloquence but alas
such ideal trust in human nature! his own pure, spiritualized nature
his oracle. What wings he lends the soul! I trust *not* Icarian!

March 18, 1840

. . . Got thinking too much of my coming bereavement.

March 27, 1840

My courage failed me as the parting hour drew nigh, so resolved
to go with them to Worcester. Arrived there at five and explored

[8] She and her husband sailed in April.
[9] Ezra Stiles Gannett (1801–1871), Dr. Channing's assistant.

town in mud. Looks *mesquin* enough in winter. Very nice hotel, comfortable parlor and quiet. Passed a sleepless night and such as I trust will be rarely repeated in my life. *Ora pro nobis.*

March 28, 1840

Tore myself away with aching heart and crushing fears from my darling sister and dear brother at seven. God grant this separation is not eternal and strengthen me to bear this heavy burden. . . .

March 31, 1840

Flying light and shadow—fresh, exhilirating air. Tom's twenty-eighth birthday! Made few calls and *flanéd* with Prof. in Beacon Street. . . .

April 5, 1840

An eloquent sermon from Mr. Gannett on the glorification of Christ. An audacious announcement by Dr. Channing that a sermon before Abolition society is to be at our church. . . .

April 18, 1840

. . . A longish visit from Prof. L[ongfellow] tells of a Portland blue who reads Plato in Greek! . . .

May 3, 1840

A good sermon from Mr. Gannett on the true interpretation of redemption, with his belief that our material bodies exist hereafter —glorified in some way. Vain meddling with unfathomable mysteries. . . .

June 3, 1840

Read aloud to Fanny *Faerie Queene* all morning. Una's lion most lovely episode, and her life among the satyrs—the personifications so wonderfully complete and yet never annoyingly so. . . .

June 4, 1840

A charming long letter from my darling Mary announcing safe arrival in England after short and pleasant voyage. . . .

June 15, 1840

. . . Read *Faust* (Hayward's translation, got up at Lowell!). Can't discover yet why it is so *very* famous. . . .

June 16, 1840

. . . Finished *Faust*, vague, unsatisfactory, chaotic, as seem all Goethe's writings to me, not to mention their vile coarseness.

June 26, 1840

. . . Drove with Tom to Mr. Allston's. Saw his wife and last most lovely picture, Amy Robsart, an angel in costume so divinely fair with red-gold hair. Also showed us beautiful sketches, Titania, etc. Dear old man!

To Isaac Appleton Jewett

Newport, R.I., July 6, 1840

. . . We have been reading the first number of *The Dial*, a magazine got up by our Transcendentalists, and as you think such things fit testers of the spirit of the times, try to get it. You will like the astonishing concentration of thought therein for so few pages. Some of the poetry resembles the "Psalms of life" and I think it is much more creditable than these patched-up Brobdingnag newspapers. . . .

To Emmeline Austin

July 16, 1840

. . . The drive I mentioned above was the return from a delightful visit to Dr. Channing in his lovely little nest, so like an English parsonage in its sweet seclusion from the highway, pretty arrangement of shrubbery and lawn, flowers peeping out in unexpected corners, and old-fashioned, vine-draped house, more picturesque than comfortable, with its low ceilings and "zoölogical smell of mice," as Lady Bulwer says. I like so much to see him there, looking like an old rat himself mousing about in its quaint nooks, moralizing so poetically on the gentle influences about him, so much more in harmony with the refined delicacy of his nature than those midst the shock of men, and appearing less physically feeble and contemptible in his easy dress and large straw hat than when in his mummy-like city bandages.

(JOURNAL)

July 24, 1840

. . . Read tonight *Widow Barnaby* by Mrs. Trollope. Admirable, *mais quelle femme!*

July 26, 1840

. . . Read Fénelon, which probed my innermost soul, now lacerating, now healing. Cried and prayed myself into composure. Read last book of first volume of Spenser—Temperance overcoming all trials.

August 23, 1840

Went not to church but read in our cove by seaside Socrates' glorious Apology to his Judges. So like Christ's before his. Such *serenity* of faith and purely Christian spirit, looking upon himself as heaven-sent, to improve his race, so shrinking from no trial. Fit forerunner of the Savior as John. . . .

September 9, 1840

. . . Read aloud in evening last half of *Much Ado About Nothing* and the whole of *Gentlemen of Verona,* one of the least interesting plays, I think. Valentine's cool resignation of his lady to bring about Julia's discovery miserably forced.

September 25, 1840

Read Macaulay's gorgeous essay on Milton; such strength of judgment and language, universal knowledge aptly used, and admirable illustrations, which when good delight me inexpressibly. . . .

To Isaac Appleton Jewett

Boston, October 3, 1840

. . . Fanny Ellsler has excited all the enthusiasm which always leaps up here to welcome first-rate excellence. She has had crammed houses, selling tickets always by auction, and more discriminating applause, she says, than in any other city. In the warmth of her good German heart has actually insisted upon bestowing a thousand dollars for Bunker Hill Monument. This latter noble and generous proceeding has not a little worried some of our proprietors and patriotic dames who dislike receiving such a sum from a foreigner for such a national purpose and especially from a pirouetter of doubtful (or rather too well known) character. I was present at the performances by which she gained the sum. She never cast her glamour over me so completely in Paris, having there such a rival as Taglioni and being comparatively lost in the bewildering magnificence of the *Diable Boiteux*. Our small theater and miserable corps de ballet are good foils to her enchanting grace, beautiful dressing and finished steps. She began that evening with the Sylphide, which is so created for the sublime spirituality of Taglioni and her pensive manner (prophetic in this prettiest of French poems of the sad finale) that she of course clings a little too much to earth but danced it admirably too and floated me back to Paris on her Psyche wings; then came the majestic *Cachucha* in which she is unrivalled (for Taglioni has not the *weight* and coquetry to dance it), then the *Cracovienne,* a spirited military dance, in which her joyous German smiles and coquettish grace when she makes the military salute to the audience or when clicking her golden spurs, would drive you crazy. She finaled with the prettiest little speech (imagine a dancer with a *voice* in Paris; our atmosphere draws out speeches like corks), pronounced with a sweetly timid accent, ending thus, "There are two monuments which will rise together—one of granite on Bunker-'ill, the other of gratitude in my heart," which word was emphasized with a distinct energy as if straight therefrom. "A touch of nature makes the whole world kin," as Shakespeare beautifully says, and the thunders and thunders of applause which followed this *bon-mot* seemed to break down the patriotic demurring. . . .

What a mere stump orator Mr. Webster is making himself, wandering all over the country stirring up dormant Whiggery, talking with such undignified egotism, though sometimes with much wit and effect. He has been censured so much for coldness and formality that this seems a hard push for popularity. This Harrison fever, as you say, is a ludicrous, piteous spectacle. Youths behind counters wearing log-cabin brooches and gold cider barrels upon their shirt-bosoms and infants in Whig cradles squalling to the tune of "Tippecanoe." My old nurse's child I found decorated with a Harrison medal and exclaiming thereat she said all the girls at school wore them. This approaches the loyalty to Royal Charlie, but this seedy military veteran is only worshipped as the visible representative of Whig principles, I conclude, and his individual claim is as secondary as that of the ass in La Fontaine's fables, who carried the Madonna and thought himself the cause of the adoration of passers-by. . . .

(JOURNAL)

October 31, 1840

Raw east wind searching through the marrow of one's bones. Read Balzac stories—such dissections of human and feminine nature. *Hélas!*

TO ISAAC APPLETON JEWETT

November 8, 1840

. . . Before rejoicing with you in the downfall of Locofocoism (confirmed by today's news from New York), I call upon you to rejoice with me . . . in having become . . . an aunt. A fact brought by the last steamer. On the eighteenth of October last, this interesting event took place (his mamma's birthday, for it is a little cockney nephew that has entered this contentious world to remind me how old I am growing). . . .

There is much purity of thought and lofty morality in this Transcendentalism, I think, and I don't think either would evaporate, as its disciples seem to, if it had more body to it . . . to nourish as well as exalt people's heads and hearts.

They might be called spiritual Grahamites, and I should imagine were so in daily life too, for there is no roast-beef smack in these vapory offsprings of green tea and vegetables. . . . 'Tis a reaction from this material age and as such must have its little day. . . . The poetry is, as you say, most miserable-Helicon diluted by weak tea, a sloppy, sickish beverage, not strong enough, like Taunton water, to run downhill.

In the way of poetical nourishment I have had such refreshing draughts from two lectures by Mr. Dana,[10] our poet and a genuine one, with a heart which throbs and gushes in all his words, a living spring within a half-dead frame. Amidst this mechanical factory of business men and politicians, buying and selling in machine-like masses . . . the breathings forth of a true, independent heart and soul . . . are as glad a discovery to a woman nature like mine, sick to death of Harrisonism and Abolitionism and Locofocoism (though I have given my share of interest and rejoicing to the success of the first because it was better than worse), as can be. John the Baptist in the wilderness could not stir and warm the souls of his hope-barren heavens more effectually than was mine the other night on hearing this voice of human nature through this chaos of brass and iron and tin nature. . . . I am not extravagantly enthusiastic now, I assure you; his last was a magnificent lecture. Coleridge could not have delivered a better—such admirable philosophy and such a lavish luxuriance of true poetry. . . . Our lectures open their *bouches beautés* like lions seeking whom they may devour, but I shall only patronize my friend Dana's. His son, perhaps you know, has gained great fame by a book of sea experiences [11] among the lovers of facts and longitudes. "He has a much more useful talent than his father," as an old proser said to me when returning from the lecture of the latter, as invigorated as if new blood had been poured into my veins! Yes, manly and simply good like *Robinson Crusoe*, and probably the son will give weight to the father's reputation as children think six brass cents worth so much more, especially if new ones, than a single silver fourpence! . . .

[10] Richard Henry Dana I (1787–1879).
[11] *Two Years Before the Mast.*

I am much amused at your account of my fame in Cincinnati, and shall take care never to go there, 'twould be such a pity to disenchant it. My vanity is not flattered because it is all for the heroine of *Hyperion*, who is as unlike me as most creations of the fancy transcend flesh and blood. Don't feel bound now to flatter me, 'cause it's no use, and I prefer to be entertained with anything else. Your letters are too gallant already; don't think because you are writing to a woman she must be dosed with sugar-plums. I hate sweet things—that is, too many of 'em. . . . Have you seen the Prof's last attempt, "The Country Blacksmith"? *very* good, especially the children looking in and the daughter singing. . . .

January 25, 1841

. . . I am having a very nice winter on the whole. The cold braces and invigorates my nerves, which are not as sensitive as yours, and as I am every day plunging into the very depths of the "Inferno," looking in on the fiery sepulchres, where the nobly grand Farinata glares, "*come avesse l'inferno in gran dispitto,*" or admiring the majestic flame which enwraps Ulysses like a cloak, I snap my fingers at Jack Frost. . . . As I have touched upon Dante I must give my enthusiasm vent a while, for this is like the opening of the seventh seal to me, this book—a new revelation (I have never read it before as a whole), and truly it may be called "a page torn from the Apocalypse," as Motley says of *Faust*—such supernatural language and conceptions it flames with. If an Italian I should believe it like the Gospel, its stern simplicity and majesty have such a stamp of divine authority, more than Milton, I think, with his poetical vagueness. It is like the testimony of an eye-witness, and if not executed so wonderfully, its formal arrangements would shock the imagination. I read it with a warm-souled Italian [12] who explains admirably to me the different allusions, and many charming little flights to *bella Italia* are we tempted to thereby. But this is too gigantesque a subject to be *emballé* in a letter. It is too awful a one for the life I lead, and shades in therewith strangely; after descending, with Virgil and Dante from bolge to bolge, in an atmosphere

[12] Pietro Bachi, instructor in Italian and Portuguese at Harvard, in Longfellow's department of modern languages.

trembling with eternal lamentations and on a soil drenched with unceasing showers of tears all the morning, every evening, lately, I am in a ball-room where flourishes the whip-syllabub of life, as if under our feet yawned no such realities. But I can chameleonize myself and enjoy all. . . .

This last number [of *The Dial*] is "beyond beyond" for absurdity: some verses by Emerson on the Sphinx which you would think could only have been written in Bedlam. . . .

(JOURNAL)

March 4, 1841

. . . Inauguration of William Harrison as President of these United States. A simple-hearted, right-minded, good old man, like the patriots of the olden time, say friend and foe. May he adjust our chaotic tides! . . .

On May 1 Fanny sailed from Boston, with her brother Tom, on the British steam packet Columbia *to visit her sister Mary in England. Comparing this passage with the earlier crossing in 1835, she missed "the beautiful shifting and exhilaration of a sailing vessel" but was impressed by "the marvelous quiet. There is none of the constant bawling of orders . . . nor racket of ropes, nor rushing about of sailors, nor wearisome creaking of masts. . . ." She saw a whale, porpoises, and, to her great delight, icebergs. On this voyage, she enjoyed the society of the British actor-family, the Vandenhoffs, whose performances she had witnessed in Boston, and who were now returning to England. As before, Fanny was an excellent sailor and the captain profoundly attentive!*

On May 15 she landed at Liverpool and the next day "railroaded it to London." On May 19 she "Reached St. Catherine's by twilight and found my darlings well. Ronald smiled at his new aunt. God be thanked for this meeting."

On May 18 she "was introduced to Carlyle," who "talked humorously with strongest Scotch accent of divers things, laughing all over. Soft eyes emitting heart and mind light—shaggy exterior—very unlike preconception." In a letter of May 25 to Emmeline Austin, she described him further: "His face disappoints at first, as does that of most renowned personages, but there is genius enough in his eyes, which have that lustrous, dewey clearness, belonging to a liquid heart and brain and betraying them. . . ." On the same date she described him to her father: "He has a heavy farmer look with rough features and hair, a slouchy manner but eyes soft and clear like Burns' and talks after a humorous fashion." On June 3 she met him again, and he "poured forth many amiable sayings but some sharp ones of Wordsworth's vanity, etc. Said Emerson was the most living man in America. Called The Dial a ghost of a book, and whether it would ever attain a body was doubtful, without which it could do little in this world. Like more and more his speech and temper."

Again as on her previous visit to Europe, Fanny was in no danger of neglecting the theater. On May 21 she first encountered the magnetic being whom her husband-to-be always considered the greatest actress he ever saw.

(JOURNAL)

. . . saw Rachel in *Bajazet*—wonderfully impressed with her Oriental beauty and astonishing fire of action. Thrilling voice and noblest conception of part—a juvenile Siddons. Tiresome formal drama only redeemed by her genius.

To EMMELINE AUSTIN

Woolwich, July 2, 1841

. . . Today it is soft and dampish like Newport, and such gushing melody from the birds: the air is positively *all* song. I have not heard nightingales to recognize them much, though this grove near us is a pet home of theirs but have been so enchanted with skylarks. Their song is all Shelley and Wordsworth declare: their throats seem too small to give vent to such a fully gushing tide of joy—they are half strangled by it, and you hear the quick and irregular pulsation of a heart in it, a human heart, for we know no other, yet it must be a child's human heart, 'tis such pure, unalloyed, boundless, trustful outpouring of delight, the *natural* voice of a creature to its Creator.

It puts to shame our feebly-uttered praise and attained happiness through suffering. I vainly look for the bird when I hear this; being overhead it surrounds you like an atmosphere, *fills* the sky. . . .

Other experiences of the summer are reflected in further letters to Emmeline. There is more about Rachel in another letter to Emmeline Austin, merely dated "July."

. . . After this came *Les Horaces*—Rachel as Camille, much more beautiful and touching than in the two other fierce characters in which I saw her but which could not be surpassed in their kind. Her delicately-formed head, simply bound with a white fillet, her grace of motion and attitude, increased by the snowy classic folds, made her acting so many statues, and she seemed the very embodiment of Psyche to me, bending, shuddering beneath mortal woes, but firm and upheld withal by the strength of purity and divine aid. One fainting scene when she hears of the death of her lover or brothers, I forget which, for I could not always follow the elaborate French speeches, and dissolves upon a seat was nature itself, inexpressibly touching and graceful; in the last act she threw the audience into groans of wonder and admiration by the inspired energy and passion of her tones and attitudes, and her extreme youth adds great effect to this. Inspiration is to me the startling quality of her acting: no stage tricks of tone and gesture but the uncontrollable "outcome of a noble soul," as Carlyle would say. A most interesting creature with her former life and present destiny; her Jewess blood and look, so young, yet having had power to resurrect this long-defunct drama, and what is more, bring it over to London and retain breathless listeners there for a whole season. What a triumph for the French! I hope sincerely she won't be the victim of her success, but one shudders for her.

On September 16 also, Fanny wrote Emmeline Austin that her sister, whose health had been somewhat uncertain since the birth of her child, had decided to return to America with her. But before the end of the letter she is doubtful again.

When Fanny writes her father next day, Mary is still uncertain, for "*she is just in that state that dreads a decision or likes to post-pone it as long as possible.*" Her husband desires a diplomatic post, but Mary has "*such a repugnance to its necessary evils, wandering into outlandish parts.*" She "*has been of late unable to study out what position would best content her but will now, I hope, make the effort.*" So unsettled was the whole situation that Fanny had even considered remaining with Mary in England through the winter, though without her father's consent.

Instead, she sailed without her sister on the Columbia, on October 5, arriving at Boston on October 21. But on November 7 she wrote these words in her journal: "*Britannia in at noon bringing us a joyful surprise: Mary, Rob, and Ronald. All looking well in spite of tedious passage of seventeen days.*"

Shifting her scene of activity from England to America did not wholly cure Mary's tendency to hypochondria. On December 21, Fanny wrote Emmeline from Beacon Street:

. . . Mary is looking much better, which is some comfort to me, but her weakness seems almost to have become a lasting portion—she is often depressed at the prospect of falling into what she calls the slough of invalidism for life but takes courage again at any natural feeling of former days. I hope on about her as a duty and because I need something to hope about.

Emmeline was in New York to consult Dr. Samuel Elliott about her eyes, and on Christmas Eve Fanny wrote her again:

. . . Tomorrow is hallowed by Christ's love and on its eve mine for you is a fit prelude. In my heart a tree is upborne, as tonight in all German parlors the tree of my life rises up, and though many boughs droop darkly, on the upper bright lights shine and gay gifts sparkle; happy thoughts, cheerful hopes placed there by your dear influence. Every year may they grow wider and brighter till the whole is illumined, even the Past made blessed! The prayer of this night is that I may shed as much light over your life as you already have on mine; may God grant it! . . .

I have been, in the way of dissipation, to one of Emerson's lectures, a very beautiful flowing of sweet sounds and thoughts, and like some strain of music with fewer confused or sharp, startling staccato notes than his wont, though among them was this assertion—"The first man that called his neighbor a donkey or a puppy was a poet"! . . . The Professor has a creamy new volume of verses out—rather meagre *selon moi*, the cream of thought being somewhat thinner than that of the binding. . . .

The next day, Christmas, Fanny had an important religious experience, which she recorded in the special journal she kept for such things.

Today, for the first time, I knelt before the altar and received the sacrament. I have often longed to partake in this touching and holy ceremony, which, if not enjoined upon us as a sacred duty, yet was addressed to our hearts in tones of thrilling entreaty to which all must hearken. A friend's dying request is sacred in our eyes, how much more then one of the last which passed the lips of Him who bestowed upon us life eternal. "This do in remembrance of me" has ever stirred my conscience when I have seen the Communion table spread, when I have prayed to draw nearer the well-beloved son of the Father, but I have shrunk back as too impure to handle those holy things, as not hungering and thirsting after righteousness alone, fearful of committing sacrilege should earthly appetites regain their wonted sway in my soul after it had tasted of that bread and that wine which typify the body of the blessed Redeemer. But today, this holiest Sabbath of the year, this birthday of the world, for Christ was born to bestow true life on all, in this church sombre but cheerful with boughs and wreaths from the woods of winter, beautifully in harmony with the spirit of the religion which decks the soul in its days of gloom with the never-dying garlands of hope and faith, the chanting of the Christmas anthem, with its words of healing benediction, all the hopes the heavenly choir sang, the infinite love of the Creator for his children swelled my heart with irresistible emotion and drew it to the altar. I felt no dread, no superstitious terror, but overwhelming tenderness and joy. When the clergyman (Mr. Greenwood) offered me the bread with the words "Eat this in remembrance of Christ," I trembled violently, and the Catholic faith in transubstantiation rushed over my mind—profound awe followed it, and I seemed already to myself a new creature, that new strength was vouchsafed me, almost a new life; the wine completed this belief. It did not diffuse itself through my human veins so much as through those of my innermost soul, warming, reviving, recreating its existence. Happiness too deep for speech or thought succeeded— a blessed, blessed peace, that very peace angels on this day promised us. Only once or twice before can I remember this peculiar feeling of serene, yet fervent, joy—the Father's love encircling us like an atmosphere, pressing evenly on our whole being like light. We do not desire to pray audibly, or frame thought into language; we feel that our soul is pouring itself into his ear, that he can never be nearer, that Heaven is where He is, and its health around us here.

I chronicle this event so minutely because it is one of the few which make life memorable and death happy. I rejoice that I have been enabled to do this of my own free will and choice. I could not have died contented without it, and now life seems more sacred to me than ever.

How beautiful and touching was the whole scene—the silence, the gently gliding steps of the guests of that simple, but soul-nourishing banquet, the affectionate manner of the clergyman, recognizing the brotherhood of humanity as it were around a Father's table, the silver-haired old men kneeling at the altar—it is enshrined in my memory for life.

O most merciful Father, receive the overflowing love and gratitude of thy child for this crowning blessing of her heart. Let her not henceforth become unworthy to partake of that precious nourishment which is the type of that thou hast vouchsafed to the the soul in thy Love.

May his divine influence abide with her, feeding every craving want, refreshing her often-fainting hopes, renewing a right spirit within her. Let her never hunger or thirst for Him again. And oh, above all, may she never mistake the living fountain. Graciously cleanse her heart that it may be worthy for the indwelling of thy Spirit. Teach it how near thou ever art.

The year 1842, the last of Fanny's maidenhood, does not seem to have been a very happy one, and it produced little significant writing. Yet it began gaily enough.

To Emmeline Austin

January 2, 1842

. . . I had an amusing peep at the Transcendental strata Thursday evening at Anna Shaw's, an impromptu gathering for Mary Channing and Eustace, but the very lights burned blue. Miss Fuller and Emerson sat like the old philosophers in the groves, each with a swarm of disciples as a halo. I got introduced to the latter and told him of Carlyle and Milnes, etc. etc., his out-of-drawing face breaking up into meaningless smiles and a feeble imitation of his lectures breaking forth in his speech. I never thought him so small a man but so is the greatest often in society. We scuffled, not danced, on the oil carpet in the hall. Maria White was there but I did not get a fair look into the well of her eyes. Lowell did. . . .[13]

Evidently Fanny had not yet forgiven Longfellow for Hyperion, *for the same letter records the "heavy visitation" of New Year's Day calls from "Frank Jackson, John Codman, and the Prof. . . ."*

The following is again from the religious journal, summing up Fanny's spiritual experience for this year:

With what strong joy and comfort do I come to this marred chronicler of my soul's history! . . .

I have often indeed since my earliest childhood heard God walking in the garden, but generally alas! like Adam, have hid myself at the sound, have mourned in bitterness of death over my fall, but have not been able to discern afar off the redemption. How truly every man lives the history of all. . . .

Visible things have become more real and yet shadows beside the invisible; all things are transformed, transfigured. Phrases, words

[13] James Russell Lowell married Maria White on December 26, 1844.

which were once dead, or living only as flowers may be said to live, now do indeed breathe and move instinct with life. This expression "a new life"—how really alive it is, how the Bible speaks as no human voice can speak; inspiration truly is there, a spirit clothed in sounds, feeding the soul as manna dropped from heaven upon the starving children of God. . . .

The Father does not reveal himself to all men; the Deity does, but the knowledge of the Fatherly heart of God is a wisdom we can never attain of ourselves; hence our blindness. Christ came to grasp our hands as brethren with one hand, pointing with the other to his Father and our Father, sent as a connecting link to lead us from the desolation of orphans, but in spite of his tender grasp, his fraternal voice we forget our birthright: *to each heart separately, in God's appointed time alone,* so I believe this truth is brought. . . .

This have I gained in part but what humiliation and contrition attends the discovery. I once thought if I could feel God daily I should be happy. But when I begin to feel and know Him as my Father, ever with me, ever loving and blessing me, the awful fact betrays itself that I am not worthy to be called his child, that the relationship is not recognizable in my erring, feeble nature, that I am perpetually marring the lineaments he gave me. I am penitent and know my duty better than I did, suffer more keenly from every neglect of it, have a conscience which warns as well as punishes, have much less excuse than formerly for wrong doing yet do so very, very little right. . . . Let me patiently await further fruits enjoying the blossoms of righteousness with a thankful, joyful heart, but no idle peace. There is no *rest* where there is *life*—on, on must I strive and toil, God helping me and his Son teaching and cheering me to make it a labor of love. Amen, amen.

CHAPTER IV

The Wonderful Year

1843 was the annus mirabilis: *in April Fanny and Longfellow finally resolved their differences; in May they were engaged; and in July they were married. From Longfellow's point of view all this occurred with startling suddenness; how long Fanny had been preparing for it in her heart nobody will ever know. Reconciliation began at the Andrews Nortons', where the two chanced one night to meet before one of Tom Appleton's frequent departures for Europe, and it was Fanny who took the initiative, for she told Longfellow how lonely she expected to be after her brother had gone, and added, "You must come and comfort me, Mr. Longfellow."*

After this broad hint, Longfellow again ventured to call at 39 Beacon Street, where he was received with sufficient friendliness so that he was encouraged to persevere. On April 17 he wrote her a letter to which she replied in the following terms:

To Henry Wadsworth Longfellow

Beacon St. Monday p.m.

I have just received your note and I cannot forbear telling you that it has comforted me greatly. I trust with all my heart that it is and will be as you say—that a better dawn has exorcised the phantoms for aye, that its cheering, healthy beams will rest as in a perpetual home within those once-haunted walls you speak of. I could not well disguise, I own, how much some of your words troubled me. I should never have ventured to speak so frankly to you had I not believed the dead Past *had* buried its dead and that we might safely walk over their graves, thanking God that at last we could live to give each other only happy thoughts. I rejoiced to see how calmly you met me until Saturday, when I trembled a little, as we are apt to do for a long cherished hope, but I will put aside all anxiety and fear, trusting upon your *promise.*

Tom has been reading me some farewell lines which caused many foolish tears to flow—therefore your friendly note was very welcome to dry them somewhat. . . .

She accepted him in a note written on May 10, and he walked forthwith, "with the speed of an arrow," from the Craigie House to Beacon Street, because he was "too restless to sit in a carriage—too impatient and fearful of encountering anyone!" He walked that day "amid the blossoms and sunshine and songs of birds, with my heart full of gladness and my eyes full of tears! . . . Oh, Day forever blessed; that ushered in this Vita Nuova *of happiness!"*

On May 16, Fanny wrote her new-found happiness to a beloved aunt.

TO MARTHA GOLD

May 16, 1843

Dearest Aunt Matty,

Rejoice with me in my great, inexpressibly great joy! I am engaged to Henry Longfellow!

This news will astonish you doubtless, as it is just beginning to many others, but it is nevertheless true—to me a *true dream*—brighter than all my fictitious ones. How it was gradually brought about you shall hear by and by, or rather what is there to tell but the old tale that true love is very apt to win its reward. My heart has always been of tenderer stuff than anybody believed, and it needed not many propitious circumstances to set it visibly flowing. It is too full of gratitude to Him who has moulded it to the reception of his choicest blessing to speak much to you yet, and words are not needed; the fact that a nature so noble and gifted and gentle and true has been bestowed upon unworthy me is eloquent enough. Good bye.

Your happy and grateful Fanny

Her brother Tom received the news in London.

To THOMAS G. APPLETON

May 24, 1843

I hope the important news we send you has not already reached your ears, that I may be the first to ask you to rejoice with me upon my great happiness in being engaged to the Professor. I think you saw symptoms enough of such a consummation before you left not to be altogether astonished, but doubtless you did not expect so soon to hear that my destiny was decided.

The heart does not reveal even to itself the gradual filling of its fountains, but a time arrives at last when the stone must be thrust aside which has sealed them up and they gush forth wondering at their own abundance. To speak more plainly, though not more naturally, it is only to be marvelled at that this blessing did not manifest itself to me long ago, but we have both come to the comforting conclusion that it is best as it is, that our characters have been ripened to appreciate it and receive it with fuller gratitude than if the past experience had been spared us.

My whole nature is more than satisfied, is enriched beyond its most exacting demands, what more can I say to reveal to you what I feel? With less sympathy I should never have been happy, and thankful am I to God that I have never been tempted to accept, in the craving for love which often misleads both men and women, an affection which would have caused a great famine somewhere in my heart. God grant, dearest, that you may be as wise and as blissfully happy as I am, and as I feel a strong assurance of being throughout time and eternity, with such a soul to lean upon for strength, joy, and the peace which perfect harmony bestows.

This event was decided just before the *Hibernia* left, but I did not venture to write it to Mary until she was stronger, and therefore thought it best to keep you all in ignorance thereof.

If you are now with her, she may show you my letter, but what are confused words to utter what is untterable. I hardly know how to write a sentence properly; the high festival within has made even Judge Reason tipsy enough to reel about very suspiciously. . . .

Fanny's first, charming letters to her husband's sister and mother were written three days later.

To Anne Longfellow Pierce

May 27, 1843

Dear Anne, For so my heart prompts me to address one it loved upon faith before it received the assurance that hers had made room for a new inmate, your warm affectionate greetings are more grateful and precious to me than I have words to express, for what but the voiceless swelling of the heart and the "happy dew" its overbrimming fountains send to the eyes can fitly reveal the depth and nature of the feelings such a welcome calls forth? My happiness seemed too infinite to be increased until your dear letter arrived, but how much it is enriched by your tender, sisterly sympathy I leave to your woman's nature to interpret. I have so recently entered into my new world that I still stammer poorly its alphabet of love and feel a child-like diffidence in uttering in syllables what if you were by me the "natural language" would better and more fluently make known to you. The holy trust I repose in your brother's long-tried affection, the inexpressible joy which fills my soul in seeing him so happy in mine, after all the pain it was my misfortune to cause him, the stars of hope which illumine the future, the gratitude even for the past, that lifts our spirits momently to Heaven, all all this claims your sympathy, and all this, I trust, we may soon talk over together, if you will grant the petition I now urge. Henry ardently longs to be at home, and cheerfully will I spare him on such a mission, but we fear his Cambridge duties are less yielding. If, however, he can slip away for a day or two, may we not hope that you will be persuaded to return with him to make a visit? If it is possible, pray give us this great pleasure without delay. Mrs. Appleton [1] joins her entreaties to mine and longs to welcome you at her hearth and heart.

Nothing in your kind letter touched me more deeply than the manner in which you resign your brother to my love and care. I

[1] Fanny's stepmother, Harriot Coffin Sumner, whom Nathan Appleton married on January 8, 1839.

have lost a sister by marriage, and I know how hard it is at first to surrender to a stranger the cherished duties and privileges which have grown with our growth and make up a portion of our own being. . . .

To Zilpah W. Longfellow

May 27, 1843

I cannot answer your daughter's precious letter without expressing to you, also, the overflowing gratitude I felt in receiving the affectionate greetings you have sent me. A glad tide of sympathy, from our mutual friends, has been constantly pouring in upon the deep sea of our joy, but none, except that of my own family, so rejoices and satisfies my heart as my assurance that our love receives your maternal benediction.

Would that language could reveal to you how fully I appreciate the priceless blessing God has vouchsafed me in your son's affection, and how fervently I pray to become worthy of it, and to improve my character by his. If the fullest harmony in thought and feeling, and strongest confidence in each other, and holiest reliance upon Him who has guided us to this better country can ensure happiness to his creatures we feel a faith no sorrow can undermine that it will be ours. We earnestly hope that you will often witness it and bless our future home with a mother's sacred influence. I deeply grieve that ill health has been so long your portion, and must now deprive me of the happiness of talking with you face to face.

Heart to heart I trust you will always permit me, and will learn to love one who offers you a daughter's fond respect. I have been long orphaned of that holiest tie, and have suffered that "mighty hunger of the heart" which no other can wholly supply—need I say with what peace and comfort I shall share Henry's blessed fortune in possessing a Mother who loves him so tenderly?

I have urged Mrs. Pierce to make us a visit, and if it is not unkind to deprive you of her services, we ardently crave your acquiescence. But do not indulge our wishes if her absence will cause you any discomfort; if our meeting must be delayed I will comfort myself with the constant hope of it. I have no right to be selfish in my days of abundance, but when will the heart be taught, like poor Oliver Twist, not to "ask for *more*"?

Accept my warmest wishes and those of my family for the restoration of your health, and with much love to Mr. Longfellow, I remain

Respectfully and affectionately yours,

Fanny E. Appleton

The wedding was at 39 Beacon Street, on July 13. Mary Longfellow Greenleaf's vivid description of it, quoted at greater length in my Longfellow: A Full-Length Portrait *(p. 231), ends: "The couple went out to the Craigie the same night by the light of the full moon, and there they seem as happy as possible." From "Castle Craigie," as she liked to call it, Fanny wrote her father a letter just seven days later. It is of no great importance in itself, but it does give a vivid glimpse of Longfellow and his wife settling down in the house that was to be their home for the whole of their married life.*

To Nathan Appleton

Cambridge, July 20, 1843

As Henry is obliged to go to town this morning to attend to some household matters, I send by him our letters from Tom, thinking you would like to see them. . . . The last two warm days must have been delicious at Nahant; here they were not too oppressive for me, and the nights are always cool. Today is fresh and beautiful, and the river seems newly washed from the sultry mists. Felton [2] and Sumner dined with us on Tuesday and Hillard [3] passed the evening, and very agreeable they all were. . . . Our chairs arrived happily from Paul [4] but no window seats; he is very unlike the Apostle in zeal and

---

[2] Longfellow's close friend, Cornelius Conway Felton (1807–1862), professor of Greek and, later, president of Harvard College.

[3] George S. Hillard (1808–1879), lawyer, author, editor, and politician, another close friend of Longfellow's.

[4] Leading Boston upholsterer of the period.

industry. We dine below, which makes it easier for Marianne and is cool and comfortable besides. Margaret Weatherstone has commended to us a countryman as servant. He has rather a Newman Noggs aspect but is in great want of work and has been at service at home since a boy, so that we are inclined to try him for a week at least. If you see Sam Appleton tell him I am awaiting his book of patterns of Lowell furniture coverings to choose one to be purchased in town by Margaret or somebody as our sofa craves such a shield. . . .

TO ANNE LONGFELLOW PIERCE

July 25, 1843

. . . Every day I am more grateful that . . . [God] has bestowed upon me such a noble loving husband, and I long to satisfy all your sisterly fondness by a fuller and nearer survey of our happiness than you have yet had. Nothing but the great pleasure I anticipate in knowing his parents and home would reconcile me to quitting my Eden just now, but we hope to reach Portland on Thursday evening. . . . I have not seen Mrs. Greenleaf [5] since my arrival here, but intend to make her a visit before we leave; James's voice only I have heard since his return, as I was dressing when he called. . . . I am truly rejoiced you have nothing to regret in the effort you made to honor the thirteenth, and shall ever preserve fresh the remembrance of that earnest sympathy in our joy which upheld you through so trying a scene. . . . I cannot tell you how deeply your Cross and the manner in which you bear it have touched and interested me since I have seen you and know what a gentle, loving nature belongs to you. Your face reveals to me a world of suffering conquered by faith and love, and although some of its expressions gave me pain, I loved to study it again and again.[6] I must love you much, and I hope you will love me, for Henry's sake, much likewise. . . .

[5] Longfellow's sister Mary, Mrs. James Greenleaf, at this time a Cambridge resident.
[6] Anne's husband, George W. Pierce, a dear friend of Longfellow's, died during the poet's second visit to Europe.

Two days later, Longfellow and his bride arrived in Portland.

(JOURNAL)

July 27, 1843

. . . We stopped at an old-fashioned house upon a broad street, with a yard in front. At the sound of our wheels a stately figure issued forth and claimed me most kindly as his daughter. Behind him sweet Annie appeared and received me in her gentle, loving arms; half smothered in my mantilla and novel sensations, I entered the house and was greeted by my mother (oh, word sacredly buried in the past, canst thou again live for me?) very quietly and gently, so that I felt relieved from all my fears, and though I omitted to say all I wished to say, felt soon at home. Aunt Lucia [7] and Mary, Marianne (Stephen's wife) were all there, and a nice tea table was awaiting us. Found no trace of Henry in either of his parents; his brother Stephen has a slight resemblance about the mouth. Was shown his picture in Brunswick Professor gown—very interesting to me and *like*.

28th. Up late. Talked with mother of Henry's early traits—his horror of guns, like mine, etc. We three drove around the town. The views on every side of the sea, which almost encircles it, of the opposite shores, varied with woodland and pretty bays, the White Hills beyond and many green islands in the harbor are extremely beautiful and make it a noble panorama worthy more fame. Drove by the house in which Henry was born, almost upon the sea, giving a crooked shoulder to the street. My poet's first glance took in nothing narrower than the free horizon and as much heaven as earth.

After dinner called at Judge Potter's [8] and saw his daughter Eliza. She is painfully thin but has a very beautiful expression of goodness and gentleness. . . . In the evening to a ball at Judge Preble's,[9] kept a week for us. Thought my sister Mary [10] the prettiest and best-dressed person there. . . . John Neal gave me great amusement with

[7] Miss Lucia Wadsworth, Longfellow's aunt on his mother's side.
[8] Barrett Potter, father of Longfellow's first wife.
[9] The father-in-law of Longfellow's older brother, Stephen.
[10] Longfellow's sister, Mary Longfellow Greenleaf.

over point always and froths out at every pore of his face and tongue. his racy, head-over-heels speeches. His mind seems at the boiling-Introduced a dozen people to me as one would mow grass. . . .

30th. Sunday. Drizzling rain but went to church, and heard a very good practical sermon, not, alas, from Dr. Nichols.[11] My attention interrupted by eyes. . . . Had a nice talk with dear Annie, who revealed to me the joys and sorrows of her past. My heart aches for her, poor child, and trembles when I think my all is also in a perishable bark. . . .

August 1st. . . . After dinner Annie drove us to the beautiful Deering Woods, where we walked an hour under noble trees free from underwood, Henry resurrecting boyish associations and flirtations. A green snake startled me upon entering this paradise, fancied it some transformed belle, some Serpentina of the past guarding her domain from intruders. Very pretty nooks overlooking green soft meadows washed by a lazy stream. Cows feeding in deep tangled ravine. Murderous boy and man stealthily pacing these holy aisles shooting God's choristers. . . . Wish I could see the gleesome boy bounding beneath this shade.

Took tea at Judge Potter's. Annie upset the cream jug, which made a milky way over the heaven of the tea-table, a disaster borne with praiseworthy equanimity by the mistress.

August 8, 1843

. . . Returned by the Arsenal [12] and visited its armory. Sumner mistook another visitor for the guide and tried to enlighten him upon the folly and wickedness of collecting guns instead of books. Pleased Henry by calling the line of barrels organ-pipes for that fearful musician Death to play upon. Felt very warlike against war, reflecting upon the noble uses the money wasted upon these murderous purposes might be put to. Spurred Henry to write a peace-poem and discussed the errors of education upon this matter. . . .

---

[11] The Reverend Ichabod Nichols, the Longfellows' pastor in Portland.

[12] At Springfield, Mass. This visit inspired Longfellow's poem, "The Arsenal at Springfield," always a favorite with his wife.

To Anne Longfellow Pierce

Pittsfield, Mass., August 16, 1843

. . . We passed nearly a week at Nahant after we left you, having a very pleasant railroading thither, with Judge Preble, part of the way, to chat with. We had some delicious drives upon the noble beaches in our gig, and a few scramblings over the rocks, one storm which lashed the sea into a fine, foaming rage, and pleasant talks with friends. At Boston Sumner joined us and undertook to enact the part of *beau père* as far as Catskill, where my friend Miss Austin, her brother, and Dr. Lieber, an old friend of mine, enlarged our party very agreeably. There we remained a few days, enjoying the wonderful view from the Hotel (the rich valley of the Hudson and its stately river lying beneath as if seen from a balloon), and the fine wild scenery of the hills around. Our friends continued with us as far as West Point, where we passed a day to make Henry acquainted with its rare beauties, and thence steamed up the river to Hudson, where by railroad and barouche we reached Stockbridge, my ideal of villages. There we had a glimpse of my dear friend, Miss Sedgwick. We shall return to dear old Castle Craigie either on Saturday or Monday, and most happy shall I be to see its venerable walls again, although I have enjoyed greatly every step of my journey. . . .

To Thomas G. Appleton

Cambridge, August 30, 1843

. . . I wish you could see how freshly, richly green our meadows are looking; frequent rains have put a June varnish upon all the country, and our river expands at full tide into a lake. We have decided to let father purchase this grand old mansion if he will. Our interest in it has been quickened by our present guest, Mr. Greene of Rome, a great friend of Henry's and a very amiable, agreeable person.[13] He has excited an historical association, or rather re-

[13] George Washington Greene (1811–1883), the historian, a close friend of Longfellow. See my *Longfellow, A Full-Length Portrait*.

minded us how noble an inheritance this is—where Washington dwelt in every room. Under Mr. Sparks' [14] admirable guidance we explored, the other day, the Revolutionary landmarks in this neighborhood—General Greene's position on Prospect Hill, etc. and he gave us the Battle of Bunker with a graphic excellence I did not know he possessed. Cole, the painter, has been to dine with us, and I find him a most gentle, pleasing man. I shall go in town today to see his pictures. He pronounces our Copley a Sir Joshua, which I much prefer to believe it.[15] . . .

To Nathan Appleton

[September, 1843]

I suppose you have seen Mr. Dexter since he examined this mansion and have heard that his report is very favorable as to its soundness, etc.

We have duly considered and discussed the question of remaining here, and think that, all things considered, we could not do better elsewhere. The house is large enough to introduce every modern comfort we should desire, and there is no position in Cambridge that can compare with it for the views and air. It is, moreover, very interesting to us from its associations, of which we have lately had very exact information from Mr. Sparks. Of course its purchase rests mainly upon your own judgment and inclination, but I state ours frankly that you may know them. . . .

If you decide to purchase this would it not be important to secure the land in front, for the view would be ruined by a block of houses.

To Anne Longfellow Pierce

Boston [postmarked September 19, 1843]

We are on the wing for New York to consult the skilful and much praised Dr. [Samuel] Elliott, who seems to be the only oculist

[14] Jared Sparks.
[15] The picture, still in the parlor at the Longfellow House, depicts the children of the second Sir William Pepperell. Nowadays it is again attributed to Copley or to Mather Brown.

capable of inspiring much faith in these days. We have regretted exceedingly the necessity of leaving Cambridge while it is so attractive in itself and in the presence of dear Mary, whom I fear we shall hardly see again before she goes south, but as Henry's eyes continue the same, our friends fairly push us off to New York. He has been so prudent in resisting all temptation to use them since the difficulty occurred, and puts himself so early in the way of cure, that I am very confident the doctor will not find it a bad case and will, I trust, speedily release him. . . .[16]

To Emmeline Austin

New York, September 20, 1843

. . . We found New York bathed in rosy light, and as we neared the wharf beheld a spectacle which would make a foreigner believe he were approaching the promised land. From a market upon the water apparently insane individuals were emptying into the river basket after basket of peaches, until the river was covered with them. We wondered and conjectured, but Sumner, with his usual zeal to apprehend strange events, asked some loafer the cause, and found that they were not thrown away because corrupted but simply because the supply was greater than the demand—huge basketfulls selling for a quarter of a dollar. After this striking American fact, I was amused, in Broadway, with a sign which I thought would greatly excite the wonder, perhaps terror, of a stranger. This was in huge letters: "Wigs and Scalps." Imagine an Englishman finding this and putting in his note book the awful discovery that the Indian customs and barbarities in America were turned to profit as well as everything else. . . . Coming from the quiet of Cambridge, still more than from Boston, the town seems undergoing an attack of delirium and looks very much as if it needed a keeper or it would run away and do something desperate.

Will you never come to Dr. Elliott? I hear you impatiently asking. . . . Yesterday we arrived, as you know, and Henry proceeded forth-

[16] For a full account of Longfellow's difficulty with his eyes, see *Longfellow, A Full-Length Portrait*, pp. 87–88.

with (while I was trying to pick up the dropped stitches of sleep) to his mansion but found it was one of his invisible days—three times a week only and until three o'clock only he condescends to relieve his victims. This morning at 9 A.M. went all three, and after waiting some two hours, chatting with Mr. Bates, Miss Wigglesworth, Dr. Parkman (whose daughter he has brought for an examination), and finally Miss Howard, his anteroom filling gradually with other suffering mortals, the magical doors flew open, and as framed therein stood the stout doctor with shirt collar *à la* Byron and penetrating look as if he were enacting a *tableau vivant* of his portrait overhead. After Mr. Bates, entered Henry, and as I thought the consultation would be freer without me, patiently awaited the result. This was that it was not a bad case, very similar to Charley Norton's and Sedgwick's and might be cured in a month, or rather that we might go in a month, but even that, I fear, is not owre true. . . .

To Anne Longfellow Pierce

September 20, 1843

. . . We think somewhat of taking lodgings at Staten Island to escape the discomforts of this noisy city while the weather is so warm. We overlook, at present, a picturesque churchyard, but its holy silence only makes the river of life flowing against its walls more painfully audible. It is a striking *memento mori* in this Babel, and its motionless occupants must now and then arrest the steps and thoughts of the onrushing crowd. But I have never seen a city where this present life seemed so apparently the only one to all living in it. It constantly reminds me of Vanity Fair, the "everlasting Now," as Carlyle calls it, being the Divinity worshipped with all the strength mortal bodies sustain. . . .

After the quiet rational lives we Bostonians lead, for the most part, New York always appears to be undergoing an attack of delirium which forbids a moment's rest but breaks its victim on the wheel of petty frivolities. She brandishes straws, believing like the madman they are sceptres.

To Emmeline Austin

[Undated. After September 20, 1843]

. . . Mrs. Butler is here, and we are to dine with her tomorrow to meet Macready, who is also here and seems a gentlemanly person enough. We went last night to hear him in *Hamlet*, and I liked him very well in parts, the scene with his mother particularly, but he has too much stage manner and mouthing, and strove to give new points as modern actors all do, merely to freshen the attention. I was introduced to Halleck at the box door but really forget how he looked. . . .

I have been initiated into Dr. Elliott's sanctum and frankly admit that I was very much pleased with him. . . . With what a business-like way he operates. I shuddered in every nerve judging of the effect from the expression of Henry's face and fear I should administer the torture rather bunglingly. He is getting to some of the painful things and was not fit to be seen many hours yesterday. As he walked home with me I thought people would suppose I had been making him very miserable and that he had been crying his eyes out in consequence. . . .

Willis [17] I half like in spite of myself, and his manners are greatly changed since he went abroad; they are more natural and gentlemanly. It is amusing to read his gossip in the *Mirror* as we get it *au naturel* first. We have a stately, sullen-looking bride here he thinks very elegant and high-bred and beautiful, to which his wife says, "I always qualify Willis's very beautiful." Generally he is pretty discriminating however. . . .

To Thomas G. Appleton

October 14, 1843

. . . Henry's eyes are, we trust, improving under Dr. Elliott's experiments. He ventures to read a little and patiently submits to all manner of dosings and blisterings. . . . Macready is here and we

[17] Nathaniel Parker Willis.

have seen him in *Macbeth* and *Hamlet,* in which he lacks genius but has great art and finish. Henry dined with him and Bryant at Mrs. Butler's table . . . and found him very gentlemanly and agreeable. I have seen Halleck, who seems quite a man of the world and full of humor and gaiety, cocking his eye most drolly at a joke. . . .

To Zilpah Longfellow

Cambridge [postmarked October 25, 1843]

It gives me great joy to announce to you that we are once more under our own roof, which is doubly dear to us because it is to cover us always. We arrived at home yesterday, having returned from New York by the way of New Haven, a beautiful town I had been long wishing to see. I wish with all my heart I could say that Henry's eyes were wholly restored, but I trust you will not be disappointed to know they are only somewhat better, for a month, after all, cannot do much for an evil of this nature under the skill of even such an experienced oculist as Dr. Elliott.

He always spoke of Henry's case as a very simple and very common one, and I have full faith, myself, that with the continued application of his remedies (which I have been instructed to administer) and with obeying the admirable rules he has given him for exercise, etc. that he will gradually find the difficulty to disappear entirely. He can already read a few pages without pain, which is something encouraging.

His health is otherwise better from the amount of exercise he took in New York, and he has resumed his duties this morning very gladly after so long a pause. . . .

To Thomas G. Appleton

November, 1843

. . . Young Lowell, the poet, dined with us yesterday and talked in a very Swedenborgian way of spiritual sympathies. He asserts most distinctly that he has been long in the habit of seeing spirits and will not consider it a disease but a very natural phenomenon, that is, that we *feel* the presence of a spirit spiritually, but always investing those of our friends with flesh and blood, our imagination converts it to an apparent *visible* reality. He says he had a distinct vision one bright afternoon in his easy chair of Maria White's face, and when he saw her was drawn to her by the resemblance. His mother is crazy, and very possibly his organization is, therefore, peculiarly sensitive to wonders. He is about publishing a new volume of poems, much better than his first, he thinks, but no longer himself as he has already left the thoughts which inspired them behind. He has grown much more manly and I think promises much, being certainly pure in heart and aspiring to do good. . . .

To Anne Longfellow Pierce

[Postmarked November 10, 1843]

. . . I have no eloquence equal to expressing our delight in being at home again: the silence here is alone such a blessing that I often stop to listen to it as to the most exquisite music, or as Leigh Hunt says when removed from noise to rest, "I drink in the quiet at my ears as if they were thirsty." As Henry does not like the trial of lamps, we accept no evening invitations, and thus can continue our reading regularly with no interruptions but the very welcome one of some dear friends. He has begun boxing lessons as Dr. Elliott says his frame demands a great deal of exercise, and finds them greatly to his liking. I shall spur him on, likewise, to long walks, which I consider quite magnanimous as I cannot accompany him. . . .

To Mary Longfellow Greenleaf

December 26, 1843

. . . Henry and I have just returned to our own hearth, having eaten our Christmas dinner in town. We remained the next day also and have driven home in a gentle, beautiful snow-storm which is "knitting up the ravelled sleeve" of Mother Earth's *robe de nuit* and giving her a very cheerful aspect. . . . I have been a good deal confined to the house of late, as thaws have rendered the walking intolerable, and find my piazza a great comfort, as I can pace there in nearly all weathers with dry feet. I think of inventing india-rubber gaiters for country wear, or of adopting the ballet-style of petticoat, as long skirts are a very abominable fashion for *country* ladies. . . .

We had a very pleasant visit from Alick,[18] which we persuaded him to prolong after your visit until he was summoned home. He aided Henry with his engineer skill in drawing maps of our *estate,* which we decorated with rustic bridges, summer-houses, and groves *à discretion!* They contrived together to plant a linden avenue in which my poet intends to pace in his old age, and compose under its shade, resigning to me all the serpentine walks, where, in the abstraction of inspiration, he might endanger his precious head against a tree. This runs along the northern boundary, and it is to be hoped will be useful, moreover, in screening us from any unsightly buildings Mr. Wyeth may adorn his grounds with. Henry has ventured to transplant four very sizable elms, to replace the murdered ones [19] in front, and I hope they will take kindly to the soil and be pleased with their new prospects. Out-of-door work is sealed by the frosts until spring, and consequently within doors it begins to flourish. Henry is very busy with his work of translations from ten nations,[20] and I enjoy greatly aiding him therein. My eyes and fingers thus far take the place of his, and I trust they will answer for the whole book unless he is restored to his natural rights. . . .

We passed Christmas evening at Mrs. Ticknor's at a large family party, where was displayed a beautiful Christmas tree, decorated with presents from one relation to another. As it was the first I had seen, I was as much excited as the children when the folding-doors opened and the pyramid of lights sparkled from the dark boughs of a lofty pine. . . .

[18] Longfellow's brother, Alexander Wadsworth Longfellow.
[19] Killed by canker-worms during the occupancy of the house by Mrs. Craigie, who, despite Longfellow's remonstrances, would do nothing to protect the trees because she believed that our fellow worms had as much right to live as we.
[20] *The Poets and Poetry of Europe* (1845).

To Thomas G. Appleton

December 29, 1843

Many thanks, dearest, for your poetical note with its sketch *à la Hogarth* of your *appartement*, in return for which I think I will give you our interior at this present. The Library, you remember, with its cozy fauteuils, heroic bust of Greene, and goodly bookcases, topped by plaster worthies, its tiled fireplace, old-fashioned mirrors, etc. A few feminine changes alone have intruded, but it is mainly the same. So, for our salon beneath, which has been *crée* entirely since my entrance into the mansion. Behold, then, its modern aspect but most comfortable withal: curtains of drab ground, gay with flowers, a flowery paper likewise, between the front windows a mirror in which are reflected, from the paneled wall opposite, our Christmas garlands and the graceful figures of a dame with falcon on wrist and a youthful hunter blowing his horn in *papier maché* through a spruce miniature grove. These are of drab and gold and rest upon Gothic brackets. Between the two windows opening to the east, upon a Gothic stand of dark wood, merrily ticks my pretty French clock, which, it seems to me, told the time more wearily when it spoke from my bedroom at home; below it is the *prie dieu*; at its left your sweet Dutch Girl looks modestly down upon her new life and upon a charming miniature of Il Violino by Mrs. Greene. In one corner is a pretty chiffonier like Aunt Sam's not unadorned with knick-knacks, and over the piano, reaching to the ceiling, stand Sir William Pepperell's two fair children, the boy with his pale face and drooping eyes, seeming conscious of the sad destiny in store for him,[21] and his sister blooming with full English health and looking able to endure any fate that might befall her. Fancy Henry playing a nocturne while I lounge by the fire in a comfortable fauteuil and you have our afterdinner look to the life.

But I have a picture perhaps more interesting than this to paint for you, viz. Allston's great one,[22] which Mr. Dana [23] civilly permitted us to see last week with the proprietors only. With no slight

[21] He died young.
[22] *Belshazzar's Feast.*
[23] Richard Henry Dana I.

feeling of intrusion and of taking advantage of the helplessness of death, I entered his sanctum, from which every eye was excluded while he lived, and while this picture was unveiled, and at first I could hardly enjoy it missing so sadly his musical voice and gentle presence. It is well named his *great* picture. No other shows half as much power of conception and execution; it is indeed a new revelation of his great genius, and is worthy, unfinished as it is, of the best days of Italian art. Belshazzar is alas! hidden under a veil of white paint, but his foot and hand are noble and give hope that the veil can be removed and his perfect figure released. The Queen is finished and very grand, with a countenance stiff and pallid with fear and yet able to bear proudly any interpretation Daniel may disclose. He stands erect in the center of the picture and is complete excepting one hand. Nothing can be more majestic than his figure draped in full folds of brown, his face so serenely noble and inspired, not unlike Jeremiah's. The group of soothsayers is full of power and gorgeous coloring but very unfinished; some of them are like hideous masks, so harshly are hate and scorn depicted. Nothing can be finer to an artist and a poet than the contrast of the pure, effulgent light from the writing upon all the faces in the foreground, and the sickly, lurid glare from lamps before a gold image in the remote background beyond columns and steps innumerable, as if the false pagan atmosphere was shrinking before the celestial and true. Some of the female heads are very beautiful, one especially prostrated in adoration at Daniel's feet, her golden hair and neck bathed in light from the writing, also another earnestly listening as if life or death were in his words. It has a more antique mellow look than his others even and required much cleaning before it could be shown. It is now framed and they think of exhibiting it. I longed to have the freedom of his studio and get a peep at all his sketches, which remain as he left them. . . . The two first sketches for the great picture are very interesting; gloriously colored in parts and having figures which he had better retained. The ominous words which gleam from his canvas seem sadly prophetic of his own doom. *His* empire is over and to be scattered far and wide but only in an outward sense. Lowell has just published a volume of poems.[24] Many are very beau-

[24] The volume, which was called simply *Poems,* was dated 1844.

tiful, more manly and finished than his former and as full of a pure and Christian spirit. . . .

At the beginning of 1844, Fanny looked back over the past year and recorded her thankfulness in her religious journal.

January, 1844

In looking back upon the record of my last year's life, and in thanking my heavenly Father for the blessed gifts of this, how utterly false and vain seem the measurements of time, one twelvemonth being but the dull twilight of chaos, stirred into transient life by a few rays from Heaven, and the next—"a new created world"—"sprung up at God's command." From the tenth of May to this hour there has been nothing but eternity within my soul, for love is the master-key of Heaven, and what heart was ever blessed with greater love than mine, given and received! It is too full for utterance even now, and is so rich in happiness, in hope, in experience, that it cannot recognize its former self, looks back upon it as upon a stranger with whom it parted some centuries ago. Since my hand traced the words on the other page what life-changes! what new and opposite relations and realities have established themselves within me! what buoyancy of hope instead of that trembling fear which regarded the future with tears in its eyes, the past with remorse only, the present with patient but cheerless submission. What an unlooked-for revelation of God's infinite love for his children! How little did I dream what was awaiting me. Poor and starved in heart, I labored in my allotted place and was suddenly hailed as the possessor of a boundless inheritance, a beggar upon God's earth, fed only by manna from above, transformed to its wealthiest citizen, the lord of a human and a poet's heart! Rejoiced am I that I had almost killed all hope of this, had so resolutely stared starvation in the face, content to bear it cheerfully if God willed. A thousandfold more blissful, therefore, was his priceless gift and the pang of unworthiness less cruel.

O Father! with my whole soul and heart and life let me thank Thee, and for his happiness, my husband's, infinitely more fervently I thank thee. Preserve it, we pray thee, and may it draw us nearer to Thee! We thank thee for all the Past as for the Present.

January 14, 1844

. . . After dinner a starlight walk with Henry. "The cool cisterns" refreshed me. Spoke of that noble poem of his;[25] says he cannot believe now he was ever unhappy enough to crave peace so fervently. What joy this gives me. . . .

TO ANNE LONGFELLOW PIERCE

January 17, 1844

I promised, dearest Annie, to report to you, without delay, Dr. Elliott's opinion of the present state of Henry's eyes. He was here last evening and examined them carefully and pronounced them much better and likely to be fully restored before long! His report also of his general health was most favorable. He is to continue the same remedies, and as Dr. Elliott says, the nature of Henry's pursuits sends much blood to the head and consequently to the eyes, exercise is especially essential to his and their well-being, by equalising the circulation. . . .

Our book flourishes bravely, and fortunately my health continues so good that I am able to forward it a little every day while Henry dictates his gleanings from his own rich mind or from the books of others and is able to read what he requires in tongues where I cannot aid him. . . .

I referred above to my health in a way which may puzzle you. I will explain myself by informing you then, in plain terms, of what you have a right to know, viz., that somewhere between May and June I hope to give you a little nephew or niece, for you to exercise all your auntly capacities of affection and interest upon. You can read our hearts, although so much separated from us, and therefore need not to be told how grateful we feel to God for this promised addition to our happiness. . . .

(JOURNAL)

January 19, 1844

. . . In evening Prescott as usual. It has the fascination of a romance and cannot be left. A romance would be thought too ex-

[25] "Hymn to the Night" (1839).

travagant even that should bring out such marvels as truth does here. Nothing in history is stranger than Montezuma's weak surrender of himself to the Spaniards—they but a handful of men and he in his own splendid capital, the despot of millions. His munificent spirit and patient submission to destiny he believed foreordained interest one much in him, and his voluntary imprisonment seems less cowardice than obedience to the, to him, divine will. The audacity of Cortes in demanding it is unparalleled. He too seems to act, like Napoleon, as a man of destiny and to have trusted some superior power to preserve him and his army. The religious motive which shared their hearts with avarice is the only excuse for their conquest. The human sacrifices were so horrible one can't help wishing for the success of the Spaniards, and then again one feels for the poor Indians whose hospitality is so barbarously requited. How vivid and beautiful are the pictures of the valley of Mexico and the lake! it seems like some of the enchanted lands that enraptured the knights of old. Mr. Prescott seems to have seen it all with his own eyes as he makes his reader.

January 20, 1844

. . . Young Lowell the poet came at tea-time to see us, looking very picturesque with his shapely beard. Talked *à la jeune Amèrique* of the great reforms this country is to display—the order of society to become more radical yet, and men of all classes to know each other and love each other in communities, etc. His pure and Christian notions are finely carried into everything with him—remarkable in a youth of imagination. He considers that beards should be worn or God would not have given them, and intends, when old, to sport one of patriarchal length.

January 25, 1844

. . . Read Henry's journal of past days. How I wish I had the record of every hour of his dear life. I am thankful to glean any part of it that was lost to me—how much through my own strange blindness. It is intensely, painfully interesting to me to see how his great heart rode over the billows of every cruel experience, as over the sunny sea which I trust it will now never lose. I regain my birth-right in him, as it were, by reading these faithful pages. . . .

To Thomas G. Appleton

January 31, 1844

. . . For more than a week the thermometer has clung to zero, and here *has* been twelve degrees below it! Poor Mother Earth looks fairly dead and laid out in a tattered shroud of snow and ice: the sky over her is as hard and chill as the walls of a sepulchre; the trees resemble skeletons adorning them and the houses coffins. The ground groans under every wheel as if it suffered from their pres-sure, the Moon's nose is evidently frozen white, and the poor stars tremble as if weeping from the cold, like many poor earthly chil-dren. There must be dreadful suffering among the poor. In fact, we have heard that a mother and three children actually perished with the cold in Broad Street! It is horrible to think of such a catastrophe in Boston, where help is always to be procured. . . .

How painfully interesting it must have been to you to explore the dreadful haunts of crime you speak of. It must seem like a hideous nightmare in your memory, and your assertion that Eugène Sue has colored *under* life is a great grief to me, for I cannot believe that such hells of infamy exist in the souls God has made. There is a frightful fascination about that book.[26] I have many times resolved to look no further into its horrors, but am irresistibly drawn to finish it.

To turn to a pleasanter subject. Have you seen Dickens's *Christ-mas Carol?* He sent it to Felton in its English garb, with capital woodcuts and a nice clear type. It is a most admirable production, I think, and has had great success in England, comforting people for the tediousness of *Chuzzlewit.* It is evidently written at a *heat* and from the *heart,* and has a Christmas crackle of glow about it, besides much pathos and poetry of conception, which form a rich combina-tion. The sketch of the poor clerk's dinner is in his best manner, and almost consoles one for the poverty it reveals. There is a most

[26] *The Mysteries of Paris* (1842–43).

touching song by Hood, in *Punch,* on the low wages for shirt-making, which seems written in blood, it is so vividly "rammed with life," or death rather. . . .

Our book flourishes bravely: we are now among the Danish poets, having despatched the Anglo-Saxon and Icelandic. I write in it every morning, the red-haired *diable's* knock summoning me to deliver up "copy" daily. It is a great undertaking, which Henry half repents, but will be a valuable gathering of stray poems, and of literatures almost unknown to any but scholars. I only lament it should take the time from original poetry, but Henry thinks happiness does not inspire his muse; perhaps she is jealous and sulks. He has some fine things in petto which will flow out when the time comes. . . .

(JOURNAL)

February 2, 1844

. . . How much time I wasted over Latin grammar and Caesar's Commentaries which should have been given to English grammar and English history, but I do not repent the aid Latin has been to me in other languages and in my own. . . .

February 6, 1844

Felton came early and read us the remainder of the abusive article in the *Quarterly.* The mob that claim our Parnassus are hardly handled too severely with their patriotic, but not poetical pretension, "forever thrusting the national flag in your face." Dana and Sprague do not receive justice, but Halleck, Bryant, and Emerson do. Henry, the Reviewer says, is "unquestionably the first of American poets." How I love to hear him praised! and after all how little of the noble proportions of his character is known. . . .

February 7, 1844

A heavenly day! Walked under a spring sun, and then, in a little open sleigh, swept merrily through Brighton and Brookline, our hearts chanting aloud the beauty of God's world. In so mild an air such a drive is next to the exhilaration upon a good steed. All the houses were decorated with clothes taking the air, often festooned under the drawing-room windows! Did no work today of any kind. The sun pronounced it a holiday and we could not gainsay it. . . .

February 9, 1844

A girl in New York has stabbed her seducer (not dangerously) but has been acquitted from the universal sympathy for her wrongs. It is cheering that men begin to feel for women in these matters, and allow them a little justice, but when will the law recognize the moral murder as great a crime as the physical? . . .

February 21, 1844

Stopped with Henry for dressmaker. . . . I have outgrown my wedding dress, and it will no longer cover one beating heart only! O Father, let the child but be as happy, and far better, than the mother and I pray for no other boon. Feel sometimes an awe and fear of myself, a fear that my heart is not pure and holy enough to give its life-blood, perhaps its nature, to another. What an awful responsibility already is upon me! God alone knows how much my thoughts and temper may mould the future spirit. Let me strive to be all truth and gentleness and heavenlymindedness, to be already the guardian-angel of my child. . . .

March 17, 1844

. . . Read Henry in evening the ancient epic of Germany, the *Niebelungenlied* in prose and verse. What a wild but vivid picture of the olden time, with its gorgeous, savage splendor, its gleams of true love through black tempests of war and murder. The first part has much grandeur, humor, and beauty, but after Siegfried's death, horrors on horror's head accumulate till one grows sick with blood. The age of the heroine is evidently quite overlooked in the great number of years the poem covers, but her character is most masterly drawn, as well as that of every active person in the piece. . . .

To Mary Longfellow Greenleaf

March 22, 1844

. . . Henry is in excellent health and spirits, and has lately commenced a set of lectures upon modern languages which I sometimes fear will be too severe a trial for his eyes, although they continue improving. I have proposed, à la Portia, disguising myself in male attire to hear them, but have now resigned myself to getting a rehearsal only. He has been also occupied with writing a few poems, which will appear in *Graham*, in May and June probably, and are among the best he has ever written. I trust one of them upon peace will carry conviction to many hearts. . . .

How do they feel in your part of the world about the annexation of Texas? Here there is great excitement and indignation, and many that have been cowardly about slavery are warmed by the occasion into a clearer expression of abhorrence. Heaven defend us from an act so foolish and wrong!

Graham has flattered Willis as much as he slandered Henry in his portrait gallery, but it is as little of a likeness on the better side. If he cannot find more truth-telling artists he had better resign publishing this species of falsehood throughout the country.[27] . . .

To Zilpah Longfellow

April 3, 1844

. . . I constantly regret that you should only know me as a daughter in name, but if the college holds us chained to Cambridge the greater part of the year, may I not hope this separation will be softened by frequent visits from you and father. I know I ask a great deal, but I long to persuade you that it is, after all, a short journey, and that a resting-place in a daughter's house is wholly different from any other kind of visiting, which, to an invalid, must be more or less irksome. In the autumn, when our repairs are completed, and

[27] This refers to a particularly inept drawing of Longfellow—"the most atrocious libel imaginable," he called it; "a very vulgar individual, looking very drunk and very cunning," which, in spite of all his efforts to prevent it, appeared in *Graham's Magazine*, May, 1843.

I can hope to make you comfortable under our roof, I shall claim the happiness of welcoming you here as a daughter's dearest right.

Henry continues very well, and very busy, having resumed his lectures, from which he reaps golden opinions among the students, I hear, but he wishes he had a little more leisure to indulge his poetical vein, which struggles to free itself from the bonds of these more practical duties. I am a pretty active spur upon his Pegasus, and wish it were possible for a poet, in this age of the world, to surrender himself wholly to his vocation, as the Minnesingers of old. He has written a poem lately upon peace [28] which I am sure will give his mother's heart a throb of great joy and pride, if his wife's has a right to prophesy from its own experience. It will appear in *Graham's Magazine* of May, and I hope will unseal many eyes and touch many hearts. I especially love to have his beautiful spirit occupied in subjects which must better humanity and freshen men's memories with the whole meaning of Christ's everlasting truths of love and mercy, which are so much mildewed by prejudice and the bad customs of nations. So many have already blessed him for the light and strength his words have given them that I long to have him always inspired by the responsibility of his holy mission—of poet.

To ANNE LONGFELLOW PIERCE

Good Friday evening [April 7], 1844

. . . Many thanks for the kind "pricking of your thumbs" in my behalf. My little wardrobe is filling up fast, but any additions your sisterly (or auntly) interest may suggest to your nimble fingers will have an honorable place therein above all the other Lilliputian offerings. These prophetic wrappings excite sensations which must be "felt to be understood" as yet seem more real than the frame they are to serve, and not a little presumptuous to me. I wonder if Eve, despite her fig-leaf teaching, provided herself seasonably for little Cain? . . .

(JOURNAL)

April 13, 1844

May ever as bright a sun and such warm, genial influences rest upon this day, a day ever precious to our hearts, for it is the anni-

[28] This was, of course, "The Arsenal at Springfield."

versary of the birth of all our happiness, of a certain evening party
at Mrs. Norton's, of a certain talk in a window-seat which broke the
spell of long separation and silence. O Father! for what a year of
infinite joy do we thank thee with voiceless but overflowing hearts!
Make us worthy to deserve another like unto it!

All the afternoon in the warm air on the piazza listening to the
quiet breathing of the happy, sleeping world. Interrupted by a
Yankee pedlar of books who wanders from Canada to New Orleans
as if it were a day's trip. *Graham* arrived with the Peace-poem in
print, and a capital story by Hawthorne,[29] which we read.

April 18, 1844

. . . Carey & Hart wish to publish a handsome edition of . . .
[Henry's] poems with choice engravings. I trust it will be really well
done, and that in fine or humble attire they may reach every heart
in the country. . . .

To HARRIOT SUMNER APPLETON

April 28, 1844

. . . Under Mr. Warren's auspices our externals are beginning to
look a little tidier. He has planted us some vines to screen the
eastern piazza and is mending the paths, etc. A famous Turk's
turban of box dignifies the front doorsteps, generously bestowed by
our *very* near neighbor, and roses are to bloom behind them. Within
doors are very welcome symptoms of a remove. Mr. Worcester's
study is cleared and washed, and ready for papering and painting,
also the bedroom, which fortunately needs only a carpet (which is
making at Lowell—the same as in my present room), and by the end
of next week we expect to take free possession of all the premises.
Fearful reports come from Mrs. Worcester of the ravages of moths,
but we flatter ourselves by filling up the cracks in the floors, now
yawning widely, and pasting paper over them to put a veto on this
kind of consumption. . . .

29 "Earth's Holocaust."

(JOURNAL)

May 10, 1844

What can I say of thee, thou birthday of my new life of love and blessedness? Scaredly and silently must thou be honored in my heart, as is the day of its freedom, through death, to a spirit in Paradise.

This was indeed my marriage-day, although another bears the title. He who can alone create the mystery of two hearts fused into one was the only witness and priest of that holiest, happiest union.

May this day ever bring Him nearer then to our hearts than any other.

Walked through the little lane and sat under a tree, sending joy into the blithe air like the birds, the insects and every living thing. Alone alas! for though Henry stole this day from college last year, he dutifully returns the theft this.

May 15, 1844

. . . Read Em Mrs. Butler's poems, which are "rammed with life" and suffering, but too bitter and morbid for a Christian woman and wrong to publish, so many sickly souls will sharpen their griefs upon her thorns. Less poetical than I expected from her geyser-like soul.

May 21, 1844

Passed the day in town and the evening in hearing Ole Bull. He is a divine musician—another Orpheus, and puts a soul into a violin almost angelic. Vieuxtemps and all other scrapers play from the head only, he from the heart chiefly, with deep pathos and sometimes drollery as in "The Carnival at Venice." "A Mother's Prayer," composed by him, was next to the "Miserere" for touchingness—such pleading, pleading tones, deepening into more *passionate* appeals at the end, as if a mother's heart was really speaking through them. He is young to my surprise. A vast crowd and vast applause. Saw returning home a dozen moons instead of one—intoxicated by this music? Charmed this morning by Crawford's "Bride of Abydos," "the music breathing from the face" truly.

May 25, 1844

Hawthorne, Hillard, and Tom dined with us. Hawthorne has a fine manly head but is the most shy and silent of men. The freest conversation did not thaw forth more than a monosyllable and we discussed art glibly enough. I really pity a person under this spell of reserve—he must long to utter his thoughts and feels a magic ban upon so doing, as Dante's poor sinners could not weep through their frozen lids. . . .

May 28, 1844

Harriot brought Em and Mrs. Blake out in P.M. and divers Lilliputian garments from Tom. Shall feel more comfortable with Mrs. Blake in the house. Henry took his sunset row on the river. Sat at window and followed the flashing of his oars with my eyes and heart. He rowed round one bend of the river, then another, now under the shadow of the woods and now in the golden sunlight. Longed to be with him and grew impatient for wings he looked so far away. How completely my life is bound up in his love—how broken and incomplete when he is absent a moment; what infinite peace and fullness when he is present. And he loves me to the uttermost desire of my heart. Can any child excite as strong a passion as this we feel for each other?

CHAPTER V

Wife and Mother

The question Mrs. Longfellow asks herself at the end of the pre-ceding chapter did not have to wait long for an answer. From 1844 until the tragic end of her life, she found, it seems safe to say, as rich fulfillment and satisfaction as any woman has ever experienced in love and motherhood.

TO ZILPAH LONGFELLOW

June 8, 1844

I must make the attempt to write a few lines of remembrance to you before I am prevented doing so by an event which, somewhat to my surprise, has not yet occurred. As I am looking for it daily, and have had my nurse for more than a week in the house, I suppose this will be my last greeting to you for the present. I patiently abide the appointed hour although I must confess to a good deal of curios-ity and anxiety to behold the expected stranger. I hope it will prove worthy of the interest already excited towards it by its parents and their numerous friends.

On the third page of his wife's letter, written next day, Longfellow adds:

Sunday afternoon

Dearest Mother,

I break open Fanny's letter to tell you that she has a son, born at one o'clock this day. Both are very well, and had a pretty easy time of it. The boy is a stout little fellow, with a large mouth, and a dark-ish complexion.

Affectionately yours,
Henry

Fanny's first letter to her father following her confinement was written a little more than a month later, and the next day she took the baby for his first drive.

To Nathan Appleton

July 12, 1844

I think you will be glad to know from myself that I can no longer be considered an invalid. I have taken my meals since last Saturday in the library, and am only waiting for some rain to lay the dust to drive out. . . .

Homeopathy has cured my lameness, and I now walk through our spacious rooms very comfortably, though rather totteringly as yet.

The baby thrives apace and is growing fatter and heavier every day; all the household are devoted to him and are wretched if he cries; that is the *lower House.* He is very good on the whole but keeps his bright eyes open longer than Nurse Blake likes in the day time but shuts them like other folks at night; he "trains" now and then (nurse phraseology for screaming) but only from hunger—his health is excellent. . . .

(Journal)

July 13, 1844

The anniversary of our wedding day. Celebrated it right joyfully by my first drive abroad with baby, Henry, nurse, and Tom, and our first dinner in the new dining-room. Hillard joined us. Charles provided a handsome bouquet and resurrected for the occasion some of our wedding-cake whose existence I knew not of. What a year this day completes! What a golden chain of months and days, and with this diamond clasp, born a month ago! I wonder if these old walls ever looked upon happier faces or through them down into happier hearts.

With this day my journal ends, for I have now a living one to keep faithfully, more faithfully than this.

Fanny meant exactly what she said. She made a few more entries in her religious journal, but the only new volumes she ever began

Fanny Appleton Longfellow
From the painting by G. P. A. Healy

Maria Theresa Gold
Appleton

Nathan Appleton

Mrs. Longfellow's parents, after the paintings by Gilbert Stuart

Fanny Appleton (right) and her sister Mary, from a miniature on ivory by Jean Baptiste Isabey

Fanny Appleton

from a marble bust by Lorenzo Bartolini

Henry Wadsworth
Longfellow

from a photograph made
about 1852

Henry Wadsworth
Longfellow

from a photograph
by Brady, 1859

Henry Wadsworth Longfellow

105 Brattle Street, Cambridge, Massachusetts, which was the home of the

Edith (left), Annie Allegra (below), and Alice Longfellow, daughters of Henry Wadsworth Longfellow and Fanny Appleton Longfellow, from the painting by Thomas Buchanan Read

Charles Appleton (left) and Ernest Wadsworth Longfellow, sons of Henry Wadsworth Longfellow and Fanny Appleton Longfellow, from a pastel by Eastman Johnson

The children of Henry Wadsworth Longfellow and Fanny Appleton Longfellow

Mrs. Longfellow, from a
crayon drawing by Samuel
Worcester Rowse

Mrs. Longfellow in later
life, from a photograph

Fanny Appleton Longfellow

*were, as we shall see, two little books which she called "Chronicle
of the Children of Craigie Castle." Except for these, which she devoted entirely to the sayings and doings of her children, we shall be
obliged to rely almost entirely upon her letters for the rest of our
story.*

To Thomas G. Appleton

October 15, 1844

. . . Last week the young Hyperion became a Christian. Mr.
Gannett baptized him, and he bore the ceremony with truly Christian resignation. Instead of crying he laughed, at times chuckled
most indecorously. We gave a sit-down *déjeuner* afterwards, and
drank his health in the crimson and gold goblet. His name is simply
Charles, it being long enough with that. . . .

*One cannot call the year 1845 uneventful for Fanny, since it
brought her, on November 23, her second child, Ernest Wadsworth
Longfellow. But it has not left us extensive literary remains.*

To Mary Longfellow Greenleaf

January 4, 1845

. . . Cambridge is muddy and quiet. Nothing has been going on
but lectures on Shakespeare from a Mr. Hudson,[1] an original genius,
who is a curious mixture of roughness and culture, giving forth, in a
most awkward way, an eloquent flood of very admirable and profound and dainty thought. . . .

Lowell was married the day after Christmas, and has proceeded
to Philadelphia with his bride, to pass the winter. She did not look
as charmingly as was expected, her dress being exceedingly simple
but not well arranged. . . . Lowell has just published a volume of
Conversations on the Old English Poets, very beautifully written,
with many charming quotations. Henry's *Waif*[2] is very successful.
One edition is already sold though it was not out until New Year's
day. . . .

[1] Henry Norman Hudson (1814–1886), the well-known Shakespeare scholar
and editor.
[2] A small anthology of fugitive poems which Longfellow had edited.

To SAMUEL LONGFELLOW

February 13, 1845

. . . I am now writing Henry's Preface,[3] wishing, as I began the book, to finish it with my own hand. His labors are, therefore, over, excepting this slight one, and if Felton is diligent in taking Portuguese lives,[4] it will be completed in a few days. . . . If you see the *Mirror*, you know how shabbily Willis tries to excuse Poe's insolence.[5] Have you seen a curious poem by the latter entitled "The Raven," most artistically rhythmical but "nothing more," to quote its burden? . . .

There is another reference to The Poets and Poetry of Europe *in an undated letter of Fanny's to Longfellow, written at a time when he had had to go to Portland without her. Since she speaks of reading proof for a volume which was published in June, the letter must date from the first half of 1845. It may, therefore, be given here.*

To HENRY WADSWORTH LONGFELLOW

To be taken in small globules, for the eyes

Wednesday ev'g. ½ past 10

I am sitting in the Library, best beloved, after giving my little bird his dream-like repast, and have seen him sink away into his nest with hardly a note, and now, naturally, turn to thee to bring thee, if possible, nearer this solitary night. Little Em has disappointed me, thinking it undutiful to leave her Father for so long a time, but promises to pass tomorrow night and the next with me. I was grieved not to see her at dinner, though partially consoled by the toughness of the mutton, but am already consoling myself more effectually for losing her as a bedfellow, i.e. upon *this* sheet I am not alone. Forgive me, dearest, such a sorry joke. Do you know this is, thank God! the first letter I ever wrote you (is not that

[3] To *The Poets and Poetry of Europe.*
[4] Professor Cornelius C. Felton wrote much of the biographical material in this work, Longfellow being severely handicapped by the condition of his eyes.
[5] In his criticisms of Longfellow's poems.

strange grammar? I am sure I don't know—my heart talks so fast I cannot tell what my pen is about) and I devoutly pray it may be the last.

Do you wish to know what I have done with my forlorn self since that merciless Ark carried you off with a whisk, as of a whale's tail, to dry land, that is toward Portland? Did you leave your carpet-bag behind expressly to comfort me with a sight of the boy that had seen you since I had?—ah, I fear no such ingenious stir of sentiment inspired him. Charley and I watched the last flourish of the tail, and then did all we could to console each other, but "ah with a difference." No magnetism told him what he had lost—so I would not.

Looking at the rainy river, and a dismal walk on the piazza, and picking lace off a gown for Charley sleeves consumed the afternoon, or that part of it out of the nursery, then came a rubbing of little fists in sleepy eyes, and a vociferous demand for "King Cole," then the bottle, and then blessed unconsciousness. Frank Appleton appeared after tea, just as I had taken to a serious dose of *Chuzzlewit*, and Sam to the big fauteuil, and with law and gossip killed the evening, a lingering death. Sam has been interrupting me with a discussion about the tendency of Unitarianism, which subject I proposed to him for a theme, so I see the brown monk in the corner has begun tomorrow's Aves, and I have *not* passed a solitary night. I have been looking over a proof sheet or two and think Felton has treated Tasso almost as badly as Alfonso did, not giving him any kind of credit for his passion for Leonora, but coolly imputing his madness to the fact that his poems were poorly published, or something of the sort. Owen could have said nothing more.

Good night beloved—bring Annie if thou canst—Love to all.

Forever and ever
thy F.

To Francis Lieber [6]

March 10, 1845

I hope you have not thought me very unmindful of your request for my husband's verses upon the ancient city of Nuremberg, but I

---

[6] This letter is reproduced by permission of the Huntington Library, San Marino, California, owners of the manuscript.

have been vainly waiting for leisure to copy them, and only yesterday lighted upon them in a compacter shape—in print.

I trust they will pleasantly remind you of the fine old city and its rich associations. I cannot read them without a yearning to behold its venerable grandeur, for I was never there, and while my eyes are daily annoyed by the stiff, barren deformities of American architecture, I long to refresh them with antique quaintness, so full of feeling and thought as well as dignity and grace.

I have an extreme enjoyment of the true Gothic; nothing in art but Beethoven's music touches and elevates me as much, and I often feel how much more devotional I should be if I only lived near a cathedral, for while our souls look out through the the senses we must lean upon them for help. It is a serious affliction to this country to possess no architecture, and though they are doing something in New York to give our people an idea of what a church was, yet, after all, no money can purchase antiquity for us, or countless associations, which are the true riches of such a building. *You* must feel the barrenness of the land, so fresh from soils overladen with treasures of art, but I hope your life will not seem more wearisome by the contrast than it did before. . . .

Since Texas was annexed my patriotism has almost died a natural death, but I hope you return with undiminished affection to the land of your adoption. . . .

To Mary Longfellow Greenleaf

April 18, 1845

. . . Alex brought with him from Washington a huge lion skin, a gift from the Commodore,[7] and it was a pretty sight to see little, rosy Charley playing upon it and fearlessly grasping the claws and tail. This infant Hercules has developed a tooth at last and has been promoted into shoes and short petticoats, so that he creeps about the room like a spider and is beginning to stand up alone with the help of a chair. His physique flourishes with ever increasing vigor, and he is hard at work upon something from dawn till dusk. I rejoice to

[7] Commodore Alexander Scammel Longfellow, Longfellow's mother's brother.

see him so well, but sometimes sigh for a little more sentiment and repose in his nature!

In August Longfellow went to Brattleboro, Vermont, to take another treatment from the hydropathist, Dr. Robert Wesselhoeft, whose patient he had been in Germany in 1842. The following letter gives a glimpse of the Spartan regime to which he was subjected.

To ANNE LONGFELLOW PIERCE

Brattleboro, August 7, 1845

. . . [The water cure] is a slow process, and the doctor is rather tried by having patients go away after a short trial, thereby spreading the impression that he makes no cures. Henry's eyes cannot probably gain much, but I think his general health will undoubtedly, he enjoys the perpetual bathing so much, and is tempted into so much exercise and appetite. He is summoned every morning at *three* o'clock, and I see, half in my dreams, a wavering of lights, and hear a mysterious whispering in German, steps descend the stairs and cross the road, then all is silent. He goes for convenience to the doctor's opposite, and is there swathed in wet sheets with blankets over them, and after reposing until the perspiration is brought about, is plunged into the bath. He then returns to breakfast, and between nine and ten walks to the douche, which is on the opposite side of the ravine, there tries divers baths and, drinking at every spring, walks till dinner-time. At five in the afternoon he has another bath and walk and thus concludes his labors for the day. The female hydropaths wear large straw hats, and of course are not very elegantly attired, so they appear, wandering over the hill-sides, not unlike Swiss peasants, in keeping with the scenery! . . .

To MARY APPLETON MACKINTOSH

Cambridge, December 31, 1845

A very, very happy New Year to you, my darling, to Robert and your little ones. I trust you are by this time rejoicing, as I am, in a nice new baby, and will soon be as well and comfortable as I begin to find myself. . . . I had no idea your expectations were so near a consummation, you had been so silent about them, and feel very anxious to hear that all is going well with you. When we meet again it will be like the meeting of Jacob and his brother, who parted single and returned with a caravan of camels, children, et ceteral . . .

Tomorrow is dear little Em's [8] wedding day, and I expect to get to her wedding, having been out to drive now for a week. She is to have quite a large number present, having such a host of friends. . . . I wish I could feel as happy at this marriage as I hoped to when my darling left her solitary life for a wedded one, but I cannot crush a crowd of fears which at times have almost tempted me to forbid the banns. She is not the least in love with Wadsworth, but builds her hopes of happiness on faith in his excellent qualities and the success of others in a like situation; she consoles herself with believing such a marriage as mine is very rare, and though I believe it must be as regards the full sympathy of tastes and tempers, etc., yet I cannot think many venture on such a union without the ardent love which can alone fuse all differences. . . .

Henry's *Belfry of Bruges* is out; a piece on Charley and one suggested by me on the old clock at grandfather's seem to be much liked.[9] . . .

The year 1846 begins with a summary and a prayer in the religious journal.

Two years more of perfect happiness have gently departed, leaving behind them two blossoms of eternity—our darling boys. O holy Father, when my soul turns to thee it becomes all gratitude, glowing like a mirror in the sun, and is it not ever turned to Thee? That is a question I tremble to answer. Thou seemest, at times, so near me, so encircling my every thought and desire that the peace which ever emanates from Thee flows through my whole being like its blood of

[8] Emmeline Austin, who married William W. Wadsworth. Fanny's fears for her friend's happiness were justified in an unexpected way when Wadsworth's health failed permanently not long after his marriage.

[9] "To a Child" and, of course, "The Old Clock on the Stairs."

life, a tide which cannot ebb; then alas! how sadly often the petty
scaffolding of my external existence, with its slender, intricate
fibres, obscures the sky and shuts me in its prison. The blessings and
cares and anxieties of my home, though warmed by Thy light, O
Father, engross my hopes and conceal the hand which gives them. I
sometimes fear that because I am upheld by so many more joys than
formerly, I lean less confidently on Thee, and yet I would humbly
believe I have ever loved Thee for Thy own sake mainly—from no
selfish need alone. . . .

O Father, let me never become blind to Thy presence, let me
never feel the air cold from loss of thee, nor, in the darkest night
mankind receives, forget that thou wearest darkness itself as a
mantle.

To Anne Longfellow Pierce

January 16, 1846

Henry's unexpected presence among you will seem a very speedy
fulfilment of your gently uttered wish to that effect. I console myself for these yearly absences by picturing the joy written upon each
face of the family circle as he appears to greet them and heartily
wish I could sometimes witness it with my own eyes. I trust he will
find you all well and able to enjoy his visit.

He must tell you what a charming gift God has graciously given
us. Charley so completely filled my heart that I felt as if I could
never have a child I should love so well unless it were a little girl,
and I am ashamed to say, welcomed this darling with a slight pang
of disappointment, but it was *very* short lived. He has won upon me
as much as Charley did in the same time—perhaps more, as I comprehend better how to take care of him, and he is more constantly with
me, by night as well as day. He sleeps by my bedside in his little crib,
and is so quiet and good that the touch of my finger is sufficient to
rock him gently asleep after each meal. I have nursed him entirely
until this week (when I found myself obliged to give him a draught
of the bottle), and he has thriven famously. He promises to be a
great beauty. His eyes are very large, and he observes people and
things as much as a child twice his age, besides cooing and laughing

very deliciously. His head is better formed than Charley's was but is quite as bald. I think he looks exceedingly like Henry, particularly in the shape of his head and eyes. So much for maternal portrait painting.

What shall we call him? Our minds are somewhat divided between Henry and Ernest. Can you propose a better than either? but I imagine you will not care to go beyond the first. . . .

To Emmeline Austin Wadsworth

June 16 [?], 1846

. . . Possibly you would be interested . . . in my brother Sam's [10] first preaching here Sunday before last. It was the first public performance I ever witnessed of any one connected with me, but apart from that, except my marriage and first communion, I cannot recall a ceremony which ever moved me so much, gave me such deep, delicious joy. He prayed and preached like a young apostle with such tenderness and fervor that I could not help shedding tears. He has just the right spirit for a preacher—most firm and courageous and independent, shrinking not from rebuking public, as well as private, sin, and yet with a gentleness which is all subduing. His style is very simple and manly too for a beginner, and his heart makes it eloquent as well as his imagination. You know this is not exactly like praising my own brother, so I can do it with a better grace. I confess that I am very proud of him and feel as if he were destined to do much good. . . .

Charley is now quite a talker and exclaims "where is the papa?" all day long. . . . Erny also grows apace, and being promoted to short petticoats is very vehement in his gymnastics. . . .

December 23, 1846

. . . We have all been ill with the prevailing influenza. First Henry was taken down, and before I had done nursing him, Charley and baby were seized very violently, particularly the latter, who

[10] Longfellow's brother and official biographer, Samuel Longfellow (1819–1892). See Joseph May, *Samuel Longfellow: Memoir and Letters* and *Samuel Longfellow: Essays and Sermons* (both Houghton Mifflin Company, 1894).

narrowly escaped a lung fever and made us very anxious for a few days. He was so drooping, sitting on my knees a whole day without moving, that I sent for the doctor, who found him in so high a fever that wet cloths were immediately placed on his chest, where was the greatest inflammation, and, though wrung out in ice-cold water, they became perfectly dry in a few minutes, so great was the fire in him. These were renewed every half hour for a few hours, and then the fire was fairly put out, and he fell into a perspiration and quiet sleep. So quickly quelled was the danger by this blessed treatment. . . . As soon as these recovered, my turn came, and I have rarely felt so ill with a cold, or I should have written you before, but I have had such a raging headache I could not look at white paper. . . .

We have . . . [Sumner's] portrait by Johnson, as well as Henry's and his sister's now. Sumner's is most excellent, with his softened, best expression. . . . [11]

We had a visit of a night lately from Slidell Mackenzie.[12] I like him in the main, but it seemed to me like child's talk (so long have I been out of that atmosphere), his military exultation in our Mexican achievements. It is to me so strangely barbarous to hear a man of years and sense find any glory in that wholesale butchery and murder, and he really seemed to feel glad of this war as a proof that we had not lost the tiger and wolf nature wholly during so many years we had been sensible Christian citizens! War is to me, now, like the fair enchantresses of old, when one disenchanted of their false show, simply wicked and disgusting. A warrior is not so respectable a man to me as a butcher, and quite as unpleasantly associated. . . .

January 2, 1847

. . . I hear of no new philanthropic movements of peculiar interest. "The league of universal brotherhood" is not only gaining new

[11] Crayon drawings of Emerson, Hawthorne, Sumner, C. C. Felton, and Longfellow himself, all by Eastman Johnson (1824–1906), still hang in Longfellow's study at the Longfellow House; the same artist's portraits of both Anne Longfellow Pierce and Mary Longfellow Greenleaf are in the dining room; in the parlor is a drawing in color of Charles and Ernest Longfellow, which is reproduced in this volume.

[12] Alexander Slidell Mackenzie (1803–1848), naval officer, author of *A Year in Spain* (1829), etc.

signatures in England and America, but stamping itself into new hearts from month to month, an undercurrent to purify the future despite this thundering of cannon in our present ears. "The learned blacksmith" [13] has sent Henry, as he requested, a pruning-hook made by his own hand, by way of autograph, and wants him to set going a peace society among Cambridge children, to match one he has founded in old Cambridge, England, as in many other towns there, to get the next generation, if possible, into Christian harness. The anti-slavery fair I declined assisting this year on account of its helping lectures to denounce the Union rather than slavery, a melancholy perversion of good intentions. . . .

January 11, 1847

. . . You ask me for new books. What do you think we have been reading? The *Iliad*, in Chapman's rugged translation!! And after wading through its sea of blood till fairly sickened with details fit only for a dissecting room, . . . we exploded the other night, at our little whist club, upon poor Felton, aided and abetted by Sumner, who was there, on the shocking immorality and disgustfulness of Homer, which the hearty Greek received with Olympian serenity. . . . He made a faint attempt to put us down by asserting it sounded very differently in the original, which was an argument we were weaponless to wield. . . .

To THOMAS G. APPLETON

January 31, 1847

. . . We took Willie and Hatty [14] yesterday to see the Viennoise children, they exhibiting Saturday afternoons for juvenile audiences. It was a charming sight, by bright gaslight in this very pretty theater —the children in the boxes so flushed and eager, and the swarm of little butterflies on the stage, with their most finished and swift

[13] Elihu Burritt (1810–1879), self-educated linguist, internationally known reformer and peace advocate.

[14] Fanny's stepbrother and sister, Nathan Appleton's children by his second wife, Harriot Sumner.

evolutions. The last dance, with the whole forty-eight in it, was very lovely, half being dressed as little black slaves and forming morning-glories with red and white scarves in every stage of bloom. Many of the philanthropic here are quite troubled about the future of these girls, as their heads will probably be turned by such an education, but they are from the lowest poor and have now a happy life enough; perhaps they are not in more danger of ending badly than if starving in the streets or toiling in factories. . . .

We dine with Papa, next week, to meet the Swiss geologist Agassiz, who has finished his lectures here but remains to dissect Father Neptune's subjects, of whom he has a fearful amount of knowledge. Tadpoles and eels are his bosom friends, and a mere glance at their brains tells him their whole history.

Sumner has been arguing off minors from serving in Mexico. The suppression of the war is more loudly demanded every day and I trust ere long will be accomplished. Dickens's *Battle of Life* shows he is waking up with the rest of the world to a knowledge of the truly honorable victories and can distinguish between a hero and a butcher. . . .

To Emmeline Austin Wadsworth

February 2, 1847

. . . Henry went to Portland last week for two days, and Sam came to cheer my loneliness. I believe I shall never outgrow the thousand fears that beset me when he is absent, nor learn to bear better that wretched sense of a constant want—the hunger of the soul, which I once could endure *tolerably*, but now, through much pampering, get very heartsick under. . . .

To Zilpah Longfellow

February 19, 1847

Your charming little mats were exceedingly welcome, and I should have thanked you for them long since. It is a great pleasure to me to have pretty things about me associated with a kind remembrance, worked in love, and not the cold purchase from my own purse which so many must necessarily be. They furnish a room almost with living faces, the noblest kind of furniture, and make one feel always within reach of friendly hearts. I wish I could make some such return, but alas I am not much skilled in handicraft, and before I was married rarely ever had a needle in my hand. Being much alone, a book was a better companion, for I think one desires society while sewing.

To Thomas G. Appleton

February 28, 1847

. . . You will see how universal the sympathy for the sufferings of the Irish [15] has been throughout the country, and what relief is offered. Ships loaded with flour barrels are a nobler fleet than if stuffed with gunbarrels—to preserve life and not to destroy—yet lately the latter were seriously thought of for this same country—but the heart of man is not, thank God, so "desperately wicked" as the catechism teaches, and, like a true instrument, gives out a pure tone when rightly touched.

I am sorry you think Sumner was wrong in condemning Winthrop. The country is fast agreeing with him, and more than one manly eloquent voice has been raised in Congress for the recall of the army and the cessation of supplies. A Polk cannot make an unjust war righteous and fit to be carried on by a Christian people. . . .

The following letter, which is preserved only in part, is undated, and the recipient cannot be identified. But it is too interesting to be omitted, and since Blanche Lowell died in March, 1847, it clearly belongs here.

. . . Poor Lowell has lost his little girl, who was, you may remember, about a month younger than Erny. Rapid teething overcame her. Such a blow must soon sever, I should think, the mother's slender hold upon life, and the poet's future darkens sadly before me. Henry saw him yesterday, and found him calm. They are, as yet,

[15] In the terrible famine caused by the failure of the potato crop.

sustained by that strong Faith which makes separation impossible and feel their child is ever with them, but mortal weakness must shatter this soon, at least for a time. . . .

Have you yet read Emerson's Threnodia on his child? It is a cry of the soul such as has rarely been so well uttered before, and is, in parts, Miltonic in richness of expression. Despite his faults, he is a great poet to me. His creative power would alone set up a dozen others. . . .

Henry has gone to college to lecture on Dante, carrying with him my Francesca by Scheffer, to charm the young eyes of his hearers. I am reading along with him in ever-fresh delight. Hillard's lectures are very beautiful, I hear, and he gives them great richness and variety by showing all sides of Milton's life and character; the last, on divorce, Summer says, made him tremble, it touched so nearly upon Hillard's own wounds. That reminds me that Emerson does not live happily with his wife; how many alas! wear a bleeding side under their cloak. "What influence we preferred elect"—to such a transfigured destiny is often the deep thought of my heart when I see what others are called to bear and forbear. And yet, will you believe it, Lowell heard some unknown individual at Northampton coolly assert that Henry and I were among the unhappy slaves of the matrimonial oar!! It is frightful to me that anybody could ever conceive, or fabricate, such an impossibility, and when I heard it gave me a fit of misanthropy to think what calumnies and lies may be circulating about us while we fancy ourselves living peaceably secure from the nagging of a malicious tongue. . . .

To Thomas G. Appleton

March 31, 1847

. . . Ralph Waldo looked in on us yesterday with his falling voice and shoulders. He was very pleasant, and more communicative than usual, on the strength of a very complimentary note Henry wrote him on his poems, whereby hangs an amusing tale. In it, Henry says, "I fear my wife will never read my poems again, she is so fascinated with yours," etc., which the solemn Alcott reading, and construing *au pied de la lettre,* goes about asserting Mrs. Longfellow no longer reads her husband's poetry! . . . Emerson was charmed with the Raphael cartoon which we brought down from the nursery where it hangs, for him to admire. He delighted in the free marks of the pencil, and said, "I see now a fine picture must always impose silence like a cathedral." . . .

CHAPTER VI

The Growing Family

Though Fanny fortunately did not know it, she herself was only a year and a half away from the same sorrow that had overtaken the Lowells. For the present, however, the emphasis was all upon joy. Her first, passionately desired daughter was born on April 7, 1847, when Fanny herself became the first woman in the Western world to bear a child under the influence of ether.[1]

To ANNE LONGFELLOW PIERCE

[Cambridge, Friday]

Many thanks for your warm sympathy in my new joy and etherial bravery. I am very glad to be able at length to confirm Henry's accounts of my well-being with my own hand, and to assure you all that I never was better or got through a confinement so comfortably. It *must* be a tedious thing at the best, and I am rejoiced to be about again and to be strong enough to enjoy my new treasure. She is as charming as these fresh spring days, which really seem to me a resurrection after the lifelessness I left the world in before I was ill. Our clumps of lilacs are perfuming the air, the apple-trees in fullest blossom, everything very late but coming out finely; as I escaped watching the slow change, therefore it bursts upon me as a miracle almost.

My little darling promises to be as quiet and good a baby as Erny, and has a sweet little face just beginning to show there is a soul behind it. She has very dark hair, a lock of which I have preserved, but blue eyes as yet though of a deep dye. I think she will be like Henry. She is very fat, and I make a better nurse than ever before. . . .

I am very sorry you all thought me so rash and naughty in trying the ether. Henry's faith gave me courage, and I had heard such a thing had succeeded abroad, where the surgeons extend this great

[1] *The circumstances are described in my* Longfellow: A Full-Length Portrait, *pp. 242–243.*

blessing much more boldly and universally than our timid doctors. Two other ladies, I know, have since followed my example successfully, and I feel proud to be the pioneer to less suffering for poor, weak womankind. This is certainly the greatest blessing of this age, and I am glad to have lived at the time of its coming and in the country which gives it to the world, but it is sad that one's gratitude cannot be bestowed on worthier men than the joint discoverers—that is, men above quarrelling over such a gift of God.[2] As one of my brother's lady friends abroad, a pious, noble woman, says, one would like to have the bringer of such a blessing represented by some grand, lofty figure like Christ, the divine suppressor of spiritual suffering as this of physical. . . .

TO SAMUEL LONGFELLOW

June 11, 1847

. . . The last steamer brought my brother Tom, as you must have, by this time, discovered, just in time to hear the last opera, which was *Norma*, and very beautifully sung and acted by the Tedesco, although she is no Grisi; the music I enjoyed exceedingly, and the moonlight scene, with "Casta diva," etc., was better done than in Paris for picturesque effect. One excited individual threw twice, in the course of the evening, his hat and cane upon the stage at her feet, having nothing else but himself to throw, which I thought would follow. I also saw the *Mosè in Egitto*,[3] which is magnificent in music but very unpleasant in design, the burning bush and invisible voice appearing on the stage, with Moses very visibly coiffing himself with his twin horns of gold when entering the former! Also his solemn prayers before each miracle were very disagreeable to me, and the final glorious one was written, it is said, to keep from laughing the French audience at the ludicrous crossing of the sea by the Israelites and subsequent tumbling in between pasteboard

[2] The reference is to the long-continued squabbles as to who really deserved the credit for the great discovery. When that incorrigible punster, Oliver Wendell Holmes, was consulted as to whether the monument in the Boston Public Garden should be erected to Jackson or to Morton, he suggested that it be dedicated to "ether," which was done. See Eleanor M. Tilton, *Amiable Autocrat* (Henry Schuman, 1947), pp. 186–89.

[3] By Rossini (1818).

waves of the Egyptians. Despite the prayer, laughing was not to be restrained here. This opera took place during the ministerial week, and I wonder greater horror was not expressed at such an improper performance. I heard it without Tedesco, who was ill that night, but had not courage to go again, the fiery rain, which actually caught the scenery, seeming to me so dangerous. It was afterwards suppressed. This Italian gulf stream of song, however, so far warmed the Puritanic ocean from its natural chill that, actually, from allowing the *Moses* to be acted as an opera on Saturday afternoon, they accepted it as an oratorio Sunday evening itself. To my simple Unitarian judgment, instead of a religious piece it was quite the reverse, for taking Moses, as Mr. Prescott says, as "only a historic character of some note," there is something revolting in this mimicry of the divine interposition by cold-blooded actors.

To Emmeline Austin Wadsworth

July 2, 1847

. . . Mrs. John Bryant has an etherial baby, another girl, which is the latest and best news, I believe, unless it be the unwelcome arrival of the President,[4] who was as famously douched as Tyler, the favorite compliment of our sky to unpopular presidents. As he drove up Beacon Street bareheaded, Mr. Quincy holding an umbrella over him, he snapped at every frigid bow as a dog at a bone, and bestowed many upon Mr. Prescott's blooming balcony of damsels, none of whom returned them; Tom thinks cutting a President in this way is the greatest thing he has seen since his return. His reception was barely a civil one, the office claiming what the man could not, but it is said he thinks it so cordial he means to bestow himself longer upon us on his return from the east! . . .

Henry has had one most desperate love-letter—a real love letter, though the person knew he was married, as was she! but said he could have never found his heartmate, as she implied she had not! It was equal to Bettina's to Goethe for spiritual passion, if there is such a thing, but, unlike Goethe, he did not answer it. . . .

[4] James K. Polk, whom Bostonians hated because they held him responsible for the Mexican War, iniquitous in itself and doubly abhorred as certain to increase the slave power.

I suppose I can now tell you that he is correcting the proofs of a long poem called *Evangeline,* written in hexameters, describing the fortunes and misfortunes of an Acadian damsel driven to this country from Canada by the British in the olden time. It is a very beautiful, touching poem *I* think and the measure gains upon the ear wonderfully. It enables greater richness of expression than any other, and is sonorous like the sea which is ever sounding in Evangeline's ears. I hope you will like it. It will not come out till the autumn. . . .

The following letter is interesting—and amusing—for its glimpse of the contemporary reaction to the early books of a writer of whose stature and future position in American literature nobody then living was aware: Herman Melville.

To NATHAN APPLETON

Martin's Point, Maine, August 4, 1847

. . . We have just attacked Prescott, after skirmishing through *Omoo,* which is very inferior to *Typee,* being written not so much for its own sake as to make another book apparently. I understand the author is engaged to a daughter of Judge Shaw. After his flirtations with South Sea beauties it is a peculiar choice (in her). . . . Last week who should be seated next us at table but Bryant the poet and his wife and daughter. They were on their way to the White Mountains and merely looked in on us for a day. He looks very grey and thin but she fairer and plumper than I remember her. He charmed the children by planting sticks as trees for them, and other little attentions, and seemed more the poet than when seen in the turmoil of New York. . . .

The next undated letter was presumably written soon after August 18, when the Praslin murder occurred. It has been said that this crime contributed to the French Revolution of 1848.[5]

[5] Modern readers know it best through two fine novels: Joseph Shearing's *Forget-Me-Not* (1932), also published as *Lucile Cléry, A Woman of Intrigue* and *The Strange Case of Lucile Cléry,* and Rachel Field's *All This and Heaven Too* (1938). Hawthorne may have used it long before in *The Marble Faun; see* my *Cavalcade of the American Novel* (Holt, 1952), pp. 49-50, n. 23.

To Emmeline Austin Wadsworth

. . . I have been haunted night and day by the dreadful Parisian murder of the Duchess de Praslin, and hope you will nowhere encounter any account of it. It reminds me of a discouraging remark Tom once made, that despite the apparent advance of the world in Christianity, it was as likely as not the last man alive might be another Cain. We are reading Cottle's Reminiscences of Coleridge and Southey, and after that have two tempting volumes of Miss Pardoe's Louis XIV, and after that *Memoirs of the Queens of France*, and after that Prescott's *Peru*, which we have been *potting down* for winter suppers. I am always sorry to see the summer go like a pretty woman out of my sight, but rejoice to sit down again by my chimney corner for the evening, with book and spouse. . . .

(Journal)

[October 11], 1847

My little Charley is now nearly four years old, and yesterday . . . I spoke to him for the first time of loving and obeying another being than his earthly parents. From the peculiar tenderness he bears to his father I felt he might gradually learn to look lovingly and reverently upward, for the habit must be established before the mind or heart can grasp the existence of a God, and it seemed to me, suddenly, that he was not too young to begin this habit, though I should shrink from petrifying it into a form.

Upon this happy impulse I called him to me and told him, with reverent manner, he had another papa up in the sky (one must lean upon some material prop with a child, but their vivid imaginations are ready to believe all things and almost approach faith in their disregard of limits and reasons), who sent down the snow and the rain, and took care of all the little birds, and loved him very much, and Erny and his papa and mamma and everybody, and hoped he would be a very good little boy, and be always kind to Erny (whom he sometimes abuses). His dark eyes dilated with childish wonder and interest, and he said at once, "I want to go up there and see him. I want to take Erny up there to see him." I told him he could not see him, but He could always see Charley and Erny, all day and all night, and loved to see him good, and was grieved to see him naughty. He listened attentively, and most touching to me was his childlike trust in my words, though he understood them not. How truly should we thus learn from Christ of the mysterious depth of God's love, but without the child's ignorance of heart (for the heart perceives more than the reason) and the child would listen as believingly to the false alas! as the true if told by one he loves.

This morning I asked him if he remembered what I told him of his father in the sky. He said eagerly, "Oh, yes. I shall have a garden there"—then, running to the windows, "There, that is my garden down there, and I shall have another up where the snow comes from." This idea, purely out of his own head, reminded me of the Swedenborgian faith in the transplanted gardens of Paradise—that those flowers loved by the just here will bloom for them above. Thus they cultivate flowers with a sacred care.

It is with great awe and timidity I venture upon planting the first seeds of that faith which is to be the life of my child's soul forever. I never so sounded my own faith, its sublimity and scope, as when trying to compress it to a child's understanding, to place in its little hand the first clue to the infinite labyrinth of material and spiritual existence. I never taught before a virgin soul, and most holy and precious does my office seem to me. God grant me strength and wisdom to teach rightly and worthily of his delicate and susceptible creation, where a slight mistake on my part may have lasting ill effects. . . .

Since little Fanny was baptized on October 31, 1847, the following undated letter must have been written from Cambridge during that month.

To Emmeline Austin Wadsworth

. . . I am hoping to welcome my dear Annie tomorrow, who has half promised to come and celebrate Lissy's christening, which takes place some time this month, I suppose, unless you wish it kept for you. We are not yet quite satisfied to call her Fanny, though Henry generally settles upon that after proposing more romantic ones, such as Bertha, Edith, Alice, etc. I should call her Maria, after my mother, but we do not either of us like the name much, and I do not associate it particularly with her, and have besides a little cousin so called after her. I proposed as a compromise Mira, which was her signature always when writing to my father before marriage, who figures as Alonzo according to the romantic fashion of those days, and wrote not a little poetry under that inspiration and cognomen, but Henry suggests that Jane Norton's dog is so named. The more one thinks about it, the harder it is to decide, for there *is* something in a name, which one has often on their lips, though, to be sure, the most ordinary becomes winning by association. Henry's mother's name is Zilpah, which is rather too peculiar and Biblical. . . .

Henry has just purchased a charming modern antique bookcase imported by Paul, who has chairs of various kinds also, and can import anything you like. It is carved in high relief with a shepherd piping on either side (appropriate for books of poesie) and cherub's heads to be grasped for drawer-handles and is just what I coveted. He has placed it where Homer stood, and is to have two more like it, to go between the side windows, which will set off the library nicely. By taking three he gets them for $110 apiece, which is not dear considering the duties, freight, etc. The one is $120. . . .

Fanny had now become completely the wife and mother. It is not unsuitable that for the record of her activities during the next two years we should find ourselves so largely dependent upon her

CHRONICLE OF THE CHILDREN OF CRAIGIE CASTLE

"Pensa che questo di mai non raggiorna"

January, 1848

Charley

Four years old lacking a few months, is a tall boy for his age, very straight and well made and graceful in all his attitudes; has a fair complexion with very rosy cheeks, light yellow hair but soft and silky, though without curl; dark brown eyes, small and deeply set in his head, very penetrating and intelligent in expression; mouth small and firm and very fond of kissing; when taken with a fit of shyness curling up at the corners in a very droll way.

He is very active and eager in disposition, fond of exercise in the open air, dragging a waggon or wheelbarrow, and in the house constantly inventing new plays with the chairs, sofa, etc. as well as his regular toys, delighting in enacting omnibus-driver or railway engineer, or baker, or carrier, or anything in the active life of business. A wooden cricket suffices him for sled when turned on its smooth back, or boat, which he takes especial interest in, often asking "Where boats live?" He is impetuous in temper, but appeased by kind words, never by force, is very loving, and has very gentle and quiet words, though generally full of activity. Promises to have a rich and noble nature, open on many sides.

Ernest

A little past two years, is of course too young to prophesy much about, but he is now an angelic little child, of most delicate complexion, with soft light hair, large, beautiful, brown eyes, of most tender and dreamy expression, mouth rather large and constantly filled with his thumb, which he sucks whenever not engaged in his sports with unparalleled devotion. His head is very beautifully formed, with a most spiritual brow, which gives me many a sigh of anxiety, it looks so like those which only hover over this earth, as the cherubs in Italian pictures, to bear away again to their native atmosphere. His frame too is most delicate, and he has none of Charley's robust energy. He joins in his plays, often with excelling merriment and roguishness, and mimics all he does and says, but loves best to nestle in one's lap, with his thumb in his mouth, holding a handkerchief drawn up to it in a peculiarly dainty way as he does his sheet in bed, and be petted, and rest there quietly, with his dreamy eyes hardly gathering the meaning of anything around him. He is timid and tender as a young bird, but most winning in his gentleness.

Sumner calls him "the young philosopher" from his brow and thoughtful air. He promises to be the poet, Charley the man of action.

Fanny

Little Fan, not a year old, is only a round, rosy, merry plaything with dark blue eyes, a cunning little mouth, and a very intelligent, eager air. She is a good baby, more like Charley at her age than Erny. . . .

January 1, 1848

Charley came into my room saying, "Happy New Year" (but what knows he of Time?), with radiant face, dragging by the hand a pretty baggage wagon, his papa's gift—Erny also happy with a cart and horse. . . .

January 8, 1848

Took Charley in omnibus to town to see Em's little baby. Had a nice long chat with her. Charley much interested in boys skating on Frog-pond, and very ambitious to do the like. Brought Erny a cake to console him—his little face pressed against the nursery-window to welcome our return.

January 23, 1848

All still sick with colds—poor baby very wretched, wailing in a way that racked all my nerves. Inarticulate distress is most trying of all: we know not where to apply the remedy, and it is so painful to work blindly. Papa ill too—had a rough day of it, with only nervous Sarah in the nursery.

The following undated letter refers to Samuel Longfellow's ordination, which took place at his church at Fall River, Massachusetts, on February 16, 1848. The poem referred to is "Hymn for My Brother's Ordination." Longfellow's indisposition was due to the fact that he had not yet quite recovered from a minor operation.

To Anne Longfellow Pierce

I am extremely disappointed, as is Henry himself, that he has not recovered faster, but there is one little point which has not yet healed, so that he cannot comfortably dress himself and go out, but is still sitting in his dressing-gown, unshorn and unkempt, and has not tried a descent to the dining room. Therefore I much fear that I cannot hold out any hope of his being able to go to Fall River. . . .

I enclose you Henry's hymn thinking the home-circle would like to see it. It is very simple, but I hope you will agree with me in thinking the "unseen Christ" is a striking association with such a ceremony. Henry wrote it one sleepless night in bed, where he carries his portfolio for bed-fellow (I sleeping in the next room with open doors) and writes down in the dark what comes to him. . . .

The "Chronicle" is resumed:

February 17, 1848

While Henry and I were driving this morning with Charley through Newton, poor little Erny was found by Mary in his crib in convulsions, from teething. She and all greatly terrified, but, thank God, he got through this severe crisis safely. Dr. Hoffendahl came out and gave us a preventive medicine. Watched by him most of the night, slept pretty well though feverish, and began to look like himself.

February, 24, 1848

Colder day and Erny full of glee. Charley made me tell him "Jack and His Beanstalk," which I altered from original version, as he was troubled at "the naughty man who didn't like little boys," and made out instead a Paradise for children in the land above. . . .

March 12, 1848

Chicks greatly interested in a little mouse who lives behind the chimney. Put out crumbs for him but they could not catch a sight of him.

A picture of wolves pursuing a sleigh with two children and their mama fascinated them—also Santa Claus with pockets stuffed with playthings.

April 21, 1848

Charley busy after dinner shovelling gravel with his barrow. I went down to village with Henry, and we saw, to our dismay, the two boys demurely pulling their wagon, having run away from home. Charley went up into the Post Office and asked for letters "for his mama and papa"!! They came back with us but a loose horse terrified me with thinking of the risks the truants ran.

June 9, 1848

Charley's birthday. Mary [6] brought him pretty presents from town, and we exhibited the magic lantern which elicited immense applause. He is four years old and a big boy of his age.

June 11, 1848

Warm day. Out with chicks on hay after dinner. They fatigued themselves out, and Charley went to bed very feverish. I drank tea with Henry and Sumner at Julia Howe's but could not enjoy it fearing my boy was ill. Found him so hot and restless on returning that removed his crib into my room and held his little hand all night.

June 12, 1848

Charley better but Erny very feverish, so potent was yesterday's sun. Amused him and the others with catching fish with a magnet from basin and exhibiting Charley's "Logical garden," as he calls it. Better at night, thanks to aconite.

June 17, 1848

Flags flying for Battle of Bunker Hill. Ronny asked what it meant —was shy of telling him—who could explain a battle to a child for first time? I wish mine need never know such things have been. . . .

July 10, 1848

Nahant. . . . Children much afraid of a little brown dog who is unhappily fond of them. Charley is a great coward. Erny also be-

[6] Mary Appleton Mackintosh, Mrs. Longfellow's sister, who, with her children, was visiting in Boston and Cambridge at this time.

cause delicate. Baby alone lets him come near. She dances on her toes along piazza singing merrily. She is very affectionate and very coquettish. . . .

August 23, 1848

Commencement day. Took children in carriage, with Papa in his gown, to see the procession. Thought of the time when my heart would tremble like some of the mammas there to see my boy stand up to spout before that awful audience.

August 29, 1848

. . . Poor baby drooping today, and at night very feverish with symptoms of dysentery. Dr. Hoffendahl wrapped her in wet bandages about the abdomen, also one on her head. I watched her all night and the fever yielded to these good measures.

August 30, 1848

Very hot. Darling baby very feeble though without fever. She is as quiet and patient as possible, uttering no complaint. Very restless and wakeful all night.

September 1, 1848

Baby confined to her bed and lying there so sadly patient, with her poor pale face and hollow eyes—such a contrast to her usual exuberant life, I can hardly bear it. Thank God the disease is no worse however.

September 2, 1848

The Doctor thinks baby decidedly better today, and my heart is lightened a little. But she is so thin and feeble, and lies upon her pillow almost without consciousness. Kept up the wet bandages on the abdomen.

September 6, 1848

A very anxious heavy day. Poor baby seemed to have much trouble in her head, and the doctor feared congestion of the brain. She was quieter after a wet towel on the head, and had a tranquil night. Nursey Blake watching her, who has come, much to my comfort.

September 7, 1848

Doctor thinks baby decidedly better today. The bad symptoms in her head have gone away, but she is very very weak, so that she can hardly bear being moved and does not seem to know me, which is very hard to bear.

September 8, 1848

Baby no worse, though needing a little mercury. The doctor does not venture to check the disease at once on account of her teeth. Poor darling lies perfectly passive, with her large hollow eyes looking up so pathetically, but never a smile or a word. My courage is almost broken. . . .

September 9, 1848

Baby showed some pain today, which went through all my nerves. Pretty good day on the whole. She looks to me like mother, her sharpened features giving her a much older look.

September 10, 1848

A day of agony unutterable. The doctor evidently shocked at baby's state, and hope almost dies within me. Another physician watched with us through the long, long night, giving no sign of cheer.

September 11, 1848

Sinking, sinking away from us. Felt a terrible desire to seize her in my arms and warm her to life again at my breast. Oh for one look of love, one word or smile! Mary was with us all day. Painlessly, in a deep trance, she breathed. Held her hand and heard the breathing shorten, then cease, without a flutter. A most holy and beautiful thing she lay and at night of look angelic and so happy.

September 12, 1848

Cut a few locks from her holy head, placed her in the library. With unopened roses about her, one in her hand, that little hand which always grasped them so lovingly. Dr. Francis spoke over her, and she was carried to Mt. Auburn. Struggled almost in vain with the terrible hunger of the heart to hold her once more. Every room, every object recalls her, and the house is desolation.

September 13, 1848

Cannot keep despairing now of the other children, and thinking how they will look when dead. Their gleeful voices agonize me. Charley told Nurse Blake "Sissy was up in the sky," and when I told him yesterday, he said, "Oh, I want to go too." When Death first enters a house, he throws so long a shadow—it seems to touch every one.

September 14, 1848

A cold, dark day in sympathy with our gloom. . . . She is every-where. In the garden I see only her merry steps and little hands grasping the flowers with glee and shouting "Pretty," and then I see her with them in her cold hands. But she is playing with the flowers of Paradise, I fondly trust.

September 16, 1848

How dear is "every plot of ground Paced by those blessed feet around." The little white bonnet is at my side out of doors and at night. I fancy a cry in the nursery and listen thinking she must be there. But I thank God all tears are wiped from her eyes and that she can never know such grief as mine.

To Anne Longfellow Pierce

[September, 1848]

I have been wishing from day to day to thank you and dear mother for your notes of affection and sympathy, but I have had quite a number to answer, which was so painful to me that I thought you would excuse the delay. Only one who has entered within the sanctuary of a mother's sorrow can understand that peculiar form of suffering, but all sorrow has a sad resemblance, which makes the sympathy of the afflicted soothing and strengthing to us and gives us a strong bond of union with them.

We feel that it is a blessed thing to have a child in heaven, to unfold its powers within the unchanging sunlight of God's love, and to be taught only by holy spirits, and it is a deep comfort to us to dwell upon its life, so happy here, expanding without a pang into far greater happiness. I feel it also a lofty privilege to bring so pure an offering to the Redeemer's feet, and am happy in the thought that it is forever safe within his arms, but we cannot always "keep heights which the soul is competent to gain," and at night the old longing will still come back

> for the touch of a vanished hand
> And the sound of a voice that is still.

In the garden she is ever at my side, but now it is a comforting presence, and has given me a love for it I never had before. I see her many steps in the paths, and her eager hands grasping the prettiest flowers, and strive to fill my heart only with the thought she is now happier yet, playing with the flowers of Paradise. The whole house is consecrated, likewise, by her memory, and I love to live over and over again the whole of her little life. I talk with the children often of her, that they may not forget her, and they receive with undoubting faith whatever I say. . . .

My remaining blessings are dearer to me than ever, though I feel I can never henceforth call them mine, and at first saw nothing in their faces but the awful Shadow which had entered our home. I am calmer now, and mean to enjoy them as long as they are granted to me.

The following are journal entries.

September 26, 1848

Beautiful day but one of wretchedness to me. Went to town and saw Harriot and the dentist. The glare and noise bruised all my wounded nerves.

Little Erny breaks up all my rest at night by nestling against me, and then

> Like a calm vessel next a hideous rock
> My heart heaves near this one idea—
> I feel *her* embrace no longer.

October 14, 1848

Very weary and wretched. I seem to have lost interest in the future and can enjoy my children only from hour to hour. I feel as if my lost darling were drawing me to her—as I controlled her before birth so does she me now.

October 22, 1848

. . . Felt much happier today, i.e. more tranquil and resigned. To be patient is the hardest of all lessons, I find, in either physical or mental pain.

Henry has so much more than I!

October 25, 1848

Drove in with nurses and children to see the great show of the entrée of water into Boston.[7] They broiled all day on the balcony in a hot sun amused by part of the procession and the crowds of people. Just before dark the huge fountain rose like a spirit from its prison. Very fine fireworks lighted it at night and the small heads were glad of their pillows.

October 30, 1848

Misty, muggy weather, destructive to nerves. Charley struck me with a stick and the pain made me cry like a baby. He has grown very insolent, but a few words from his papa softened him and he begged my pardon very penitently.

[7] From Lake Cochituate. The fountain was on the Common. This celebration marked the establishment of Boston's public water supply system.

November 1, 1848

Lovely day. Lost it all by visitors and packing for Mary. Felt ready to cry like a child, a good day is so important to me physically and mentally. I am all down again this week. Em's baby upset me. I devour my children's faces as if looking my last upon them, and shrink with cowardly terror from the possible future.

November 5, 1848

Rainy day. Went to church and at communion all the gates broke loose and I was overwhelmed. I seem to gain no permanent strength, only an outside crust, which is soon shattered, but my grief is softened, though not lessened.

November 30, 1848

Thanksgiving Day. Went to Chapel to Father's quiet pew and heard a graceful sermon from Mr. Peabody on gratitude and a happy home. He does not boldly venture upon the great sea of Truth, but plays well on the shore. Was overcome by allusion to the lost of the year. Thought how my little Fanny came tripping in after dinner last Thanksgiving. Took walk with Charley and Henry round Common greatly interested in lamplighter.

December 9, 1848

Cold winter again. Erny has taken cold, very feverish at night. Had his crib in my room—a night of agony and anxiety listening through the hours to his short breathing from the very crib in which my little Fanny breathed her last. Aconite expelled the fever towards morning and he slept quietly with me.

December 12, 1848

[Eastman] Johnson began a drawing of the children in pastel. He thought Erny would make a lovely one. They sat very well. Charley vastly tickled with the idea. . . .

December 31, 1848

Clouds hang on. Erny very feverish at night. Took him into my room and had an anxious night, hearing the soft footfall of the New

Year without being able to give him a very hearty welcome. Another giant sorrow for me may be hidden under his cloak.

Before leaving this terrible year, we must look at a portion of one undated and unaddressed letter fragment. Lowell's Fable for Critics *was published on October 21. Ten days later, Longfellow noted in his journal that he had "nearly completed"* Kavanagh.

. . . Have you seen the *Fable for Critics?* Is it not very clever and witty? The author you will easily guess. . . . Henry has finished a tale called *Kavanagh*, which, however, I hope he will enlarge before printing it. It needs more filling out, but has passages of extreme beauty on a background of plain Yankee life. I doubt if it will be as popular as *Hyperion*, for Germany is Henry's native country. . . . Still it is well for him to try his hand at painting our raw beauty, for no one else can give it such a charm.

He passed a few days with Emerson at Concord, and met Alcott, Channing, Thoreau, all Emerson's "gossips" as he calls them. They seemed very quiet, impressive people, he says, but he had little chance to hear them roar. He rather spoiled his day by going so late, instead of taking the early train, as Emerson wished, and then he could have had a satisfactory talk with the sage before the others arrived. He, Emerson, has been here once and was quite changed, I thought, by his foreign, social life—much more lively and talkative and like a man of the world, told us of Tennyson, whom his friends wanted Emerson to take to Italy, and of Bailey, who devotes his life to *Festus*, improving and enlarging it and never meaning to write anything else. I have no doubt it has shaken the kaleidoscope of his brain into many new figures, this handling of society, and the result I hope we shall see. . . .

The 1849 records are much more abundant than those from 1848. We begin with the second volume of the "Chronicle of the Children of Craigie Castle."

January 5, 1849

. . . Charley very cross and violent, had finally to be punished by his papa. It breaks my heart to see these demonstrations of temper, thinking what pain it will give him in after life, but he has a very tender conscience and a very loving nature, and is as angry with himself as with others, so I think it will be easily subdued. It is chiefly imitation, too, of the older boys he has seen. He thinks it manly to repeat their saucy phrases. He has no sulkiness fortunately—a flash and all is over. Little Erny flies, like the dove of peace, to comfort me when Charley abuses me—he is an angelic little child, so gentle and good always. He sits in his small rocking chair at my side as demure as an old woman.

January 9, 1849

. . . Dreamed my darling Fanny was restored to me; sitting quietly by my side, she said she had been in heaven. Dream caused probably by seeing baby in omnibus, which gave me a hysterical feeling, and a story I heard of one coming to life when the last sad offices were performing. . . .

January 14, 1849

Both chicks in study after breakfast, a pretty picture, sitting on the same cushion, looking at their little books, their rosy faces and fair locks touching. Out throwing snowballs with Uncle Stephen after dinner. Told them story of the little boy (my version of Jack and the Beanstalk) who planted bean in the garden and it began to grow, and every time he did a good thing it shot up higher, and when he was generous and kind a beautiful flower bloomed on it, and when he was naughty the flower died, and it grew shorter again, and the leaves turned black and dropped off. And so it grew up and up to the sky, and he found he could climb up it, putting his feet on the leaves as steps, and when he reached the top the last flowers sprang to his shoulders and made little wings with which he flew among the clouds till he reached a lovely garden, where all good children lived and flew about, taking care of flowers, feeding little birds in nests, and doing a thousand kind and loving things, and the poor naughty children wandered outside, hearing their voices and longing to see the garden but could only peep through chinks in the wall until their beanstalk grew tall enough for them to look over the wall, and the more they were good the faster it would grow, etc. etc. They listened delightedly to my moral lesson and seemed to understand it.

January 17, 1849

Told children of my adventure last night returning from Julia Howe's dinner. The omnibus ran against the carriage and broke the traces, so we descended on the bridge and took shelter in the tavern nearby, warming ourselves by the cooking stove in the kitchen, where divers lean but hospitable females were preparing supper for uproarious teamsters. The damage was soon repaired and we reached home safely. . . .

February 1, 1849

Charley begs warmly for the story of the beanstalk and listens to it with great solemnity. If I change an accustomed phrase, or make an addition, he is in an agony, and still more if I laugh. He apologizes if he laughs himself, and says, "I did not mean to." It is to him too true and earnest not to be received seriously. I love this reverential spirit and am very unwilling to wound it or have it wounded. It is the best shield he can bear through life, and never, never I trust may he be ashamed of it. It is the very shadow of God's presence in his soul.

To EMMELINE AUSTIN WADSWORTH

February 14 [1849]

. . . Mrs. Butler continues her readings to the delight and wonder of her crowded audience. I have been to all but two, and have considered the last always the best, though, perhaps, *Lear* is a more astonishing proof of her power and pathos than any. *King John* was very fine, Falconbridge, Arthur, and Constance so beautifully portrayed, and I hear her Queen Catherine was most touching—so much her own story, a stranger resisting her husband's divorce and pleading for her daughter. She wept and everybody else. Last night was

Macbeth—very grand and ample, especially the second witch scene, where the "hell broth" seemed boiling before your very eyes, she gave it such motion with her voice. You can have no conception of the sonorous clangor of her voice, nor of its infinite compass and exquisite sweetness. Then such lines as this she gives so beautifully, "The crow makes wing to the rooky wood." She has read parts of *Hamlet* to the enormous audience of the Tremont Temple and gives it us tomorrow. The enthusiasm about her is as great as when she acted here, but she will not repeat her course. She reads once or twice in Salem, once here, and in New Bedford, and then to New York. . . .

March 2, 1849

This has been a week of dissipation, or I should have written you earlier. . . . On Monday evening Mrs. Butler read to the admiring Cantabs [8] *The Merchant of Venice* and was escorted upon the stage by Henry. It was a very crowded and appreciating audience, and she read it with her usual power and skill. I sat directly under her and thought her face never was so beautiful as in Portia's speeches, etc. When it hardens to Shylock it becomes so altered it is like a different mask, suddenly slipped on. She came home with us afterwards, and we had a very nice little supper with Hillard, Sumner, Stephen, and ourselves only. . . . She was in great spirits, as she always is after reading, and seemed to enjoy it much. At the close I presented her with a bouquet and Henry with a sonnet,[9] which he read. She was much overcome and could hardly recover herself. Her affectionate nature is easily touched by kindness, and the tears flow at once. She seemed to take a great fancy to the house, and I was much disappointed she could not stay all night. . . . I saw her Tuesday evening at Mary Dwight's, . . . and she sang one of her old songs and danced and seemed much more at her ease than usually in a party. . . . The next night she read at New Bedford and will begin her course at New York tomorrow. She promises to return in May, so you must stay to hear her. It has been the highest of all public pleasures, and I feel that after her interpretations of the

[8] Cantabrigians, i.e. inhabitants of Cambridge.
[9] "Sonnet on Mrs. Kemble's Readings from Shakespeare."

great poet I never shall wish to hear him from less gifted lips. And to listen, night after night, to such wonderful creations has made him loom before me as a greater miracle than ever before. He has left nothing unsaid. . . . The *Hamlet* was, I think, the one that gave me the most intense enjoyment. I never before heard it as I imagined it, and the reading of his father's ghost was something miraculous—the clear, unearthly tone melting away like mist. . . .

To Samuel Longfellow

March 18, 1849

. . . *Kavanagh* is coming on bravely, and will probably be out in May. It is a story within a story. A poetical village schoolmaster wishes to write a romance and remains wishing, though one passes before his eyes. There are therefore two heroes. This is all I shall tell you of the story. I am sure you will be charmed with it. There are many very beautiful thoughts in it and a background of Yankee life humorously depicted without the vulgar element. Emerson dined here the other day with Lowell, and lately gave his lecture on England, which is full of shrewd observation. . . .

To Thomas G. Appleton

March 20, 1849

Since you disappeared as suddenly and mysteriously as a juggler's chicken from the astonished eyes of Edward Austin, leaving as in like cases, nothing but an *empty box* behind you,[10] I trust all has gone well with you and that you are fast recovering health and spirits in the balmier air of *outre-mer*. I have been much disappointed to see so little of you this winter but it seemed hopeless to entice you into our quiet from your gayer life. I do not like to feel so separated from you during your short visits in America, so cut off from all familiar intercourse and sympathy. For a few words exchanged in a hurried visit I do not call intercourse; they merely glance upon the surface of life and reveal nothing of the inner his-

[10] He was supposed to dine with Julia Ward Howe but went to Europe instead. Fanny's anxiety over her brother's restlessness of spirit is often expressed.

tory. I should have been glad to have your confidence more entirely, to know all you were feeling and suffering, but as opportunities have been difficult to find for this free overflow, and you sought to make none, I can only hope you were happier in being silent or had nothing to reveal. . . .

(JOURNAL)

April 12, 1848

. . . a night of wearing anxiety with Erny. His last double teeth are coming through and he woke from his morning nap with great fever and weight upon his brain. He did not recover from this oppression until four in the morning when he put his hand to his head (being in his crib at my bedside) and said in his natural sweet voice, "My head is cool now—got all well; you are very glad, aren't you, Mama?"

Such nights of anxiety as I have had this week between Stephen [11] and Erny seem to add ten years to my life. Julia Howe was here *à cheval* yesterday afternoon wishing for the *intense* in life. What more can she desire than the extremes of joy and suffering in domestic life? Life has been too intense to me this year. I should welcome calmer repose, to heal my wearied brain and heart.

To CHARLES SUMNER

[July, 1849]

. . . I read yesterday Emerson on war. How good it is to have been written so many years ago! I wish he would write something as useful now and not absorb in clouds what should be fertilizing the earth and feeding his hungry brethren. Where has his humanity gone, I wonder, for this article proves he once had some. It is very sad to me to see him, like Goethe, a mere "looker on here at Vienna," but perhaps I do him injustice. He has written against slavery, etc., but when I meet him he is like a ghost to me. I never feel he cares, from his heart, for any human being. They are merely singular

[11] Longfellow's older brother, now approaching the end of his troubled and ill-managed life. He died in 1850.

phenomena, not brothers, to him. But enough— He thinks he is working in the best way doubtless, and I have no right to judge him.

(JOURNAL)

July 4, 1849

Passed day in town. Henry in Portland to see his father who was very ill, he feared dying.

Charley sat up to the fireworks and was highly delighted and excited, wished the rockets would hit the sky and said, "I could sit up two nights to see them."

TO HENRY WADSWORTH LONGFELLOW

Study—9 o'clock Monday [July 9, 1849]

I trust to hear from you today beloved, or tomorrow certainly. Sumner will take this into town in a few minutes, and I hope you will get it tonight that you may know we are all well.

Sumner came out Saturday evening just as we were locking up, went to church with me yesterday, to hear William White preach a very dull sermon, and had Felton to dinner. I consoled them for your absence by a bottle of rose champagne! After tea we walked to Mrs. Follen's and returned by the warm twilight to hear Curzon (which came from the Book Club) the rest of the evening, Sumner reading aloud. He is fascinated with it and has been reading it this breakfast also. Yesterday was a very warm day and this promises to be like unto it.

The chicks are gay as usual, and send many kisses to papa. They still talk of their charming day at Aunt Sam's and the fountain which delighted them. We remained there to tea, and they were very good all the time, Maria [12] amusing them with all manner of pretty things.

I showed Felton your list for examination, but there was only the Spanish. Shall I make some out for other languages? Sumner says he will conduct the whole matter for you if you are prevented returning, if you will write what you wish done.

---

[12] Maria Goodwin, companion to Aunt Sam.

Two editions of *Poems* and three of *Kavanagh* of similar size have arrived from the Liverpool publisher.[13] He says a recent law prevents a foreigner from obtaining a copyright in England, or a publisher for him, but he will pay you $100 for the manuscript of your next volume. I mean to have it early, before printed here.

There is a letter here for Read, directed to your care, which I suppose he will call for. Nothing else has come.

Mrs. Todd wants Anne.[14] I shall part with her, as I suppose our movements [15] will be soon decided.

I trust you have been spared, darling, all the pain possible and will be cheered through the trial, whether it is long or short. How I long to know all you have been suffering. My thoughts have been momently trying to penetrate the curtain between us, so strange and oppressive to me. A long, long kiss just here.

Ever thy
Fanny

TO EMMELINE AUSTIN WADSWORTH

Portland, July 13, 1849

You will be surprised to see Portland instead of Newport at the head of this note. It was a very sudden change of plan, caused by the illness of Henry's father. He has been very feeble all winter, and within the last ten days has seemed to be failing so rapidly that Henry was twice summoned here by telegraph, and finding he was likely to linger in this state some time, or drop away at any moment, we decided to give up Newport and take up our abode here for the present. I am very glad we did so, for even if he should rally from this apparent giving way of the vital powers it will probably be his last summer on earth, and Grandmamma takes such pleasure in having us and the children near her that, for all reasons, we did best.

We have very comfortable quarters in a large and well-kept hotel very near their house, and although the heat has been excessive the three days we have been here, it is so unusual in Portland, we shall

---

[13] John Walker.
[14] A servant.
[15] I.e., summer plans.

not probably long have reason to complain of it. It is extraordinary weather—the nights are so warm we sleep with every window wide open, a thing I never ventured to do in Cambridge. The children feel it a good deal, and go about with nothing but their drawers and petticoats! Though it seems rather city-like here after Cambridge, there are so many fine, shady streets they will make out very well for walks, but it is rather hard work to amuse them through the heat of the day. We have a private parlor communicating with our bedroom, and that with the nursery, which is very convenient, particularly as Henry must sometimes leave me to take his turn as watcher.

His father has happily no pain, and lies perfectly tranquil, dozing nearly all the time, and rarely recognizing anyone. He has been an invalid many years, having ruined his constitution by too close application to his profession, and has been so depressed by his loss of activity that it will be no pain to him to leave his weary body. He has the dignity and courtesy of the old school, added to a gentleness and sweetness of disposition all his own. He has now the comfort of seeing all his children about him, Mary having fortunately arrived within a few days from New Orleans, and Alex within a few weeks from southern bays where he has been all winter surveying. Annie is therefore relieved from her great responsibility and care, and mother, though at first brought to her own bed by the sudden trial of her feeble strength, is now cheerful and composed, and is prepared to meet her loss with a Christian confidence. Her character is a very beautiful one to me, so gentle yet so strong, so cheerful and patient and child-like. Henry has drawn from both his parents what I am sure I am not partial in considering his almost angelic disposition, his strength under trial and constant consideration of the happiness of others. You will forgive me this slight effusion on the anniversary of your wedding day—the *sixth*—can it be possible? And yet I have lived a great deal in that time. . . .

To Charles Sumner

July 19, 1849

Many thanks for your kind note, which I believe Henry has acknowledged although I have not. We have been deep in *Lady*

Alice,[16] and even Curzon has been neglected for it. It has a more vigorous and natural tone of sentiment than Lamartine, without his grace of style, and has many graphic pictures of English life at home and abroad, is very interesting and very improbable and intensely Puseyistical, but a love story always has charms for us, and has pleasantly occupied some of our quiet days here. One cannot help feeling the beauty of some of Lamartine's rhapsodies, and being thrilled by his plaintive melodies, so like those of an Eolian harp, but, also like those, they are depressing and enervating, and even his religious emotion is to me too much mere emotion, not a self-controlling power. I only speak, of course, of the impression of his writings. He has shown himself manly and trustworthy in action. But it was not of him I wished to write. I have finished here your address, and I wanted to tell you what joy and hope it has given me, what a sisterly pride I take in the author of words so strong in truth and wisdom. "Truth is mighty"—this thought has been with me ever as I read, and also the feeling how feeble are bayonets and even serried ranks of men, armed with the strongest gifts of earth, and marshalled by human intelligence, beside this overwhelming force of well-arrayed, throughly disciplined truths—words I should say, which win every outpost by a *coup de main* and occupy the citadel before we have thought of resistance. . . .

Poor Rome! I watch her fate with intense interest.[17] I wonder the nations do not remonstrate as protectors of antiquity and art. They might, for the relics that belong to all, and say, "Rome belongs to Christendom; no one nation has a right to injure her. Let it be considered parricide." If they could be got to acknowledge that paternity a still holier one might follow.

Henry's father has had no perceptible change since we came, for better or worse. . . .

[16] Presumably *Lady Alice, or The New Una,* by Jedediah Vincent Huntington, published by Appleton, in New York, in 1849.

[17] In July, 1849, a French army under Marshal Oudinot, defeated Garibaldi and captured Rome, destroying the republic which had been set up in February and re-establishing papal authority.

July 27, 1849

A Temperance procession with music, many little boys belonging to it, interested the children by their gay yokes and ribboned caps. Erny said, seeing them forming, "There goes a soldier. I call him soldier because he is *red*." A good definition! the gay dress being to many all that makes a soldier, forgetting the weapons of murder that dress conceals. . . .

To Mary Appleton Mackintosh

August 6, 1849

. . . Our painful anxieties and long watching here are now over. Henry's father is at last at rest, after many years of suffering and depression which made life almost a burden to him. He died on the third at three o'clock in the morning, most peacefully. The day before I was with him all day. He was evidently dying, and no longer recognized any one, but it was a great comfort to see so gentle and natural a departure: he met death as a friend and not as an enemy. If he could have recovered sufficient consciousness to have spoken a few words to us, it would have been an additional consolation, for during this last illness he has not spoken at all beyond a greeting, but we rejoice his spirit is peacefully released from the "body of death" it has carried so many years. He was a most pious, excellent man, beloved and respected by all, and it is touching to see the general interest of all the citizens here. I shall never forget his affectionate greeting to me as his daughter the first time I ever came here, and his tenderness ever since. It has been a great satisfaction to me to help nurse him, and his memory is very dear to me.

Henry was his favorite son, and has loved his father with all the warmth of his heart. He feels his loss keenly, but is comforted by the thought of his release. Annie has nursed him so constantly for so many years that his death will make a great change in her life. He has never been out of her thoughts, and she was never willing to leave him for more than a day or two. I fear she will be much broken down now, after the first excitement is over, but she has a strong Christian faith to bear her up. His countenance had a beautiful expression after death; it had recovered the look of his youth, and the sadness it has worn of late years was forever obliterated. The funeral took place yesterday afternoon. Dr. Nichols (the Dr. Channing of Portland and a very remarkable man) made a very beautiful and appropriate prayer at the house, which was filled with old and young. About fifty members of the bar preceded the hearse, a voluntary tribute of respect. He was buried in a cemetery overlooking a beautiful landscape of woods and water, just at sunset—one of nature's many symbols of the resurrection. . . .

There is a gloom and depression of the nerves about such an occasion, despite one's radiant faith that life flows on forever like a river and that death is but the shadow of its shores, which makes me today too weary to write you all I should like about this good and admirable man. He always reminded me of Grandfather in his appearance and character, and like all the family was overflowing with love and gentleness. When Charley was a baby he used to place him on his pillow (if too ill to be up), and caress him, repeating "Grandpapa's comfort" again and again. He always had them on his knee or would amuse them with his tool chest constructing something for them. They little know what a friend they have lost. . . .

August 13, 1849

The children longed to go to Deering's Woods, "where papa played when a boy," so we gave them a picnic there, a lovely fresh afternoon. Grandmama drove with us but did not venture to get out. A flock of sheep just within the bars fascinated Erny, who would have kissed, I believe, the dear little "baa lambs" if they had not run away. The shady, solemn wood, carpeted with beautiful moss, excited them highly, and Charley in his admiration walked along so fast he tumbled over upon his basket of cakes and hurt himself not a little. When we emerged upon the bright turf beyond, he chose an old oak tree for the canopy of his table-cloth, saying, "It is so beautiful under the tree; here it must be." After our long confinement in town the sight of nature exhilarates the children as we older people, and they see its beauty afresh. We rambled about admiring the lovely light between the trunks, the soft, silent water and radiant turf and crystalline atmosphere. . . . We then strolled again through the wood, picking up acorns and the calumet flower, nature's own pipe of peace, and so met the carriage, Erny grieved not to see the pretty sheep again but consoled by a beautiful oak garland made for him and Charley by Aunt Anne. They wore them on their hats to show Grandmama and then on their sunny hair, looking like infant Bacchantes. They begged me to preserve them carefully in memory of "the beautiful wood."

August 24, 1849

Returned to Boston. Chicks highly excited at starting—the cars, etc. Charley looks at all machinery with peculiar interest. Had their daguerreotype taken the afternoon before leaving. Charley was very reluctant, but at last relented and gave a laughing likeness. The fountain at Aunt Sam's, where we dined, charmed them with its gilt ball dancing up and down. Poor Grandmama will miss much their lively ways, while they turn to fresh objects with a delight which hides the past. . . .

To Thomas G. Appleton

Cambridge, October 9, 1849

. . . There is not much news in Boston, I believe. Hillard's speech at the Whig Convention is much praised. It is eloquent and candid and gives a high tone to the Whig party I should be glad to think it possessed. Still it is strictly conservative. It proposes nothing to be done to stay the mighty evil and simply stands still. I confess I like the idea of the Free Soil party to put the federal government distinctly on the side of freedom in all future acts, but as the New Yorkers have proved unfaithful (though they think they can convert the old Hawkers by joining them), they will have much to contend with. . . .

The greatest piece of news is Margaret Fuller's marriage to an Italian marquis, poor as herself—a secret marriage of a year's standing, and a baby is actually alive to confirm it! This somewhat accounts for her ardent sympathy in the Italian cause, her nursing, or rather talking, in the hospitals, for she naïvely confessed she had rather talk with the convalescent than nurse the wounded. Crawford says, however, hers is the only true account of those days, of the universal desolation of the people, and all can share her enthusiasm. Louis Napoleon deserves a St. Helena as well as his uncle, except that it would be doing him too much honor. He simply deserves a vigorous use of the toe of the *boot* he has abused. May his own pinch him well! I fear his letter to Ney was only a theatrical flourish. . . .

Mrs. Butler is at last divorced with her own consent, her husband giving her a yearly sum and two months of the children. She is now reading in Philadelphia as Mrs. F. A. Kemble. . . .

There is a fuller discussion of Margaret Fuller's marriage in an undated letter, evidently written at nearly the same time. Margaret Fuller's attitude toward Longfellow's poetry had given Fanny no reason to love her.

To Emmeline Austin Wadsworth

. . . I suppose you have heard the wonderful piece of news from abroad—Margaret Fuller's secret marriage to a young Italian Marchese, and her actual possession of a living baby a year old! Why she concealed it is a mystery not as yet explained. Perhaps she was ashamed to have her surrender known after the rather grand position she had taken about marriage; perhaps she had a latent spring of romance which was fed by this secrecy. She writes that he has saved enough from the wreck of his fortune to pass one winter in Florence and then they come to America, where she flatters herself with her talents, her boy can never starve. Think of the dry, forlorn old maid changed into a Marguerita Marchesa d'Ossoli! Mrs. Craw- ford says she saw this youth often there, sometimes at breakfast (after she was married to him) without suspecting anything, and as she went out with her to walk, Miss Fuller would say to him, "I shall see you again this evening"! Matrimony and maternity have, I hope, improved her, and with no personal attractions to have at- tached a young man is a good deal in her praise. She retreated to the mountains when her child was born and has kept the secret wonderfully. . . .

Charley put a wooden ring on his head today and said, "Mamma, if I am a good boy, when I go up to the sky, shall I wear a thing like this round my head like the little Jesus? He wears it, doesn't he, to see his way by night without a light?" He had seen pictures of the Holy Family with the halo about their heads. . . . He says his lessons to me now daily in the Library at a little table where his books are kept and likes to hear the little bell to summon him while Erny is taking his nap. After dinner Erny joins too and says his letters very well and counts on the Chinese counting-board. They both delight in geography as I teach it, making their fingers ships to sail to China for tea, to California for gold, to England to see Ronny, to Africa for monkeys, etc. Thus they get the products of the country and their relative positions very well.

We come to a series of letters in which Mrs. Longfellow is much concerned with one of the most sensational murders in Boston and Cambridge history—the killing (November 23, 1849) of Dr. George Parkman, uncle of Francis Parkman, the historian, by John White Webster, a scholar of reputation, Professor of Chemistry in the Harvard Medical School. Webster is the only professor in Harvard history who was ever tried and hanged for murder.

Whether the verdict was a just one, and whether the crime ought to have been described as murder or only as manslaughter, need not be discussed here. Webster never admitted premeditation. The cause was Parkman's dunning him for some money he owed him; maddened by the other's taunts, Webster, according to his own account, picked up a heavy stick and struck Parkman a single blow. Unfortunately for both men, the blow proved fatal. The panic-stricken killer thereupon proceeded to destroy any chance he might have had for mercy by dismembering his victim's body and attempting to conceal his crime.

This grisly affair is often referred to in the memorabilia of the period, and when Charles Dickens came to Boston on his famous reading tour in 1867 he insisted upon being taken to view the scene of the killing. (He had met Webster himself on his first visit in 1842.) Mrs. Longfellow's letters bring us a shocking sense of immediacy;

*reading them, we feel almost as if we were living at the time, and
the horror of a whole community builds up around us as we read.*[18]

To Emmeline Austin Wadsworth

November 26, 1849

. . . Boston is, at this moment, in sad suspense about the fate of
poor Dr. Parkman, the lean doctor. He wandered away on Friday,
with money in his pocket, and was last seen on Craigie Bridge with
an Irishman, who called him away for medical attendance. It is
feared he may be murdered. That would be a sad end for the good-
natured Don Quixote. . . .

To Mary Longfellow Greenleaf

December 4, 1849

You will see by the papers what dark horror overshadows us like
an eclipse. Of course we cannot believe Dr. Webster guilty, bad as
some of the evidence looks. But as no murder is yet *proven*, we must
hope some better light will dawn on this dismal mystery. You cannot
conceive the growing excitement since Dr. Parkman's disappearance
and the state of things in the Medical College were brought to light.
Many suspect the janitor, who is known to be a bad man and to
have wished for the reward offered for Dr. Parkman's body. He
could make things appear against the doctor, having bodies under
his control.

I trust our minds will be soon relieved, but, meanwhile, they are
soiled by new details continually. I went to see poor Mrs. Webster
on Saturday, the day after her husband's arrest, but of course was
not admitted. What a terrible blight upon her life and that of the
girls! the mere suspicion, for I cannot believe anything can be
proved.

[18] There is an extensive account of this case in George Dilnot's *The Trial of
Professor John White Webster,* which was published in London by Geoffrey
Bles, in 1928, in the "Famous Trials Series." Among numerous brief accounts,
mention may be made here of Cleveland Amory's in *The Proper Bostonians*
(Dutton, 1948).

His character ought to be a sufficient shield against such suspicions, and is with all who know him.

He has been merry and cheerful as usual the past week, and passed the evening of the day the supposed murder was committed . . . with his family, perfectly at his ease. He was much broken down by his arrest, but is now calm. . . .

To Thomas G. Appleton

December 17, 1849

The Webster tragedy still hangs heavily upon our hearts, and will for a long time. The coroner's jury, after their long and secret sittings, pronounce him guilty, and the circumstancial evidence is certainly as bad as possible, but I cannot believe, knowing his gentle and genial disposition, as we do, that there was wilful murder—manslaughter there may have been, as Dr. Parkman's family have identified his remains beyond question. People's conjectures vary from day to day: some things are cleared up, others look worse, so that the horrible excitement cannot easily be allayed. Both parties being so well known and connected, it has caused greater horror and distress than you can well imagine. Dr. Webster has been always very reckless about money, so that his family are now really destitute in addition to their mental suffering. . . .

I have just been dining at Lowell's with Miss Bremer.[19] She has been there some days and seems greatly to enjoy the quiet and benediction of the place, after the lionizing she underwent in New York. She is a very pleasing person, very gentle and caressing in her manner, with a soft voice and very small hands. She is quite petite and just upon fifty years of age. . . . She seems as sensible as she is good, and reads English, even Emerson, with remarkable comprehension and discrimination. She draws profile portraits with great delicacy, and will carry away some American ones in her little book, having already Miss Sedgwick's, Irving's, etc. She is so gentle and

[19] Fredrika Bremer (1801–1865), Swedish novelist. She was in America 1849–1851, and made many friends among Boston literati. Bruno and Petrea are characters in The Neighbors (1837) and The Home (1839), respectively. As Mrs. Longfellow surmised, the latter was patterned after the author herself.

quiet I can hardly believe such romance as Bruno's and others once stirred under her voluminous cap. Her nose is longish and red, and I think Petrea's trouble about hers was probably drawn from her own experience in her younger days. . . .

The following letters, both undated, were clearly written in December.

To Thomas G. Appleton

. . . I do not know why you abuse *Shirley*.[20] I think it wonderfully good, and agree with all the *Examiner* says in its praise. A Yorkshire girl the authoress must be. Why is she not known? She must be worth hunting out. Ticknor's book [21] (1st volume) is at last born, and looks learned and readable, with a tremendous falling bib of notes, but as lively an infant as one could expect. Dana and Lowell, as well as Henry, offer new poems for Christmas—the former only a new edition, but he is causing a furore in his old age at Philadelphia by his Shakespeare lectures; crowds go away unable to get in. It must warm his disappointed heart cheerily.[22] Poe died miserably, you have doubtless seen, and rang his own knell, as it were, in a Bell-poem which should bear the bell for happy imitation of sound. . . . Emerson is among his pines at Concord, with his usual familiars about him, like the grotesque forms on a German illustrated poem. Miss Bremer passed a day with him and seems much interested in him and Alcott. Holmes was lecturing over Dr. Webster's room the very time the murder was committed if done there. Sumner has been vindicating in court the rights of a little black girl against the city of Boston for free admission to the free school, to be able to go like white children to the one nearest her home, and not forced to traverse the town to an African school, with

---

[20] By "Currer Bell" (Charlotte Brontë).
[21] *History of Spanish Literature.*
[22] Longfellow's new poems were *The Seaside and the Fireside* (dated 1850, but perhaps published in time to catch the Christmas trade); Lowell had no new volume of poetry at this time. Richard Henry Dana I (1787–1879) brought out under an 1850 dateline, a two-volume edition of his *Poems and Prose Writings.*

its ban of caste. . . . Agassiz is, for the present, happier with Miss Cary [23] than an ondine—perhaps her relationship to Mother Carey's chickens suggested pleasing associations. . . . [Henry] has a poem on Tegnér's death,[24] wild and mystical, like a northern rune, and as incomprehensible, probably, to most people. The "burning ship" typifies his madness, and the accursed mistletoe his fatal love of drinking. I let you into the secret in case you should puzzle over it. . . .

TO EMMELINE AUSTIN WADSWORTH

. . . Our hearts are, if possible, heavier than ever as our hopes are withdrawn. There seems no escape now from Dr. Webster's guilt, monstrous and impossible as it appeared to us. His family are quite destitute and have long wished to support themselves. The truth has been much softened to them fortunately, but sooner or later it must come with crushing power. All gaiety in Boston is stopped by this tragedy—the community is stunned, and cannot easily recover, nor should it. . . .

Christmas, 1849

The children woke up eagerly to see what Santa Claus had left them. Charley found a funny little man who hopped out of his box when opened and Erny a baby in a wagon, which charmed him. Driving into town, Erny said in his little soft voice, "If I was God I would make it snow all the time."

Dined at Grandpapa's and in evening made merry with about thirty other children, Charley in a picturesque crimson and black sack with Spanish drawers of the same. A Christmas tree very charmingly brought them some beautiful toys, Charley a gayly-painted steamboat and Erny a horse and wagon bearing meal bags, also a little sled apiece from "Mamy" and two fine toys from Aunt

[23] Elizabeth Cabot Cary, whom Agassiz married in 1850.
[24] Esaias Tegnér (1782–1846), famous Swedish poet. Longfellow translated "The Children of the Lord's Supper" and a portion of his masterpiece, *Frithjof's Saga*. The poem is "Tegnér's Drapa," originally called "Tegnér's Death." Longfellow wrote it in 1847; it was included in *The Seaside and the Fireside*.

William. They kept brisk and awake until ten o'clock, when we drove home over the frozen road under the frozen moon. Erny was wretched because he was hurried off to bed without putting his things in order, and to appease him was taken up in nightgown to do it, then went to sleep very happily, the starry tree and the little girls probably shining through his dreams like some celestial vision. . . .

The Webster tragedy moved, crescendo, into the new year.

To Emmeline Austin Wadsworth

January 14, 1850

. . . Henry went to see Dr. Webster Saturday and thought he appeared very much as usual. It is said his counsel feel cheered by the report of the inquest at last given them. There are so many false stories it is impossible to know what to believe. . . .

To Mary Longfellow Greenleaf

February 14, 1850

. . . Dr. Webster's trial is now, I believe, to take place in March, and it will be almost a relief to have it over, whatever may be the results. The lawyers are of opinion, I understand, that the nature of the evidence cannot convict him, strong as it is, but I fear people's minds will never clear him unless some wonderful revelation in his favor turns up.

His poor family are struggling to support themselves in various ways. One of the girls teaches drawing, another music, and they take in sewing, but of course this barely pays their daily expenses. Mrs. Webster keeps very retired—no one has seen her, I believe, but the girls speak freely of their father, of his beautiful letters to them, and are so sure of his innocence that, although they have seen the details of the accusation, they do not seem dismayed by his position. They were much annoyed at one time by anonymous letters offering to reveal the true murderer for a certain sum, which raised momentary hopes, to be crushed by the certainty that they could only be sent to extort money.

If acquitted, I should think it impossible for the doctor to remain here—so their future is a most uncertain one.

We are passing the vacation very quietly at home, enjoying just now Mrs. Kemble's readings, which are as wonderful and thrilling as ever. A few nights since she read before the Mercantile Library Association Henry's "Building of the Ship," which she has desired to do ever since she came. She prefaced it with a few words stating the wish she felt to read it to a Boston audience, then gave it with magnificent effect. Her genius and feeling seize always every good point and give them the fullest expression, and the music of verse is always rightly rendered. It was a rather trying occasion for me, sitting in that immense audience of 3,000, but I got through it better than I expected and so did Henry. She stood up and delivered it off with great spirit. . . .

To Thomas G. Appleton

February 18, 1850

. . . Mr. Alcott has issued cards for a "Parliament of the Times" to be held by himself, and Mr. Emerson, with a room full of invited guests. Poor Mr. Emerson knew nothing of it till the evening came, nor how he had been used as decoy duck. Sumner gave us the funniest account of it. It was a lamentable failure. Mr. Alcott led off, and Mr. Emerson helped him now and then, and a few others trotted out their hobbies, Garrison, as usual, on his thundering war-horse, and insisting a portrait of Carlyle in the room should be taken down or its face turned to the wall, whereupon Mr. Emerson tried to excuse, said "mocker at humanity," and thought now he had said his say on slavery and Ireland, he would come round to better feeling and use his "frolic words" to better purpose.

There were several ladies there, and Miss Bremer made a few gentle remarks, but Alcott's hope of pumping them into easy and wise conversation was balked, and his wife said next day to Miss Bremer, "It was a failure; we cannot converse in this country." Poor

Alcott longs for academic groves and tractable pupils, and Emerson is really hungering for society, but knows not how to get it, followed as he is by such a sorry set of bores. As if people could be made to talk as water-pipes, when the stop is removed, to flow! I wish you were here to help him to some kind of sociable, agreeable club. He is evidently weary of the weak, watery reflections of himself that surround him, and longs for fresh minds and pastures new. Miss Bremer seems to have found in him her ideal, he is *the* American man to her, and interests her intensely. Henry called on her the other day and heard Mrs. Alcott, a gaunt, grim woman in a sacque, say to her, "Miss Bremer, do you think a woman has fulfilled her mission until she has become a mother?" Poor Miss Bremer replied with spirit, "Indeed, I do, for all children are hers." She will have the drollest idea of Boston society—such strange varieties has she seen. . . .

Henry has gone to town to have Miss Bremer's hand cast for me. It is very small and I wished it for a souvenir, a kind of autograph! He is often tempted in now by the railroad, which in ten minutes lands him at the Haymarket! It is luxurious too, with purple velvet and rosewood, and far surpasses omnibus comfort except in not landing you at your door and carrying you to an undesirable part of Boston. . . .

To Nathan Appleton

March 8, 1850

. . . Wednesday evening, despite a pouring rain, we drove in for Mrs. Kemble's last reading—the first part of *King Henry IV*, which was admirably delivered. Redoubled applause at the end brought her back to give some farewell words, which with great emotion she faltered forth, saying she should never have the pleasure of reading in Boston again.

I found her in tears below, and she said, "I believe I love Boston better than any of you. I like to ride to Dorchester Heights and think how gloriously you beat us." This was magnanimous from so true an Englishwoman, but she has warmed toward America much of late years.

She invited us to the Revere House and there entertained us and some dozen other ladies and gentlemen with a nice little supper, her brilliant salon decorated with the choicest flowers from Salem and elsewhere. She is now in New York. . . .

March 25, 1850

. . . All minds are absorbed now, of course, by the Webster trial, which has gone through one week, increasing in interest. There are so many witnesses on both sides I should think it would take nearly a month to complete it, and the poor judges and jury, it is feared, may break down with the fatigue and bad air. The latter were walked to church yesterday, but are kept locked up, of course, all night, and being all men of active habits must feel the change of life and diet seriously. The prisoner has maintained a wonderful calmness thus far, and some people think his mind is stunned by the blow, but he appears to take a close interest in all that goes on. There is one story about him almost incredible. A very perfect model was shown of the college, and as Dr. Wyman walked by him, after giving the most searching anatomical identification of the jaw, etc. the doctor said, "Wyman, we ought to have that model for the college. It would be a capital thing." This is like the trivial mind of the doctor, but at such a time one would think even he would be sobered. He is also said to have shaken hands warmly with Dr. Francis Parkman [25] as he passed him. There seem to be no new facts against him, as we supposed, but the old are strong enough, supposing all Littlefield's testimony true. Still, I hear there are very strong witnesses to prove Dr. Parkman was seen during the afternoon, and some of them giving him a direct course, so the interest will be undiminished to the end.

Mr. Webster's speech [26] is the next great topic. It does not find much favor at the North, and many Whigs even disapprove it. It is very Southern in its attempt to be national. This notion of enforcing the human game-laws is very Shylock-like—"the law allows it," but who would cut the pound of flesh? . . .

[25] Not the historian but the Reverend Francis Parkman, brother of the victim.
[26] The famous Seventh of March Speech, supporting the Compromise of 1850 and upholding the Fugitive Slave Law.

To Nathan Appleton

April 8, 1850

. . . We have survived the horrors of the Webster trial and its dreadful termination, but such a painful excitement will never fall again upon our community, I think. Here the sympathy for the family is deeply felt, and two papers signed by both male and female friends have been sent to them to express it. . . . The sentence was a great shock, though not unexpected, particularly by those who had watched closely the trial and saw the evidence drawing every day fatally round the criminal. In New York and Philadelphia the papers express great dissatisfaction with it, and petitions are talked of to the governor.

His wife and daughters, I see by tonight's paper, have been also to beg for a commutation of the punishment—what will be done we know not. . . .

Dr. Webster's counsel certainly put no heart or strength into the defence, and allowing the possibility of manslaughter weakened very much their witnesses for the alibi. But they had probably lost their interest in it.

Some think the only avoidance of an execution would be at the request of the Parkman family, but this is asking more magnanimity than they may possess, as the Reverend is very savage for a reverend, went every day to the court house, and now talks complacently of "the majesty of the law," which I should fear was a cloak to a not very Christian sentiment but a very natural one in his own breast. I hope this will be a death-blow to public executions here, though I think imprisonment for life would be quite as disagreeable. The doctor seems more rational since the verdict, and prays with his family very devoutly, and talks of having made his peace with God, but I doubt if there is any real repentance as yet. It is fearful to see how easily he lost his foothold in men's regard—how very little respect all classes seem to have had for him, for years. . . .

April 10, 1850

The chicks went to school today for first time. Highly elated with the idea and set off with their papa, satchel on shoulder, as merry as birds, little knowing what a weary word school will be to them hereafter. Miss Jennison, a firm maiden lady, teaches them with a dozen others in the nice old house overshadowed by the Washington Elm. They sit in little arm chairs with a fence at the side for books. . . .

To ALEXANDER WADSWORTH LONGFELLOW

May 4, 1850

. . . I received yesterday a snowy box of wedding cake from Cary Greenleaf, and was told of the wedding by Miss Hodges, as a very quiet one in church, all gaiety being given up on account of the terrible affliction of her friend, Marian Webster. Those poor girls and their mother bear up with the faith in his innocence which has supported them thus far and the hope of the Governor's pardon. If a new trial is had he may be saved, but every day his character is so blackened by new stories (too true alas! many of them) that he will have little left to live for unless to purify it. . . .

To MARY LONGFELLOW GREENLEAF

Washington, May 22, 1850

After my long silence I write you from this curious city, which may amaze you if you have not heard from Portland of our intended journey. The desire to meet my father, who was not well enough to undertake New Orleans and the West, and to escape a month of east winds, so disagreeable to me last year, induced us to accompany Mrs. Appleton here, where we have passed a week very pleasantly, not having yet found summer weather but something much better than we should have had at home.

My father arrived here a day before us from Charleston, looking very thin after his Cuba visit, and with more cough than we hoped to find, but feels well and has only bronchial troubles to contend with. Jewett has proved a most admirable nurse, for poor papa was reduced very low in strength from a bilious attack at Havana, and we all feel very grateful for his devoted care. . . .

It is very amusing here for a short time seeing such varieties of people and hearing politics discussed with such frankness and freedom. Mr. Clay has the next parlor to ours and often favors us with a chat. He is impatient to have his compromise acceded to, but there seems little promise of any speedy decision on these important matters—all dread a long summer session. . . .

The President [26a] we found very cordial, and hearing my name he darted at Henry saying, "This must be Mr. Longfellow; I remember him well," which amused us greatly as they never met before! . . .

The poor Websters we left still living upon hope of the Governor's pardon and their faith in their father's innocence. The trial has been most unfairly abused, and if a new one was had I fear the doctor would have even less chance of exciting sympathy, so many bad stories have come out against him since he has shown such frivolity and falsehood during the other. . . .

To EMMELINE AUSTIN WADSWORTH [27]

. . . [Tom] has brought us Tennyson's last volume, a series of small poems written in memory of a friend, young Hallam, the son of the historian. Such a delicious book as it seems to be, the poems so finished and beautiful, full of the tenderest feeling, doing for friendship what Petrarch's sonnets do for love. A most touching idea is it not? It is called *In Memoriam* and will be published here in a few weeks. Henry is feasting upon it with eyes full of tears, and at Nahant, with the melancholy sea chiming in as music to the dirge-like words, I shall sadden myself with it to a joy purer than joy itself. The pieces were evidently written at different intervals, and there is a higher tone and deeper feeling in them than in anything he has written, wedded to the most perfect melody. . . .

Nahant, July 11, 1850

. . . Yesterday was a sad day here as everywhere. What a sudden and grievous blow is the President's death! The good old man, truly

[26a] Zachary Taylor.
[27] This undated letter was sent from Cambridge before the Longfellows left to spend the summer at Nahant. The London edition of *In Memoriam*, which Fanny had been reading, was published June 1.

loved by all, and whose firm hand was so needed at this crisis to make North and South work in harness amicably. Boston was shouded in gloom, I hear, and all hearts saddened. It is our only comfort that Mr. Fillmore is, apparently, so worthy a successor. He looked to me like a man of calm strength, his countenance is very prepossessing, but his energies are untried, and the boldest might shrink from such sudden responsibilities at such an embarrassed session. All hope he will at least have a stronger cabinet than the last. . . .

Dr. Webster's confession is very awful, is it not? but to me credible knowing the nature of the man. . . . What a discovery for Mrs. Webster and the daughters after their firm belief in his entire innocence! What sorrow can resemble theirs! And so worthless a man to inflict such an amount of injury!

To Harriot Sumner Appleton

July 24, 1850

. . . What a sad tragedy is the wreck of the *Elisabeth* [28] with her precious freight of human beings and works of art! The poor Marchioness' fate is in keeping with her romantic history but very sad for her mother and friends. Sumner has gone to find, if possible, the body of his brother Horace, whose early loss will be very painful to him, and to his mother and sister unspeakably so. . . .

To Emmeline Austin Wadsworth

August 14, 1850

. . . Sumner has been down one or two Sundays, and the last one Whittier also came, and we all drove over to Lynn to see Grace Greenwood,[29] but found her not. I never saw Whittier before and

[28] At Fire Island, on July 19. "The poor Marchioness" was Margaret Fuller, who was drowned with her husband and child.

[29] The pseudonym of Sara Jane Lippincott (1823–1904), poet and essayist, a friend of Whittier's.

was much struck by his strongly marked face, with its fine brow and piercing eyes, giving him at times a fierce expression like an eagle, and again softening to a very sweet and tender one. He is a true iconoclast, but as a poet and man is full of gentle feelings. . . .

Tennyson is married and settled in Westmoreland. I am curious to know what his bride is like. Henry receives some charming letters from clever English girls. . . .

The next two letters—the first a fragment addressed to an unidentified correspondent—are undated. The second, at least, must have been sent from Cambridge. Professor Webster was executed on August 30. Jenny Lind landed in New York on September 1. Stephen Longfellow died on September 19. Alice Longfellow was born on September 22.

. . . The terrible Cambridge tragedy still seems to darken our sky—though it is a great comfort to know the poor doctor seemed to die penitent. He wrote a letter to Dr. Parkman (the Reverend) entreating that some softer feelings might at least be recovered towards his family, that his wife and children were wholly innocent, and that she had often expressed her gratitude to him for his (the Reverend's) help in her spiritual culture. I hear she is tranquil, but what their plans are I know not. I should think they would go to Fayal, as here they cannot move without attracting attention. . . .

What a welcome Jenny Lind is getting. I am glad of it. I like such enthusiasm for an artist and a good creature. No Queen could get it. It is pure love of excellence, though of course mingled with mere fashion. . . .

I hear Mrs. Webster is ill in bed and has been for some time—no wonder, poor woman! Mr. Everett has written a letter of neighborly sympathy to be signed by us all. The girls were seen wending their way to church on Sunday shrouded in their black veils and the deeper gloom of their dreadful destiny. What a year in those young lives! with their weekly visit to the prison which Sumner says is as dismal as any Inquisition, and this last awful memory! . . .

To Anne Longfellow Pierce

We received Alex' letter yesterday, and enter with deepest sympathy into all the anxieties and watchings of the sick-room. How unfortunate that we cannot be there to aid and relieve you.

I am urging Henry to go even for a day, to have at least the comfort of seeing his brother again, and think he will tomorrow. He is unwilling to leave me at night, for both my nurse and doctor are so far off, and I am expecting the crisis any day, but can return, he finds, in the afternoon, having some hours with you.

How soon again all these sad offices have been renewed to you, but poor Stephen's health was so shattered, and so little happiness seemed in store for him in this life, that we can hardly regret rest is at hand and an existence where his warm affections can meet with due reward. Pray give my truest love to him if he is still able to remember me. . . .

I trust dear mother and you all are sustained by every holy consolation and feel how much there is to be grateful for in the circumstances of this illness under your roof. My prayers and tenderest thoughts are with you. . . .

To Mary Appleton Mackintosh

November 2, 1850

I take advantage of the first certain link between us and your distant island [30] to tell you (if you have not heard it already) that I am the happy mamma of a very nice little girl, born six weeks ago today. I had a very expeditious labor for me (only two hours), relieved by ether, and got up remarkably well, never before with so little nervous weakness. For the first week (Goody Blake being engaged), I had a chatty Scotch nurse from Dumfries, full of stories of Mrs. Burns and the poet. The ponderous tread of Mrs. B. (Blake, I mean), is still trying the timbers of the house. She considers the baby remarkably fat and vigorous for its age. It is a great laugher

[30] Antigua, where Mary's husband, Robert Mackintosh, was now stationed as governor general of the Leeward Islands.

and has a very expressive little face already, with dark blue eyes and an inclination to look like Henry, I think. You may imagine how grateful and happy we are in this arrival, as if our secret prayers had been answered, but my joy is more tempered than it was formerly, and I dare not trust dwelling upon the future. God has been very merciful to us in so healing our wounds, and I feel this to be a most holy gift. . . .

To Mary Longfellow Greenleaf

January 27, 1851

. . . We are very quietly enjoying our vacation, having been driven out of the big library by the cold . . . to the snug study, where we feel more cozy and comfortable, though I confess when *four* cigars are puffing away at once, as they were yesterday, its dimensions are rather limited. Sumner comes out, as usual, to pass Sunday with us, and we have delightful literary and philanthropic talks into which politics will occasionally creep. He is now hanging within four votes of an election as our senator, and is likely to remain in this unpleasant position for some time, but bears it very calmly and serenely, not over anxious to enter public life and resign his beloved studies. He is far too good and pure and noble for a politician, and though he has an energy and eloquence which, as well as the times, seem to claim him for such work, I shall half regret it. . . .

To Zilpah Longfellow

February 28, 1851

. . . On Saturday the twenty-second our little girl was christened, we thinking it a pleasant celebration of the good Washington's birthday. She was named Alice Mary, the former being a favorite name of ours, and occurring several times in my father's family in the olden days and at least once in yours—Alice Archer you may remember—the Mary was added for her two aunts' sake.

She behaved beautifully, and although it was a very trying occasion to me, my spirits rallied after a while and all went off pleasantly. There was no one present but my father's family— . . . I did not feel equal to any more witnesses than I could help.[31] A little ice and a beautiful christening cake crowned with a bouquet from my Aunt Sam Appleton enlivened the close. The children will, I hope, remember this occasion, for it made a good deal of impression on them. Dr. Francis officiated as usual very feelingly. . . .

To Emmeline Austin Wadsworth

March 10, 1851

. . . We have been reading a very well written book of true sentiment—*Reveries of a Bachelor*.[32] . . . Lowell has written a very witty, rollicking poem on "the knockings" in the latest *Graham*,[33] full of puns and drolleries. Tom is almost a believer and Henry Sargent an ardent one with some strange stories. . . .

In March a telegram from Portland announced the death of Longfellow's mother, who, by this time, had become Fanny's mother as well.

To Mary Longfellow Greenleaf

March 18, 1851

How truly do I sympathize in the sudden shock the news of dear mother's departure must have given you and Alex. . . . It came likewise to us without a warning, but I can hardly call it a surprise. She seemed to me ever lowering upon the brink of that better land, and I have hoped she would thus gently leave us when God willed

---

[31] In her "Chronicle of the Children of Craigie Castle," Fanny wrote, under date of February 22: "It was very trying to me seeing her [Alice] in the gown last worn on this occasion by my Fanny but got through it as well as I could. She was truly baptized in her mother's tears."

[32] By Donald Grant Mitchell (Ik Marvel).

[33] "The Unhappy Lot of Mr. Knott," in the April number.

to release her from her weary body. In what harmony with her life was such a transition—this continuance rather than change of being. She had nothing but the flesh to put away from her: her soul was already clothed upon with immortality and assumed its natural place without effort or suffering. I trust Annie feels reconciled, and that you all will, to such a removal, without the prostration of prolonged illness, so painful to witness in so feeble a body; without a cloud upon her mind she fitly closes a long life. There is something very beautiful and touching to me in her death, and it brings the next life nearer and nearer to us. Ah, if we could all be as fine and gentle in soul as she was, as free from passion and selfishness, as fine and cheerful in doing and enduring, it would never seem afar off, and so quietly might we all be led to it.

I shall greatly miss the motherly tenderness with which she always greeted me, but am deeply grateful I have been allowed to enjoy it so long. . . .

To Emmeline Austin Wadsworth

March 18, 1851

. . . What a snowstorm is howling about us today, like those I remember in my childhood, drifting high over doors and windows and keeping all prisoners in doors. Poor Henry, however, has had to battle through it to college, for that old mill must still work on, no matter what storms block up the ways, or sorrows encumber the hearts of the workmen.

He was cheered yesterday by pleasant letters from England, from people he has cheered—from the Costello,[34] with such exclamations as "How well you understand me!" etc., all which I enjoy as much as he does, and from other damsels there. He is truly favored by women, because he does understand and reverence them peculiarly, and has just that tenderness and sympathy in his own nature which sounds the depths of theirs. Most men have a chivalric enthusiasm about women if they have any, but he, though I say it, has that tender sympathy far less common which all feel like magnetism. You

[34] Louisa Stuart Costello (1799–1870), British writer and painter.

know, I think aloud to you, and I say this with pride and joy and holiest gratitude for my most abundant share of it. . . .

The children are well, but little Alice begins to feel teething troubles. I think she is growing a beauty—so full of vigor and life, so plump and round and rosy. She dances and sings all day long, and has the devoted homage of all the household. A baby is a true queen of most willing subjects. Erny says he is to be an artist, and I half believe it; he is so absorbed in drawing, . . . giving the chairs and clocks a most Ruskin-like picturesqueness of attire and shading. . . .[35]

TO SAMUEL LONGFELLOW

March 31, 1851

. . . We have been reading a very summery book, *Nile Notes by a Howadji,* the author being an amiable youth named Curtis,[36] a late guest of Charles Norton's. It is full of glowing Tennysonian pictures, with a style well suiting the poetical subject—and much quiet humor. He is, or has been, a disciple of Emerson, I fancy. . .

TO EMMELINE AUSTIN WADSWORTH

April 21, 1851

. . . I have been dipping into Mrs. Browning . . . lately, and am more than ever amazed at her prodigious genius, so strong and yet so purely feminine and tender, so holy with the deepest reverence. Her love sonnets in the last edition I have not seen, that is not all, but the few I have are unequalled for depth and sacredness of feeling, written with her very heart's blood. I can hardly bear to see them in print, and yet all lovers will feel grateful for them. Hawthorne's *Seven Gables* is a wonderful book—of every high

[35] An interesting observation in view of the fact that Ernest did become an artist. See his autobiography, *Random Memories* (Houghton Mifflin Company, 1922).

[36] George William Curtis (1824–1892). He dedicated *Prue and I* (1856) to Mrs. Longfellow.

genius, so artistically treated and completed, and such portraits with
modern times made poetical by the subtle mysteries of antiquity,
with an awful beauty like all of his. . . .

To Nathan Appleton

May 4, 1851

. . . We have had quite exciting times in Boston since you left,
though the papers much exaggerated everything and give one a
pretty fair idea of how foreign revolutions were ever started. The
seizure of a supposed slave and his summary trial without judge or
jury and return to slavery was thought by many a great indignity in
Massachusetts, and the Court House was chained against an im-
aginary mob, and he was marched off with three hundred police-
men as guard. . . . It caused a great indignation throughout the
State, where Northern freedom is thought as important a matter as
southern slavery, though of course no opposition was intended by
force. It rather helped Sumner's election, which I fear will not give
you much pleasure, but you can feel sure that whatever he does as
senator will be dictated by a sincere conviction and an earnest desire
to do right and a statesmanlike broad view. He did not wish it, and
would gladly resign now if his party could choose a man of the same
opinions in his place, for he has no political ambition whatever, and
was more depressed at the moment of his success than during the
long and doubtful contest. I think all his enemies will do him justice
some day, for they now singularly misunderstand him, and we are
in a position to judge him with peculiar impartiality. . . .

June 24, 1851

. . . Our Class Day went off very pleasantly though so unusually
crowded. . . . But I did hear Jenny Lind at last in the evening,[37]
and her voice fully equalled my expectations, though a little husky

[37] Alice's birth had prevented Fanny from attending Jenny Lind's first Boston
concert in September, 1850. Tickets for this concert were sold at auction, a
"high" of $625 being achieved. Longfellow paid $8.50 for a gallery seat. Samuel
Longfellow incorrectly states the sum as $8.00, and I ignorantly followed him
in my *Jenny Lind* (Houghton Mifflin Company, 1931).

at times. There is a power and body to it I hardly was prepared for, and the fascination of her whole personality is very remarkable, though she has grown very thin by her hard work here.

TO ANNE LONGFELLOW PIERCE

July 3, 1851

. . . I had a very pleasant visit from Anne Sophia on Class Day, and we enjoyed the fascinating Jenny in the evening, though not together. *She* came out to see me before she left, and was very agreeable and easy in her manners and her conversation full of feeling. . . .

TO EMMELINE AUSTIN WADSWORTH

Nahant, July 14, 1851

. . . There is to me always a delicious sense of repose in leaving home, I can hardly explain, for I am not one of those terribly fussy housekeepers, but still the weight of a big house and of several servants is something so distasteful to my mind that I feel it, though to you it would be light "as a dew-drop on a lion's mane," having a genius for such management. I can rarely sit down quietly without being haunted by the thought of something neglected or forgotten, for though I arrange everything as methodically as I can, still my memory is treacherous and I dread its constant faithlessness. This occupation of the mind by petty cares, not dignified enough to elevate or interest it, is very tiresome when one longs for freedom for something better, and here I do enjoy my emancipation and can read and think like a new creature. . . .

August 22, 1851

Do not think, dear Emmeline, that I wait for answers to my letters that I write so irregularly. I abhor all such formalities and manacles between friends. . . . I write when I can, and perhaps ought to be more methodical about it, like the faithful Anna Ticknor (who, it must be remembered, is unmarried and has no children as perpetual check-strings to every action) but alas! that is not in my nature, and here our days and nights are broken in upon by continued interruptions. People call at all hours, and we have many chance visitors from town: one day a lantern-jawed Kentuckian with son and daughters, all greatly desiring autographs, another day some Italian or German refugee hoping for a little advice about their future, another day Mr. Saxe, the huge Vermont humorist, evidently expecting to pass the day, and yesterday a country cousin, or rather the husband of a country cousin of mine, the grimmest kind of Puritan, with a sweet little boy who is called Samuel, and the familiarity of Sam and Sammy he said is never practised at home! (consequently I took a malicious pleasure in calling him by the latter the whole time he was here). This is only a specimen of the odd varieties we see (though of course more and odder in Cambridge, for Henry seems to be considered a kind of Helper General to all nations, and his good nature always encourages the idea), but there I can escape a little of it—here my hospitality is more unavoidable and our one salon gives me no place of refuge—at least for writing, for my bedroom is table-less. Then walks, drives, returning visits, nursing, etc. are items of an engrossing nature. Gladly would I gossip away with you by the hour if it were as easily done as wished, but even now comes Charley with "Please, Mamma, draw this General for me, and then make a tail to my kite, and then read a nice, long story to me, for it is raining, and you know you said I mustn't go in the wet grass." Then little Erny's beseeching face is full of some urgent appeal, but I say, "Not now, my dear boys, I must write to Aunt Emmeline, and as soon as it clears up you may go to the Indian tent to see the woman make the gay baskets and then to the pebbly beach to bring home some nice large stones for baby to bite"—so off they go, resigned—for a time.

I was very sorry to hear Pierce Butler was again stirring up the old ashes of discontent and can only hope he will keep it strictly private, though that is hardly fair to Fanny, but he evidently never intends to cease molesting her. . . . She does not understand . . . that a woman cannot contend with a man; he is the strongest, and it is better for her to yield to great injustice unless she would become the earthern vessel dashed in two by the iron. . . .

To Samuel Longfellow

August 31, 1851

. . . You will see by the papers, we are in the midst of another Cuban excitement. The shooting of our invaders, who as pirates deserved their doom, is rousing sympathy meetings everywhere, though the papers, nearly all, support the government. But things look troublesome. The South is resolved to get Cuba at any hazard, but the Cubans have not courage to meet them half way.

The tornado in Medford was a wonderful visitation for so northerly a region. Houses were scattered like chaff, and everything ploughed up in its way. It is fearful to know what an enemy the familiar elements may become. . . .

To Emmeline Austin Wadsworth

September 3, 1851

Our time of sojourn here is almost spent, and I truly regret the close of our pleasant summer, our tête-à-tête walks upon the cliff, our full and perfect enjoyment of each other's society. Henry has already resumed his College duties, for several days, and in a week we return to Cambridge, which, *entre nous,* has become, outside my own house, a dreary place to me, so few intimate friends have I there, so monotonous is my life. But even this shadow of complaint is a sin while we are all blessed with health and every comfort and have such dear friends elsewhere if not very near. . . .

We have had some magnificent sunsets lately, and Sunday evening, after a very hot day, we sat upon Mrs. [William Wetmore] Story's rocks, with Emerson and her artist guests, and enjoyed one soft enough for Sorrento, the harsh coast mellowed with the richest beauty and the quiet sea all ablaze with purple and gold. Cranch, the poet and artist, is still here, with a gentle, poetical-looking wife, and they joined us, and we all sat upon the piazza late into the night by the light of a most ghostly moon. Cranch is a handsome, interesting person, very shy and silent, reminding me of Motley. I see by the papers Julia Howe has returned—I hear she was much admired in Rome and her soirees much courted. With her many resources of languages, music, and clever conversation, I can imagine how attractive she must have made them, where people really *love* society, which they cannot be said to do in America—for its own sake. How dull she will probably find it in South Boston, for she is not to be satisfied with the society of husband and children, and a social nature like hers really requires more not to consume itself. . . .

To Emmeline Austin Wadsworth

Cambridge, December 26, 1851

. . . Has the Kossuth enthusiasm of New York reached your quiet regions? To me, he is a most interesting character, historically, and I cannot help believing him an honest, devoted patriot, but in Boston there is very little sympathy in him or his cause. They have a fashion of disbelieving in all possible republics but their own, and their hearts are not easily touched by the misfortunes of any modern hero. His visit to this country saddens me because the excitement he has caused must raise in him false hopes which cannot and perhaps ought not to be gratified. We should not engage in foreign wars, and after all he will be greatly disappointed. Still, money seems to be freely offered him, and that, I suppose, he chiefly needs. . . .

February 18, 1852

. . . We have just got through reading the tragic history of Margaret Fuller Ossoli, by Emerson, Channing, etc., various friends taking up her remarkable life with their acquaintance with her. It is deeply interesting and shows forth a woman of nobler heart and brain than I had supposed. There was so much distasteful in her manners we evidently did her no justice, though her friends were of the most devoted kind. Her prophetic longing for foreign life and active benevolence were strangely fulfilled, and the Italian part is very touching, all its struggle and sorrow seeming fitly to close in the grand and solemn beauty of their united death. For it was beautiful, and life would always have been to her "too difficult" as she says when overwhelmed by its burdens.

Mrs. Ward was here yesterday and told me much of Jenny Lind's marriage at her house,[38] the beautiful character of her husband, and his entire worthiness of her noble and deeply religious nature. It was most quietly and privately accomplished, taking every one by surprise, though we all knew Jenny was furnishing a house at Northampton for the summer. Their plan is to be there but a few months and then go to Germany. She (Jenny) considers his talent as a composer every remarkable and has long known him so well that it has none of the danger of a sudden fancy.

She brought him out here with her last summer, and I was much pleased with his modesty and look of feeling and gentleness. I trust they may be happy, for so sensitive a nature as hers would terribly suffer from the reverse.

To Mary Longfellow Greenleaf

March 2, 1852

. . . I wish you liked . . . [*The Golden Legend*] better, though I think it natural it should not please you entirely. The corruption of belief and teaching in the Middle Ages is not a pleasant thing to be reminded of, but these are the true pictures, however disagreeable, and Henry wished to show that even in that darkness and corruption (for which he is not responsible as some critics seem to make him!) there was enough pure faith for the great trials of life and death. The poem is written in the truest religious spirit and is meant merely as a picture of that age, for which he takes a well known (in Germany) story of that time upon which to illustrate the "form and pressure" of the time. Lucifer was introduced not as the spirit of all evil but as the type of evil in most men, and as indispensable as a character in a religious poem of the Middle Ages.

Blackwood has a good review upon the religious part of the poem, though he, like most of the critics, has some very stupid blunders,

---

[38] Jenny Lind married Otto Goldschmidt, her accompanist, at the home of Mrs. Sam Grey Ward, 20 Louisburg Square, Boston, on February 5, 1852.

making the poor author responsible for the story as others do for the theology. Perhaps a preface was needed, and I am rather sorry it was not written, but Henry thinks if people will be so stupid they must find out his meaning for themselves. . . .

We have a good Opera now in Boston, and last night we went to see Mrs. Mowatt,[39] who is a very interesting actress full of the poetry of her art. . . .

To Samuel Longfellow

March 18, 1852

. . . Have you seen Miss Mitford's gossiping book of literary reminiscences? She spoils in it Henry's ghost story of Washington appearing on a white horse to protect the house while beset by fire on two sides, by leaving out the fire, which was the whole point of it. Fields was her authority. . . . Why do you say no more of Mrs. Browning? I hoped to hear you had cultivated her acquaintance further, despite the distance. Miss Mitford gives the cause of her melancholy poems, the sudden loss of a brother in a boat with other young people, and it is a sad enough story. . . .

I liked your critique of the *Legend,* but you make a sad mistake about Prince Henry. He tells that lie at the end, in the excitement and distress of the moment, not to deceive Elsie but the Priest, but finding it not heeded, his fully roused better nature conquers his selfishness and he rushes to her rescue. . . .

To Emmeline Austin Wadsworth

April 16, 1852

I will gladly aid you in enlarging little Austin's library and would send you those books I think good at once if I knew whether you have them not, and where you would like to have them purchased. It is not easy to find very good ones for a young child, and I remem-

---

[39] Anna Cora Ogden Mowatt, later Mrs. Ritchie (1819–1870), distinguished American actress, and author of the famous play, *Fashion* (1845).

ber, in my despair, I often thought of writing some myself, knowing so well what pleased best my own children. They liked always stories of simple truth, without being spiced with horrors or with fairy fancy, but as they get older their tastes are less innocent. I rather prefer the English books to the American ones, for these latter are so apt to have Yankee expressions or Calvinistic ideas, but the Rollo books have always had a good reputation. My children have only *Rollo Learning to Talk,* which has short stories, and they always liked it much when little. *Little Annie's First Book* is a good one to learn to read by (American). Then *Little Mary's Treasury of Elementary Knowledge* (English) is an excellent book, having many charming pictures and comprising eight books more from young lore to older. Erny calls it his Bible because it has the Bible history simply explained and so well illustrated that he has learned every important fact by the pictures. Then *Pleasures of the Country* by Mrs. Myrtle (English) is a charming book with capital stories, and if a little too old for Austin, he would enjoy the highly colored and truly English pictures by Gilbert and would soon grow up to the text.

Then *Willy's Rambles,* by Jane Marcet, is a very nice little book about the building of a house, not too old. And *Jane Taylor's Nursery Rhymes* is always a favorite, and *Rhymes, Chimes, and Jingles,* which you probably have. My children have any quantity but not many they care to hear twice except these I have mentioned. There may be newer ones I know not of.

The Illustrated Book of Songs for children is a beautiful book, adorned by Birket Foster, and among fairy books *Gammer Grethel* always holds its place.

How I wish I could see your darlings at these pretty ages. What a comfort they must be to both of you, their young life seeming to supply what is wanting from our more exhausted fountain. My whole life is bound up now in my home and children. I am spoiled by it for society, which seems to me very barren and unsympathetic, giving us only glossy surfaces or sharp corners instead of the genial depth and lofty aspiration we crave. We so miss Sumner's Sunday visits, with their free, fresh variety of topics and nice literary talks which he best loves. He too pines for them in Washington, and says a lecture from Agassiz was a great refreshment to him there—so far off is he from all science and literature. . . .

Charley Norton is a very noble youth and interests me much. The article in *The North American* upon better houses for the poor was by him, and he seems full of sympathy for the unfortunate, and not like so many of our youths sneering at all misfortune. He has not an ardent nature either, but thoughtful and pitiful. He is like an English youth, where there is now so much philanthropic feeling among the young and old too. . . .

To Samuel Longfellow

May 10, 1852

. . . From the depth of winter we have suddenly burst into full summer verdure; in three days the bare boughs were clothed with green. Kossuth's coming seems to have produced this miracle, as his genial presence makes blossom many a wintry heart and conquers many a prejudice. He was shamefully abused in most of the "hunker" papers before he came, but no one can fail to listen to him with[out] respect and sympathy, however hopeless they may consider his cause. We have seen him several times delightfully.

We first met the Pulszkys (his Secretary of State and a man of wonderful information and intelligence) at a party at Mr. Charles G. Loring's, and were charmed with them. Madame Pulszky has a face of animated beauty and is very clever and agreeable. We called upon them and were introduced to Kossuth after hearing him address a committee from Salem in his drawing-room. He took Henry most warmly by both hands and said, "Though I am not a man of genius, I know how to appreciate one." He has a fine, graceful figure and noble countenance, especially when kindled by speaking, great dignity of manner, and is usually rather grave and silent, but what he says with his deep musical voice is always freighted with thought or feeling.

We dined with him on Sunday at Dr. Howe's, quite by ourselves, and I sat next him, but felt such an awe, thinking of all he had suffered and done, I could not speak much. Madame Kossuth is tall with fine eyes, but drooping with much weeping, and her face tells a tale of anxiety and sorrow. Her health has suffered much, but the Pulszkys are full of freshness and life and seem ready to go through all again. Madame Pulszky said to me, "Kossuth is the great man of the century. I have seen him now under every variety of circumstance and always the same greatness—never a thought of self—he sacrifices everything for his country." I said, "His enemies acknowledge his greatness by their fears of him." To which she replied, "Yes, they know his ability, but not his character."

Tuesday last was Exhibition,[40] and the Pulszkys came out and went with us. Kossuth had been invited by the President, but declined, having to speak every day in some new town, but just as the oration was half through he came. We heard the roar of welcome as we sat in the Chapel. The young man paused and retired; Henry and Felton escorted him and Madame in at the North door, Governor Boutwell and his suite following. As he appeared on the platform in his black velvet frock coat and plumed beaver, such hurrahs as only students can give roared through the densely-packed room. He smiled and bowed slightly, then sat down. The young man finished his theme, "On unsuccessful great men," very appropriately handled, and when it was over, Mr. Sparks [41] descended to welcome the noble guest, and begged him to address the students. He at first declined, but being introduced to them by the President, stood forth and said a few words. He then drove directly to our house, where he remained half an hour, sitting down in the study, after being received in the library, and putting an arm around Charley and Erny, asked them to recite one of their papa's poems, but alas! it was not forthcoming! . . .

Kossuth's speeches are as wonderful as ever, always appropriate to the place and occasion, and always marked by the same trust in God and the justice of his cause. They all seem most sanguine of final success, but I wish I could have the same faith. Crushed as their country has been and is, it is hard to condemn them for wishing to raise it at any cost. Pulszky had large estates, a splendid library, etc., all now lost, but his books, which a friend has saved. I

[40] At Harvard College.
[41] Jared Sparks, the historian, now (1852) president of Harvard.

have not heard Kossuth in public, not having had courage to go to crowded Faneuil Hall, but read his speeches with the same interest as ever. The one at Bunker Hill was very touching and eloquent, and at Lowell practical and good, in which he spoke of all he had done in Hungary to promote the industry of the people and organize manufactories, now all suppressed. . . .

Another book is having immense success—*Uncle Tom's Cabin,* by Mrs. Stowe (Miss Beecher that was). It describes slavery in all its phases without exaggeration and with a graphic truth and pathos and power which all must feel. It must do much good, but is most painful to read, though varied with scenes of great humor and showing the best of such a system. It is the most American book we have had and will give its authoress great fame. Alice Cary's poetry is thought very remarkable, but to me it rings, like the mocking-bird, of too many other songsters, as do most of her sister and brother poets. . . .

To Emmeline Austin Wadsworth

Newport, August 20, 1852

I should not have allowed so many days to go by since my last without a word of love to you, but I have been suffering the last fortnight with rheumatism, which made it very painful for me to move. It still lingers a little, but I hope is about departing, though in this moist climate when once fixed it is not so easily got rid of. I got excessively overheated in dressing after my first bath in the sea, and then driving home in a strong wind naturally presented me with this unwelcome guest. . . . Ever since that severe attack I had in Boston when you nursed me so kindly, I have been subject to it when thus exposed. . . .

Our house here is now quite filled up and likely to be overflowing. Julia Howe is a great acquisition. So full of spirits and every variety of talent, her wit rouses us all out of the languor this climate induces, and her singing (greatly improved in Italy), is a perpetual delight. . . . After breakfast we sit about the hall door, looking over green fields to the sea and chat very merrily or profoundly as the humor takes us, then the bathers depart and the rest retire to their rooms to write or read until the incessant ringing of the bell announces that callers are invading our quiet (I now refuse them as I should at home, having seen enough). After dinner another chat or playing of foot ball on the lawn, even the ladies having taken to tossing it, then come the drives or the sunset walk on the Cliffs, and in the evening when no "hops" or parties draw off the gentlemen, we get up games or adjourn to Mrs. Benzon's parlor for singing, and so runs the day away. It is impossible to lead a more sensible life in all this bustle, and in this lazy air all care is softened and all thought becomes a dream. . . .

To Thomas G. Appleton

Cambridge, November 15, 1852

. . . The Lowells returned two days since [42] looking fresh and well, but James's picturesque beard succumbed to English prejudices, and its removal takes half the poetry from his face, I confess, though I am not fond of beards. They came out with Thackeray and found him very genial and agreeable on the passage. Henry saw him on Saturday but I shall not probably at present, as he goes directly to New York to begin his lectures. Clough also arrived [43] and proceeded to pass Sunday with Emerson, so we have not yet seen him. I cannot imagine what he can find to do here but hope he won't be disappointed. The *Homes of American Authors* [44] has made its appearance and makes a very charming book, with capital sketches of the various mansions and beautifully written essays upon them and their owners by various hands. The "Howadji" [45] has done ours and Emerson's and Hawthorne's with his usual grace and humor, wickedly fastening upon poor Alcott the name I gave him of Plato-Skimpole, and giving a very amusing account of Emerson's attempt at a Club. . . .

[42] From England, after a rather extensive trip abroad.
[43] Arthur Hugh Clough, author of *The Bothie of Tober-na-Vuolich*, lived on Appian Way in Cambridge, 1852–1853.
[44] *Homes of American Authors, Comprising Anecdotal, Personal, and Descriptive Sketches*, by Various Authors.
[45] George William Curtis.

December 7, 1852

Your full and pleasant letter was eagerly read, and we all rejoice
you find London so agreeable and were tempted to stay over the
grand pageant which was not a thing to omit. The *Illustrated News*
gives us the whole scene, and with a written description which quite
makes one a spectator, but the feeling of the occasion is in the air,
magnetically sympathetic from face to face, and cannot be reported.
Tennyson's Ode [46] we have only parts of, which mars it, but though
singularly modern and familiar for such things (shocking, I suppose,
to the elders fond of statlier measures), it has a simple dignity of its
own and gives the modern appreciation of duty over mere glory. . . .

Clough we see often and find very agreeable, by no means so
painfully shy as I feared. He seems full of feeling and good sense,
and I hope will succeed here, and be able to bring over his English
bride to something promising, but as yet it is uncertain. We shall
soon have Thackeray, and I hope to enjoy his lectures greatly.

The new Music Hall [47] is a splendid affair and ample enough for
the largest audience and perfectly comfortable in all its arrangements, with its forty doors of entrance from the spacious corridors.
The opening Festival was very fine, with Sontag [48] shining in pink
through the open lattice of the gallery, *vis à vis* her rival as in the
play of *The Ambassadrice* from her story. I forget if I told you the
Benzons [49] had her one evening at a select soiree musicale and that
she graciously sang a charming song. I found her very easy and
good natured in conversation, and looking a perfect German lady.
Her voice, though so skilfully managed, wants power beside the
freshness and richness of Alboni's. She was very civil to the clergymen, and Dr. Sharpe was deputed to thank her and present her a
Bible! . . .

(JOURNAL)   January, 1853

I have to thank God that the children have been in perfect health
since last date, a long time for such a blessing. In May last they were

[46] "Ode on the Death of the Duke of Wellington."
[47] Opened November 20.
[48] Henriette Sontag, Countess Rossi (1806–1854), the great German soprano.
[49] The Swedish consul in Boston and his wife.

made very happy by the arrival of their dear cousins Eva and Angus
Mackintosh from the West Indies, two very sweet, good children.
Charley celebrated his birthday and Eva's together on the ninth of
June with quite a party, and after their merry romp outdoors enjoyed his polka in the parlor. He and Erny dance very well. Miss
Davie (the governess) taught all at home in Uncle Sam's room, and
they gained rapidly in writing under her care and made a nice little
school. In July we all went to Newport, and there they bathed together and rambled all along shore from our pleasant house on the
cliff and kept up their lessons bravely. In August Eva and Angus
went with their mama to Pittsfield, and in early September we returned home. The football was much kicked of mornings. Charley
has wanted jackets open in front with shirt or white waistcoat very
becoming to him. Erny and Angus are like twins and frisk together
like a pair of squirrels. Eva is very fair with her golden locks and
refined features but almost too silent and demure. Darling little
Alice looked pale and thin through the summer but upon heartier
diet has grown fat and rosy and wonderfully knowing and enticing.
She likes to take up a book and read stories and says more cunning
things than can be remembered, is rather passionate but generally
very good and yields readily. Santa Claus' eve was a great delight to
all the chicks, and New Year's Eve at Grandpapa's with the richly-
laden tree. Baby was very lively in her little white gown and blue
sash and carried off her huge doll's bedstead triumphantly, wishing
it in sight all night. On Angus' birthday, the sixteenth of January, I
had a few chicks in the afternoon, and Eva presided at supper, with
the Wedgwood set, and Angus got the boys' ring in the cake, Fanny
Nowell the girls'. Little Mabel Lowell was present with her sweet
mama. Afterwards we got up tableaux in the nursery, enclosing the
door towards the entry—first Eva as a Spanish lady in my Spanish
dress with the mandolin, then Erny as her page, next Erny and
Angus as Turkish soldiers in the red caps, etc., then "the dull Lecture," Erny reading the big Finnish Bible with spectacles on nose
and Eva asleep with a wreath of roses on her head and one of my
smart gowns on. Angus enchanted with the snow and a sled but
poor Eva feels the cold much. . . .

To Mary Longfellow Greenleaf

April, 1853

I was rejoiced to see your handwriting again and humbly express my own remissness in writing, but for two months I felt so miserably that I could not wield a pen. An attack of influenza and rheumatism left me in a state of extreme debility, so that I could do nothing but recline on a couch, without even the privilege of talking, for my throat seemed weaker than any other part, having long been a tender one. I had the consolation of listening, however, but could enjoy nothing from the want of vitality in my veins. . . .

Mrs. Stowe's *Key* has appeared and will make a great stir, I sup pose. Its facts are more painful than the softened fiction of *Uncle Tom,* and I think the South will be sorry to have provoked such a reply by denying her statements. She more than confirms them all by fact, if not always by law, and it is written with the same fairness and endeavor to show it is the thing and not the men which is so bad. I am curious to know how she will bear the overwhelming reception awaiting her in England, for she is a little, feeble, timid-looking woman, and I should think could hardly stem such a torrent of admiration. . . .

To Samuel Longfellow

May 26, 1853

. . . I believe I wrote you of Mr. [Moncure D.] Conway, a Virginian youth of the Divinity School, and a warm hater of slavery—refreshing to know from a slave state—a very agreeable, excellent fellow. I wish you could know him. He made a reverential pilgrimage to Emerson and got him to promise the school a visit. He was amused with Thoreau, who, asking what they studied and he replying, "The Scriptures," asked, "Which? The Chaldee, Hindoo, or Jewish?" . . .

To Thomas G. Appleton

June 21, 1853

. . . We had the other day a farewell dinner for Hawthorne [50]—
with Emerson, Lowell, Clough, Norton, and Sam for guests, and
very pleasant it was. The new Consul looks quite radiant for him,
and feels no doubt the cares of life lightened for some time. He is to
give us in the autumn another volume of his charming mythological
tales,[51] the old gold in a new mould. . . .

To Anne Longfellow Pierce

June 24, 1853

. . . I feel pretty well at present, though incapable of much exertion, expecting to be confined about the first of October, a prospect
which has depressed me a good deal, and I have been very miserable (physically, I mean), all the spring. I find children such a
responsibility as they grow older, and so difficult to manage rightly,
that I shrink from further duties beyond my capacities.

Alice is a darling comfort but promises to have a pretty good will
of her own too and is fated to be a tomboy, I fear, unless she has the
good fortune to get a companion of her own sex. . . .

To Samuel Longfellow

Nahant, August 31, 1853

For many weeks we have been hoping to see arrive your sermon
on "The Word Preached," [52] and the extracts and commendations in
the newspapers have only sharpened our impatience—when lo! yesterday in feeling at the bottom of a carpet-bag Henry brought from
Cambridge about Commencement time, it appeared, having been
thrown in with other pamphlets and left there unknown to us all this
time.

[50] Whom Franklin Pierce had appointed American Consul at Liverpool.
[51] *Tanglewood Tales.*
[52] The first sermon included in Joseph May's collection, *Samuel Longfellow:
Essays and Sermons.*

Having now read it, I can no longer refrain from telling you how admirable it seems to me, how its clear, forcible style utters the Truth as the truth should be uttered, in tones of authority and simplicity. The part about the Word is very beautiful, and the whole is to me the best matter in the best words. I appreciate your style even better, I think, in print than in manuscript, and for preaching it could hardly be improved—it is so compact and earnest and rises to beauty so naturally, without inflation, and falls again so quietly to the even tread of the argument. I am very glad this was printed, for it will make you more widely and worthily known than any subject less broadly treated and such a manly voice must be most grateful to many waiting and thirsting souls. . . .

The following letter from Cambridge is not dated. Mrs. James Russell Lowell died on October 27.

To Emmeline Austin Wadsworth

. . . The Lowells . . . came to see us, and her pale, thin face and hollow cough were sad omens of her fate. She has enjoyed the country here (they have been at a farmhouse between Lenox and Stockbridge) but she has gained nothing from the mountain air, and her last hope fails her. It must be hard for her to turn her thoughts to another world leaving such treasures in this—a sweet child, a girl too, and a most loving husband. Poor Lowell, his harp, which has saddened only for others' sorrows, will have a string of deeper tone added to its quick sensibilities. I cannot help thinking, when I see her, of his prayer beginning, "God! do not let my loved one die." [53] . . .

To Mary Appleton Mackintosh

November 22, 1853

I am glad to be able to send you a line by this steamer to say that thanks to God, I am nearly well again and am every day gaining

[53] This poem, "A Prayer," is included among Lowell's *Earlier Poems.*

new strength.[54] I have not yet driven out, nor dined downstairs but once, and feel in no haste to leave my pleasant chamber. . . .

We are puzzled for a name. Grace and Rose are proposed. Papa fancies the latter, romantic as it is, but Henry thinks it rather barmaidy. . . .

When her children were very small, Fanny wrote them Santa Claus letters each Christmas. A number of these, some of them undated, are given together here.

Christmas Eve, 1851

My dear Charley,

A merry Christmas again to you, my little friend! As I peep slyly at your face upon the pillow I am very glad to see it so rosy and round, and to find you well and strong this year as last. I hope to find you as good too—much *better,* for you should keep growing good as well as strong, but I am sorry I sometimes hear you are not so kind to your little brother as I wish you were. Try to be kinder this year and more obedient to papa and mamma who love you very much and whom you love, too, I know. I hope you won't be disappointed that I do not bring what you ask for in your letter, but the truth is I do not like to have little boys play soldiers though I don't mind their playing with them, so I fill your stocking with a watch, which will make the time pass very sweetly, and I find in my bag some beautiful books your kind friend Mr. Rölker popped in as I came along which I think you will like as well.

Good night! away I go!

Your constant friend
Santi Claus

P. S. I like to see toothbrushes well used.

My darling little baby [Alice],

How are *you?* Fat, and rosy, and good as ever? Last Christmas you could only *crow* and now you can say I don't know how many words, and run about like a little mouse. You are not too little to be

[54] Edith Longfellow was born October 22.

very affectionate and obedient either, and I think you are still one of my best little girls.

I have a beautiful bird in my bag for you who will sing to you all day long but not so well as dear little Dickey and Willy. And I give you Tom Thumb for a husband and many kisses besides before I fly away.

Good bye.
Your old loving
Santi Claus

Xmas Eve 1851.

Dear Charley,

A merry Christmas to you! Is it possible I see a jacket hanging on that chair, and bless me! a waistcoat! why how you little folks do grow. But I hope you will not yet outgrow old Santa Claus, who dearly loves you though he wishes sometimes you were a little more gentle and obedient to papa and mamma.

I believe you have taken pretty good care of your teeth as I told you but I want you to keep your heart clean of bad thoughts and secret thoughts and to tell your dear mamma and papa everything you do and think. I am glad to see you have studied so well this year, but am in too great hurry to say all I would.

Your loving
Santa Claus

I forgot to give you my love and to say that I think you have been a very good boy this year.

Dear Erny,

I am very happy to see you so fat and rosy this year and to know that you no longer suck your thumb, but instead use it much better by holding a pencil by it and drawing such beautiful pictures. Why don't you try your hand upon *me* as you have taken to portraits I hear?

Good bye, darling boy. Think how many chimneys I have got to pop down.

Your loving old
Santa Claus

A Merry Christmas!

Christmas Eve 1853
Chimney Corner

Dear Charley and Erny,

I have not time tonight to write you each a letter, having so many little folks' stockings to fill and I am afraid to stay here too long for fear you should see me, for I hear you begin to find me out and that will never do until you are too big to be pleased with toys and bonbons.

I love to come and wish you a merry Christmas but I wish I could say you had been as good boys this year as the last. You have not been so obedient and gentle and kind and loving to your parents and little sister as I like to have you, and you have picked up some naughty words which I hope you will throw away as you would sour or bitter fruit. Try to stop to think before you use any, and remember if no one else hears you God is always near and you would not wish to speak them before Him.

A new Year is just beginning and I hope to find you at the end of it among my best boys.

Ever your loving
Santa Claus

Manuscript materials during the next few years are not very numerous, but enough survive to give the flavor of the family life and interests.

To Samuel Longfellow

February 22, 1854

. . . We are greatly excited about the dreadful Nebraska wickedness,[55] and Henry has gone down to the Reading Room to try to find some report of Sumner's speech. I hope it will be pungent, for I know his heart is full. He writes us that it has made him almost ill. The Whigs pretend indignation, but I fear it will be of the most

---

[55] The Kansas-Nebraska Bill, sponsored by Senator Stephen A. Douglas, and bitterly opposed by Sumner and others, which allowed the inhabitants of each territory to decide for slavery or freedom.

luke-warm kind. . . . Still I am glad the Whigs are to have a Faneuil Hall meeting separate from the Free Soilers, because it will show the amount of antislavery feeling at the North of all shades. I should have liked to hear Beecher but knew there would be no room and I have not been out in the evening. . . . Henry went to hear Theodore Parker with Tom and Bayard Taylor and Lowell, who all dined here afterward, but he did not stay for the peroration. War, Slavery, Pestilence, and Famine seem to threaten the poor weary Earth. I wish she had four as potent champions, but what do I say—a million blessed angels lackey her and there is no fear she will long be surrendered to the power of her enemies.

Henry, as you have doubtless heard, is weary after twenty-five years teaching, and has resigned his Professorship—to have time for other things and to feel free, but he will remain in the harness until the summer vacation. . . .

To Mary Appleton Mackintosh

May 8, 1854

. . . Sam Longfellow arrived to christen baby, as we were very anxious he should consecrate one of our children, and as he could not come again until August, we could not very well postpone it. . . . Sam made it so beautiful and touching . . . by his tender, earnest manner and fresh expression of its deep significance that I wished there had been more friends with us to appreciate it and to associate with it. Baby behaved charmingly, cooing gently all the while, and with her fair, sunny countenance and blue eyes answered well to her Saxon name, Edith, which Henry inclined to give her. She had a famous christening cake, covered with roses, and the chicks thought it all very fine, though it was hard to awe them into propriety with such a strictly family party. . . .

June 19, 1854

You will think I have been long silent but I missed the Boston steamer and have since been so busy with guests I have had not a moment's leisure. . . . Mr. Lawrence [has been with us] more than a week, . . . and has made a beautiful drawing of Henry which all agree in thinking the best yet taken. It is full of life and with a very lively, agreeable expression. . . .[56] Lawrence could only come now for this and a beginning of Lowell, having many New York engagements, but will return in the autumn to Boston. We have had all the pleasant people of Cambridge to meet him and have driven them about Brookline, etc. and he seems highly pleased with this vicinity, thinking it so much more finished and English. He is a very agreeable person, so quiet and intelligent and shrewd in his observations. He wishes to draw me by and bye, and I should like a good portrait of Alice. . . .

The letter from which the following fragment is taken is dated only "October 14." Since The Newcomes *did not begin its serial course until October 1853, it presumably belongs to 1854.*

To Emmeline Austin Wadsworth

. . . We are reading *The Newcomes* with much enjoyment, and I like it thus far better than any of this cruelly true satirist's. The Colonel is a beautiful character, showing the tender side of the censor's heart. . . .

To Mary Appleton Mackintosh

January 2, 1855

. . . We are getting deeper into [Sir Thomas Fowell] Buxton's Life, and are charmed with the strength and tenderness of his character, his Christian humility so beautifully spiritualizing all his manly labors. Wilberforce's first appeals to him, too, to join his holy league against slavery are so interesting. Ah! these are the men a nation should honor and bow down before, not the destroyers of their race and the retarders of civilization and practical Christianity!

[56] This is the familiar crayon drawing by Samuel Lawrence, in the parlor of the Longfellow House, where another by the same artist depicts Alice and Edith.

What power an evil thing has—this war blights even our more hopeful hopes for mankind, and our teachings to our children, for it is impossible to make them believe it sinful while every mail brings these exciting pictures of carnage. The boys are forever shouting Tennyson's battle poem, though they never before learned by heart anything so long, and the other evening, when Henry called to take Em to the opera, he found her three tiny fellows on the drawing-room floor enacting dying soldiers while one dragged the little wheelbarrow over their prostrate bodies for cannon.

We have exceedingly enjoyed our opera evenings with her. Grisi has certainly lost the freshness and power of her voice, but she still acts and looks magnificently, and her Norma was never grander. There has been great enthusiasm for her and Mario here, and our immense new theater has been nightly crowded and a beautiful sight with the gay dresses of the ladies. It is a most comfortable place, with elegant dressing rooms for the ladies, and with a staircase and hall finer than I remember abroad. She says she never sang in one she liked so well, but that of course is not to be relied on. . . .

To Samuel Longfellow

November 5, 1855

. . . *The Song of Hiawatha* will be out on Saturday. I believe we are to have some copies today. I hope you will like it. It is very fresh and fragrant of the woods and genuine Indian life, but its rhymeless rhythm will puzzle the critics, and I suppose it will be abundantly abused as [Tennyson's] poor *Maud* seems to be. Pegasus will "gang his ain gait," despite all the whips and spurs of the many who think they know so much better than the poet what he ought to say. . . .

I saw Rachel again in *Adrienne*, which was grandly done but did not somehow touch me—only intellectually as perfect acting. . . .

January 1, 1856

Happy New Year to you! How begins it in Brooklyn? With good promises as thick, I trust, as our snow-flakes, and as softly covering all the rough and gloomy places of its predecessor, if that deceased worthy had any for you. He brought me a new care but a new darling,[57] so I cannot complain of him. She is a dear little thing and considered very promising for one of her weeks, now eight. I feel really growing to be a venerable Banyan tree, with all these young shoots springing up round me, and they seem to root me more and more to one spot. . . .

Your Christmas, I hope, was as pleasant as it should be. I was housed quietly all the stormy day, but Henry and the children . . . went to Mrs. Howe's at South Boston, where they had a tree and tableaux from Thackeray's Christmas book of last year.[58] . . .

Have you had, in your warmer region, the wonderful splendor of last week here—Aladdin's garden of silver with jewels upon every twig for fruit? It lasted two days and nights through the most brilliant sunshine and moonshine, and was really the most magical spectacle of the kind I ever saw—Nature's grand Christmas tree to delight all her children, rich and poor, with the simple elements of rain and light, both heavenly gifts however. Fireworks were got out in Boston to adorn it still more.

Henry's *Hiawatha* seems to have roused all the nettles of criticism, but we don't read the disagreeable ones. The disrespect and impertinence of them strike me most, so different from the English ones—ten of these from leading literary journals are most eulogistic and appreciative and civil. . . . No one wishes another to like all styles of poetry but if the author is known and valued, he should be supposed to be *honest* and to choose even his metre with a good reason.

Thackeray and Ole Bull I lost seeing, but heard the latter's seraphic strains when he played here one evening, the former also present.[59] . . . Is not Browning rich but rugged? His letter of an Arab physician [60] is very powerful. . . .

[57] Fanny's sixth and last child, Annie Allegra Longfellow, born November 8, 1855.

[58] *The Rose and the Ring.*

[59] Thackeray spent much of December, 1855, lecturing in Boston.

[60] "An Epistle Containing the Strange Medical Experience of Karshish, the Arab Physician," in *Men and Women* (1855).

CHAPTER VII

The Last Years

The year 1856 was a trying one for the Longfellows. In the spring, their older son, Charles, not yet twelve years old, injured his left hand very seriously, destroying the thumb altogether, by the explosion of a gun which his father had reluctantly permitted him to use against his mother's advice. Of the several accounts Fanny wrote of this terrible accident, I give the one contained in her letter to her husband's sister Mary. The threat of more serious calamities in early summer fortunately did not materialize, but the twenty-eighth of June must have been a day to remember with horror.

To Mary Longfellow Greenleaf

May 2, 1856

I have not had a moment's time to write you or you should not have been left in ignorance of all the particulars of Charley's sad accident. His father was obliged to watch with him all night, for more than a week, and I was needed all day, whenever baby could spare me, so that we have been much absorbed since it happened. It has been a sore trial to us, completely unnerving us for the time, and the thought of our boy's maimed hand has been before our eyes and hearts through all the sleepless nights and anxious days. But all has gone on as well as possible, and we begin to feel more resigned, and to be grateful it was not his face, nor right hand, that suffered. He has helped us by the astonishing bravery with which he has borne all the horror and suffering, walking home more than a mile, "without crying once," as his companion said (who had the presence of mind to bind up his hand with a handkerchief and tie it tight with the cord of the powder-flask), and as soon as his hand was dressed, with the blessed help of ether, he begged us not to worry, saying, "Ah, Doctor, ether is much better than gunpowder," on which text,

you know, I could preach a sermon. The doctor is in daily admiration of his courage, for this daily dressing gets to be very trying to
the nerves, as well as painful, but he is cheerful and hardly winces,
and is now allowed to go out freely to recover his strength. It will
be a fresh blow to me when his hand is well enough to be uncovered,
but "sufficient for the day," etc. I trust he will never feel it as we
do, and that it may have a lasting, beneficial effect on his character.
The gun burst, either from being overloaded, or from being worthless, we do not know which. We feel very grateful to the older boy,
who brought him so well home, without allowing him to yield to
faintness, etc. Think what a walk for the poor fellow! He was at
Fresh Pond. He bought the gun with money he had saved up, but
Henry had told him only to use percussion-caps with it, but the
temptation was too great—he yielded and was severely punished. . . .

To Thomas G. Appleton

Nahant, July 29, 1856

. . . James thinks you have chosen the better part in going away
to a more temperate climate from these tropic heats, which, even
here, have been almost intolerable of late. The sea is of mingled
glass and fire, and the sails of silver, even in the shadows of the
sky and sea, seem one, but yesterday anything but heavenly was
their aspect for an hour—an hour which seems to add ten years to
one's life. Alice had been bathing, and her nurse came in with her,
overwhelmed with terror and grief, saying the poor child was nearly
drowned, for, while she was looking away for a moment, Alice
slipped off a rock and lost her footing and her strength, and she
rushed in just in time to save her. Before this fright had subsided
came on a terrible thunder-squall, and we watched with intense and
most painful anxiety a vessel, just upon our rocks, struggling away,
but with anchor dragging, and again hurled back again until I heard
her scrape distinctly. Erny thought Charley was in her, and I
sickened too much to look, until, by immense efforts, she ventured
a sail up and got off into open sea. In a quarter of an hour Charley
appeared, without hat and drenched to the skin with salt water and

fresh. He was in her, with the Rev. Vinton! and thus, in one day, we had to thank God for the lives of two children. Ah, they are terrible cares—you are fortunate perhaps not to know the inexpressible anxiety they cause hour by hour. One has no longer any youth after they come. . . .

To Mary Longfellow Greenleaf

August 1856

. . . We are very pleasantly situated in this snug little cottage, directly overhanging the sea, with such a superb view from our piazza of the great Atlantic, and these richly-colored rocks, and all the outward and homeward-bound sails, not to speak of the ceaseless atmospheric changes, and the ever-shifting beauty of sea and sky that Henry is quite consoled for being still a prisoner. You have been told, no doubt, how he struck his knee upon entering the rail car, and, though seeming a slight injury, it has held on in the tedious way these things are apt to. He walks about the house, but with just that touch of pain and stiffness, now and then, which warns him to do no more, but as we have Tom's nice little phaeton here (for he left us carriage, horses, coachman, all ready for use), we drive daily on the grand beach which is a great resource and pleasure for him. . . . The children are very happy here, as you can imagine. Charley and Erny have a boat, and are out from daybreak fishing and paddling about, but the latter often comes home to play fairy-land with Alice upon the rocks, collecting sea-weed and shells and arranging them in crevices. Even little Edy joins in this fun. Alice goes to a neighboring cottage to say lessons with some other little girls, and is as brown as an Indian. . . .

We have very painful news of a younger brother of my cousin Fanny Wright. He has been many years in Texas, and though I have hardly seen him since a child, all say he has had the same frank, amiable character. Fanny was especially attached to him, and has been long hoping his return. But last May or June he was murdered by Indians on an expedition, though his friends rather suspect a Frenchman and Mexicans who were with him, as the rest of the party were uninjured. . . .

To Thomas G. Appleton

Cambridge, November 1, 1856

The awful crisis is at hand—upon a breath now seems to hang the life or death of the country, and it is a moment of most painful uncertainty. The state elections from Pennsylvania were not encouraging, but since then it has looked brighter and our hopes revive. It is thought the large body of Quakers did not vote there, but will now for Frémont, caring only for the Presidential question. But the Buchananers are straining every nerve and using every fraud to swell their numbers, and we fear the state elections discouraged many who like to be on the winning side.

Sumner arrives tonight as far as Brookline, where he is to be the guest of Amos Lawrence over Sunday, to enter Boston with a grand cavalcade on Monday. In the evening they give him a banquet in the Music Hall, where I suppose he will have to say something, and the next day is the election. He is still only well enough to just come home to vote, any excitement giving him sleepless nights, but is now we trust fairly convalescing, and, when allowed quiet, quite well. The Frémonters gave a magnificent torchlight procession this week, five miles long, gay with transparencies and music, and as we drove in to Miss Mifflin's wedding-visit, we encountered it in Charles Street, the rockets darting over our heads, the cheering, and long perspective of Chinese lanterns a most exhilarating sight. . . .

December 15, 1856

. . . I am reading . . . [Mrs. Browning's] new poem, *Aurora Leigh,* and think it magnificent—the finest web she has spun yet. Get it, if you have it not, and revel in her rich, fresh fancies, and wonderful word pictures. It must be an autobiography, and gives you her deepest feeling on books and art and life, with touches of humor and sly sarcasm you would hardly expect from her. It is healthier than her former poems, the rose without a grub of her mature womanhood. . . .

To James Russell Lowell [1]

January 2 [1857]

You have so illuminated my sober candlestick [2] with that divine "light which never was on sea or land" that I feel very proud of my gift, not disinclined to believe it has some hidden, wonderful powers, like those of Aladdin's magic lamp, to bring down such a fairy palace to the sound of sweetest music. But well I know too that in this case all the value lies in the Magician—in the poet's heart and soul, which, from the humblest and most unworthy object, could summon a world of "silvery enchantment." The Roc's egg in that palace is never wanting, and as it can never fly away, any bright morning, I trust the possessor can never be wholly desolate. . . .

To Thomas G. Appleton

February 9, 1857

I wish you could have peeped into the study last week to have seen the juvenile faces when the doll-box arrived, with its fascinating contents. Charley, having been made the happy possessor of a toolbox at Christmas, was called upon for aid, and soon undid the lid, with Erny's help, while Alice and Edie stood by, dumb with expectation, their eyes sparkling like stars and their cheeks glowing like roses as I opened the inner cover and revealed the most beautiful of dolls, with all the choice paraphernalia of her toilette. Then such exclamations of delight, as they examined them, bit by bit, and rushed with them from me to Rachel, from whose arms baby was gazing wonderingly on. It was really an era in their little lives, and they will probably remember, years hence, the sensation caused by this arrival. I had told Alice, a few days before, what was coming and of the doll sailing on the sea, and discussed with her the chances of her being sea-sick, etc., so she was expecting her with quite a human interest combined with the wonder of a foreign acquaint-

[1] The manuscript of this letter is in the Houghton Library, Harvard University, and is reprinted by their kind permission.
[2] "I sent Lowell a bronze candlestick for a New Year's present and had in return a charming poem." Fanny Longfellow to Thomas G. Appleton, January 9, 1857. See Appendix to the present volume.

ance. They both dreamed of the doll that night, and the next day, the French class coming, they had a welcome opportunity to display her perfections to their little friends. I enjoy with them her charms, for it it is always a pleasure to see anything so complete and finished. The next day my box arrived, and the two beautiful dresses emerged fresh and fair as if just from the maker's hands. I have no doubt the evening one will be quite resplendent when fully unfolded, and the purple will make a very rich day costume. I am very glad it is both larger and longer than my old measure, and fits admirably. The hoop too I was glad to see, being so much more pliable and moderate than those we have here. It is a magnificent present, my dear Tom, and you were very very kind to be so generous in adorning me.[3] . . .

February 23, 1857

Washington's birthday is every year more honored, as we further depart from the nobleness of his character, and today is a universal holy day, and in the evening Mr. Everett rolls forth his sonorous sentences again at the Music Hall, the proceeds to help buy Mount Vernon from the shameless family. Mrs. Kemble resigns her reading for the occasion.

She is as wonderful as ever, and the enthusiasm and eagerness as great as on her former visit. It is as fresh a pleasure to me as ever and the genius it implies as amazing. We had a very successful supper for her the other evening and never was a merrier round table. Our guests were the Motleys, the Agassiz', the Sam Wards, Lowell and Emmeline and Sam. I only wished you had been with us to fire another revolver of wit against Motley and Lowell. They were all in the greatest spirits and kept it up till nearly morning. Mrs. Kemble was in one of her gayest moods and seemed to enjoy it highly. . . .

April 18, 1857

. . . Julia Howe's play [4] has been abused by all the papers here and in New York except in one or two cases, but she is serenely in-

[3] Some of the beautiful dresses which Tom Appleton sent his sister from abroad are still kept in the Longfellow House, and a photograph of Mrs. Longfellow wearing one of them is reproduced in this volume.

[4] *Leonora, or The World's Own* was acted by E. A. Sothern and Matilda Heron, first at Wallack's Theater, New York, then in Boston.

different and thinks it was a success. The sudden virtue of the *Herald* about it is amusing, but it is strange so clever a woman should have chosen so hackneyed a story and so wretched a heroine, and should not see there is tragedy enough in life to inspire a drama without descending to vice. It is cleverly written, and the close has a good deal of vigor, but it should never have been published. The poor Doctor must feel it painfully as a thing he cannot give his daughters to read. One hoped better from an American woman of genius, and I trust she will do something better that this may be forgotten. . . .

To Mary Appleton Mackintosh

April 21, 1857

. . . I see in Burritt's little paper a very encouraging account of the progress of the emancipated blacks in the West Indies from a speech delivered by a Mr. Thompson, at Manchester, quoting Mr. Davy. Count Gurowski[5] . . . has written a book about us à la Tocqueville, very shrewd and profound, with a capital chapter on slavery, showing the fallacy of all the usual arguments in its favor. That one eye of his is more penetrating than many ordinary pairs, and as he is an impartial observer his testimony is less prejudiced than those of most strangers. He does justice to what is good in us, and is justly severe on all our shortcomings private and public. Such fair criticism one reads with pleasure. . . .

September 29, 1857

In the bustle of getting settled at home, putting down carpets, getting the children ready for autumn weather, etc., I let slip the Boston steamer, which I usually write by, so I fear you will think there has been a long vacuum. Your last letter too claimed something cheering and comforting. It grieves me greatly you should have so

[5] A picturesque and eccentric European refugee who rather forced himself into Longfellow's friendship and showed no hesitation about advising Americans how to manage their affairs. See Le Roy Henry Fischer, "Adam Gurowski and the American Civil War: A Radical's Record," in *Quarterly Bulletin of the Polish Institute of Arts and Sciences in America*, April, 1943.

many troublesome symptoms, and I sometimes think you might be quieter and better here, but then the worry and anxiety which would beset you away from Robert and the children make me shrink from urging it. You have care and sorrow enough in your illness without borrowing any from the future, and I wish you would try to live from day to day and not anticipate life so much. The happiest and the strongest of us might easily rob ourselves of both strength and happiness if we thought, for more than a moment, of the possible loss of both. I say this in tenderest love, and I know, darling, that this is a very part of your disease, and cannot be helped, but I wish you could be surrounded by people who would cheer and amuse, without fatiguing you, and brighten every possible outlook. . . .

Alice has just had her seventh birthday, and is the best and brightest of little girls, a great pet of her papa's. Edie, though lovely as an angel, is rather obstinate and wilful, but so caressing and sweet all are drawn to her, and Annie is the sweetest little thing you ever saw. I carry her round the library and ask her the names of the busts. She says, Homer, Sophocles, etc. with amusing correctness, and is very eager to learn. Charley and Erny have commenced school with Tom Bradford, who has many boys they know, and they like it much, and don't mind the trouble of going into town in the horse-cars every day and a long walk after they get there. He is so amiable and such a perfect gentleman I hope much from his influence. Charley has now taken to football with all the fury he put into sailing, and comes home stiff and bruised, battling with even students at the game. He is studying "training" to get himself into a strong condition and insists upon all the food recommended! Erny is of quieter taste and is the devoted ally and companion of Alice. . . .

I have seen Mrs. James Russell Lowell [6] for the first time and thought her very sweet looking. All praise her to the skies. Mabel seems very happy with her new mamma. . . .

November 2, 1857

I am very glad you were able to get to Manchester in time to enjoy the treasures of Art there heaped up like the jewels in Alad-

[6] Frances Dunlap, the second Mrs. Lowell. As the next letter shows, Fanny seems soon to have altered her first favorable impression of her.

din's garden. How I envy you seeing these! Nothing I miss so much in this new world as the best pictures. Music now comes to us, but those cannot, though we are to be favored with specimens of modern English and French art regularly, but I love the "grand old masters" and care not for Ruskin's sneers at them. His school of Pre-Raphaelites miss all the poetry of the art in their foolish mania for detail, and they cannot get the saintly grace of expression when art was a religion and an act of devotion. Charley Norton has written an account of the Exhibition in our new Magazine which is a little à la Ruskin, not in style, but in theory. He thinks "the three Maries" show coarse, vulgar grief, with no elevation in it, but its genuineness I suppose touches the multitude.[7] It must have been pleasant meeting so many friends there. I hope you saw Florence Nightingale, who, I see by the paper, was there the last days. Henry has, in our new Magazine, a poem, written some time since, on her as Santa Philomena (Nightingale), which I hope you will like. There really was such a saint. . . .

We had a very pleasant little dinner, the other day, for Mrs. Kemble and Sally, Em and Lou, Mr. and Mrs. Ritchie (Cornelia Wadsworth), young Sturgis of London (Russell's son), Tom, and Lowell and his bride. The latter we were all disappointed in, as neither pretty nor attractive, and regret all the more he did not marry Jane Norton. . . .

December 1, 1857

. . . This sad financial trouble [8] seems to have shaken even the stout pillars of English capital and it at least teaches the lesson emphatically that the well being of one nation affects all the rest, a fraternal idea which should never be forgotten. Your Indian successes [9] must be some consolation, though the loss of life must have

[7] Charles Eliot Norton's long article on "The Manchester Exhibition" was in the very first number of *The Atlantic Monthly*, I (1857), 33–46. He took Annibale Coracci's picture of "the three Maries weeping over the body of the Savior"—"the most popular picture in the whole gallery of ancient masters"—as expressing all the worst qualities of the Bolognese school.

[8] The panic of 1857.

[9] After the terrible mutiny of 1857, when the government took over the administration of Indian affairs, hitherto entrusted to the East India Company.

caused much sorrow, and we hope the retaliation will be that of a Christian people and not barbarous like the heathen enemy. But it is hard to make war anything but heathen—the great Christian injunction "Love your enemies" can never be written on any of its banners.

We have greatly enjoyed welcoming Sumner back again, looking better though thinner.[10] He has dined twice with us and comes again today, for alas he must go tomorrow to Washington to commence the cares and labors of the long session. . . .

He gives us most interesting accounts of his travels and his glimpses of society which are certainly beyond any granted to any American before. The best in England have greeted him with such warmth and kindness that it makes us glad he is so worthy of the honors heaped upon him. The high civilization there especially charmed him—the thorough culture I mean rather than material luxury. . . .

Did I write you of a singular coincidence he mentioned at Stirling's [11] house . . . which he says is crammed with rare treasures of art as his fields with rare cattle (he has a bull named Hiawatha and a cow Minnehaha).

He met there the still fair Mrs. Norton, and she, speaking enthusiastically of *Evangeline,* said the two lovers passing each other on the Atchafalaya she considered so typical of life she had that word engraved on a seal, and afterwards having Leopold, king of Belgium,[12] for a guest, he speaking of *Evangeline* in the same way, said he thought that word, in its connection, so suggestive of life experiences he intended to have it on a seal, whereupon she, amazed,

---

[10] Charles Sumner had spent some time abroad while recuperating from the brutal and barbaric attack made upon him (May 22, 1856) in the Senate chamber by Representative Preston S. Brooks, of South Carolina, after Sumner's speech on "The Crime Against Kansas." Massachusetts sent Sumner back to the Senate in 1857.

[11] Sir William Stirling-Maxwell (1818–1878), Scottish author. "The still fair Mrs. Norton" was Caroline Elizabeth Stuart Norton (1808–1877), novelist and granddaughter of Richard Brinsley Sheridan. Her first marriage to the Hon. George Chapple Norton was unfortunate, and Meredith's *Diana of the Crossways* was suggested by her. She married Sir William in 1877 but died the same year.

[12] Leopold I reigned 1831–1865.

showed him hers! Singular, was it not? He brings many sugar plums to Henry, and tells him how warmly he would be welcomed at Dunrobin and Inverary. The Duchess [of Sutherland], in driving him about, with four horses and outriders, put the book in the carriage for him to read aloud to her. I tell you all this because it may amuse you, and I love to think Henry is so well appreciated among strangers. How much more would they think of him if they knew him personally, for the best of him is not in his books as it is with many poets. The overflowing goodness of his heart, his tenderness towards every human creature, in fact to everything having life, is but faintly hinted at in them.

December 28, 1857

. . . As I grow older I think I enjoy more and more my *shell*, like one of Mr. Agassiz' venerable turtles, whose physiognomies are so accurately painted in his wonderful great book, and I find it very hard to emerge from it for the attractions of other people's. We very rarely . . . go out of an evening, we so dearly delight in our own fireside, and the boys utter such a lament if we do that I have not the heart to cut them off from their nightly readings. Perhaps when my three girls are young ladies we shall be again tempted into society. . . .

Christmas eve Erny displayed a tree for some of Alice's little friends, which he got himself from the woods, cutting it down and shouldering it home, like a young giant, and all the gifts and decorations were purchased and arranged by himself, none of us older ones being much in the secret. It was very pretty and the slight gifts highly enjoyed by the juveniles. Many of these he made himself, such as baskets and paper dolls, the rage now among little girls.

Christmas night we all went to papa's and had a very merry time, although there were not many children, Harriot's young cousins having grown up into young ladies. Naty dressed up as Santa Claus, with a mask and long white beard, and a pannier of presents on his back, and was a great fun to the youngsters, though little Edie was half frightened by the motionless face. However, as he brought her a large doll as big as herself, she soon made friends with him. . . .

June 22 [1858]

. . . We had a very interesting meeting here on the 17th (Battle of Bunker Hill) of the Historical Society, and they were so pleased to come to this house on that day, that they came in unusual force, and had a great deal to say. Mr. Winthrop, Mr. Everett, Mr. Adams, etc. spoke of the associations of that time, and the former quoted Henry's lines in the poem on Charley, and they all seemed so full charged with reminiscences and facts that they could be hardly got to break up for supper. I wondered, too, they could resist the invitations of the birds to come into the garden, but they were listening to other more spiritual voices even. They refreshed themselves copiously with ice and strawberries and coffee and tea, and went off declaring, in all their annals, they had never had so interesting a meeting. . . .

On Saturday we had a boat race in Boston on Charles River, in which we took great interest. The Harvard Students rowed against seven other boats of stalwart Irishmen and others, and beat them triumphantly. Beacon Street had contributed the cup, and of course was highly elated at the result. The ladies crowned the students with flowers, and we all cheered like mad. We had an excellent place to see at Hetty Coolidge's, and Alice was as excited as her papa. Charley was out in his boat . . . and enjoyed it highly of course. He takes to the water like a duck, but I hope he will exhaust his passion for it before he grows up. . . .

How sad is all this gossip about Dickens.[13] I cannot believe the most of it, but it is a pity, since people will invent reasons, he cannot give the plain story of the trouble. I am very glad Robert has been so kind to Motley, for I know he will truly appreciate it, and he is such an excellent fellow he deserves to be known. . . .

[13] Charles Dickens and his wife had just separated, after many years of marital unhappiness. The "gossip" referred to involved his wife's sister, Georgina Hogarth, and Ellen Ternan, a young actress with whom Dickens had appeared in amateur theatricals. Nobody today seriously suspects Miss Hogarth, and, though a number of critics and biographers have assumed that Ellen Ternan became Dickens's mistress, the case has not been proved. For a careful examination of the evidence, see two articles by the present writer: "Dickens and the Scandalmongers," *College English,* XI (1950), 373–82, and "Ellen Ternan," *Dickensian,* L (1953), 28–34.

Nahant, August 10, 1858

I suppose you have rejoiced with us in the Great News of the Atlantic cable, if it only proves a reality! There has not been time yet to get the ends safely on shore, so as to bring the Queen's message to the President, and until that comes I shall hardly believe in it. We were at the Hotel the day the news came, and Henry had gone to leave our cards at the office for some one when he saw the clerk writing off a telegraphic message from Boston. It was this, so he was the first to get it here, and meeting Lord Napier [14] in the corridor we had quite a chat about it, he disbelieving it as we did at first. He said he had a duplicate of the Queen's message locked up in his desk, and that it had no sentiment nor poetry in it but was plain and diplomatic. The papers here have invented various phrases that ought to be the first sent, generally "Peace on earth, good will to men." But that is rather a mockery, where people systematically keep up armies to prevent it. . . .

Cambridge, November 29, 1858

. . . Henry has just received a charming photograph of a drawing of the bridal procession of Priscilla and John Alden. The artist who did it, Mr. [John W.] Ehninger, is to make a series for Christmas,[15] which will be very pretty, I am sure. . . . The book has had a great success, and the largest sale a book of poetry ever had, I believe. Henry needs all of it, he is so sensitive to any fault-finding, but I believe a poet never has his work criticized as he would like, that is with just praise and censure, and his idea in it understood, and the good things brought out, instead of the usual flippant, careless eulogy which is no compliment. . . .

December 12, 1858

Since I wrote you last poor little Alice has had a slow fever, but she is now getting over it though looking weak and pale. I feared, at first, it might prove a lung fever, she had so much pain in her chest, but fortunately it was not so severe.

[14] The British ambassador.
[15] Published by Rudd and Carleton, with an 1859 dateline.

As I had only just recovered from my influenza, which made me more ill than I have been for years, and from nursing Henry through his, who had it very severely, and does not feel right yet, I felt the fatigue a good deal, of watching with her for several nights. The little girls too have had bad coughs, but I hope we are now all nearly over our hospital condition. . . .

The following is one of Fanny's most important letters for the expression of her religious and theological views. It also shows the independence of her character and her thinking. Much as she revered her husband's younger brother, she would not permit him to lead her to accept a theological position she considered unsound.

The "Mr. Beecher" referred to is, of course, the famous Brooklyn clergyman, Henry Ward Beecher (1813–1887), brother of Harriet Beecher Stowe. What particular "frank confession" of Beecher's Mrs. Longfellow had in mind I do not know, but Beecher's position is clear. He professed himself unable to pray to God except through Christ.

"The parting with my old church in Federal Street" occurred when the congregation moved to its present home on Arlington Street, corner of Boylston, facing the Boston Common.

To Samuel Longfellow

March 29, 1859

. . . Your sermon I have read carefully, and think you have expressed yourself with your usual clearness and thoroughness and unflinching sincerity, but I wish I could feel that your view does not tend to an extreme as much as Mr. Beecher's frank confession. I think in vindicating the Father nobly and justly you do not give the Son quite his high place as *Son*, that is *next* in holiness and love and every divine attribute, for although we may be considered capable of becoming his brothers in some happier sphere, and in the end attain even his purity and power, certainly we are not here his equals; he is at least an elder brother, taught heavenly things as we have never yet learned them *except through him*, and now I come to what

I consider the fundamental mistake of our claim to be naturally one with him here.

We forget we have been steeped in the wonderful truths he was sent to give us, and think, because we have them, we can claim kindred with the almost divine, at least superhuman, messenger. The one difference of *sinlessness,* which the best here never dared to claim, shows that he is as much above us as God is probably above him, as he himself declares. Where have we got our Christianity but from him? Should we have invented it unaided? Did any other carpenter's son come near conceiving of a heavenly *Father,* beyond even the dream of a Plato? It is hard to put these things into words, without overstating them one way or the other.

I conceive him, shortly, not God, not man, but the link between the two, what the ancients would call a demi-God, and intended to bridge that difference by elevating us to a diviner life, and possibly hereafter to his full stature. For this he has not necessarily anything to do with the personality of God, which is a Pantheistic idea I disrelish, but is simply his Son, as we are his children, though in a lesser degree, at second remove as it were, like grandchildren, if any material scale can be applied to spiritual resemblance. There is something in your way of speaking of him which an instinct within me, for I do not know that I agree with any precise theology, revolts at, as when one we love is undervalued.

I agree with you that the Calvinist view of the Father is very low, and that the worship of the Son is as untrue as that of the Virgin by the Catholic, but why can we not give them their rightful reverence and throne? If, as you show, we can embrace the Father in our sympathy why need we fear that the Son will be too distant if we do not view him simply as a Jewish man?

The parting with my old church in Federal Street was a sad funeral to me. I was much overcome, as the past swept over me in a tide, and I thought of my mother as I remembered her, sitting upon the very spot in the pew I occupied, with the gentle refinement of her features, her rose-shell complexion, and eyes full of holiest thoughts, her admiration of Dr. Channing, though herself an unyielding Calvinist, and her willingness to listen to his ministry many years; then of him I had a vision as he sat at the side of the pulpit, with his earnest, penetrating eyes, and hair swept forehead, and the inspired fervor of his discourse, making the soul seem so out of proportion to the frail body—then his tender, touching eloquence to us children at the pulpit-foot, when we listened to him as to an angel—all this broke me completely down.

Poor Mr. Gannett faltered too in his farewell review of the past, and sobs broke his utterance. It is hard to have such sacred spots destroyed. I believe the pulpit is to be spared, but I have by me a cross, made out of a portion, which was sold at a fair, held last week for sick and incurable women (a charity proving we have an Irish Florence Nightingale among us), where they were in immense demand.

From here on we shall find Mrs. Longfellow increasingly concerned about slavery and disunion, and as the Civil War approaches somewhat forgetful of the peace principles she had professed. Wendell Phillips' "electrical speech . . . in your region" was delivered at Beecher's Plymouth Church, in Brooklyn, on November 1, 1859.[16] (Samuel Longfellow held, at this time, a Brooklyn pastorate.)

To Samuel Longfellow

November 7, 1859

. . . What an electrical speech Phillips has given in your region! Rather too revolutionary for my taste, I must say, though very eloquent. I like Beecher's sermon better, in the Christian spirit it has, although one can't help liking old Brown, so brave and outspoken, and his tragic history gives him the picturesqueness and pathos of an

[16] For the positions taken up by Phillips and Beecher, see Ralph Korngold, *Two Friends of Man: The Story of William Lloyd Garrison and Wendell Phillips* . . . (Little, Brown, 1950), pp. 253–55, and Paxton Hibben, *Henry Ward Beecher: An American Portrait* (Doran, 1927), pp. 175–76. Franklin B. Sanborn (1831–1917) was active in antislavery work and many other liberal causes. There was much sympathy for John Brown in Concord, where Emerson declared that when he was hanged he would make the gallows as holy as the cross, but Hawthorne was of the opinion that no man ever deserved hanging more.

Ugolino. This attempt to implicate distinguished men in his crazy attack must be without support, but I heard Sanborn had taken flight from his school on account of being compromised, I know not with what truth.

It well shows what it is to have "powder on board," and what an uncomfortable thing is this "blessed institution." . . .

To Emmeline Austin Wadsworth

November 28, 1859

. . . Sumner goes to Washington tomorrow, where I fear he will have a winter of great excitement, for the insane attack upon Harper's Ferry, by a brave old monomaniac Brown, who has enlisted everybody's sympathy by the staunch, Puritan, and Covenanter spirit he has shown, fully believing he has done God service by even this attempt to help the slaves, "this despised poor" as he calls them, will, of course, bring out much hostility between North and South.

Virginia has been in the most absurd panic, ever since the attempt, in which seventeen men held the arsenal for a day, and they had to get Federal troops to dislodge them, killing twelve and severely wounding Brown and the rest. Brown does not explain his plan, but either thought the slaves would be able quietly to run away, backed by him (for he seems too humane to desire an insurrection), or expected a larger force.

The Virginians have tried to implicate several distinguished names, having found them among Brown's papers, but they were merely letters written in sympathy with Brown when suffering in Kansas the loss of sons and property, and his present attempt is a mystery to his old friends. It has shown the truth of what strong stuff a Yankee farmer is made, and the whole country what cowardice and fears overhang a slave state—a good warning against increasing the number. A cow passing a sentinel, and not answering his challenge, frightens him into the idea of a great, invisible force, and the Governor posts down with a small army, and so they go on, laughed at by all the country. Friday is the day for the poor man's execution, and they dread a rescue. Phillips, Emerson, and others call Brown a saint, and he will be considered a martyr by many. . . .

February 20, 1860

. . . The fire-side is so attractive in our cozy study that I rarely like to leave it, to see what is going on, though I braved a snowstorm on Saturday to hear Fanny Kemble's *Richard III*, which is a most marvelous performance, her black eyes and hair really making visible to you the wicked, wily king, and the horrid seduction of her voice, in wooing Lady Anne, really making possible that incredible scene. Then the sweet boy-voices of the little Princes, one grave and one arch and merry, the tremulous aged ones of the old Duchess of York, Queen Margaret's fierce passion, and the mother's grief are all so truly given, but the most thrilling are those of the ghosts, in one breath banning and blessing, and changing from an unearthly scream to the most flutelike music.

She never read better, and all grieve it must be the last. The final evening we, with other friends, intend to decorate the platform with flowers. . . .

I met Mrs. Thayer, the other day, before Palmer's "White Captive," a beautiful statue but uncomfortably nude and too short and plump, but with a very fine head, taken from a Pittsfield damsel's.[17] He told Henry the body was also taken from life, a sempstress of the family, for interest in his art and not for pay, con[descen]ding to him for it! Can you imagine a Yankee girl brought to that! . . .

March 6, 1860

. . . I alternate with faith in Louis Napoleon and utter distrust, but am so glad he continues to give Italy a crumb of hope to live on that I can pardon many shortcomings, and if he could only turn Protestant! should believe all things, for Papal misgovernment is too stupendous an imposition to longer endure the light of the sun.

[17] This celebrated statue, now in the Metropolitan Museum, New York, is generally considered the masterpiece of Erastus Dow Palmer (1817–1904). As Mrs. Longfellow's comment shows, nineteenth-century people were, strangely, inclined to be shocked by it.

You have a great pleasure before you in the reading of Hawthorne's new Romance, hardly yet published, but we were favored with an advance copy. It is a most rich and fascinating book, his wonderful, idealizing fancy breathing new life into such a venerable corpse as Rome, and putting all its so familiar sights and sounds into a really new poetical aspect. It is just the country for him to describe, for he always sees everything in that magical twilight atmosphere, where fact merges into fable, which the prosiest person must find in Italy. Ah, he makes me so horribly homesick for its high delights! His story has the same painful tone, deeper even than a minor key, which all his books have, as if written by a fallen angel, but which gives great power and true human pathos, if sometimes morbid, to his creations. But, as you have not yet read it, it is useless to describe it further. It is called *The Marble Faun,* and the scene is laid in the present day. He greatly praises in it Story's "Cleopatra," which Sumner also thought a very remarkable statue. I have seen, lately, a photograph of Miss Hosmer's "Zenobia," and that must be very fine, the captive Queen treads, with such majesty, the Roman pavement, and wears her chains with such a haughty grace. . . .

May 15, 1860

. . . the English . . . think we are an oppressively gay people, which we are, perhaps, in a shallow, foolish way, but have not the regular, nourishing resources of true enjoyment. I feel this so much here. With so many men of high culture about us, yet, from lacking the genius for society in our country, we do not get the easy, delightful, daily pleasure from them we should in Europe. They are too busy, or too domestic, and hardly one of them but Agassiz is to be relied on for any social purposes. There is no promenade, no Corso where one can meet and exchange a few refreshing words, no gallery to lounge in but the dreary Atheneum, where I rarely meet a soul I know. And women are equally hard to attract unless specially invited. Henry pines under this life, being especially social by nature. George Sumner dines with us every Wednesday, and Scherb (who is a bore and self-invited) every Monday, and that is all the

relief he gets from incessant wife and children! Lowell never comes
now of an evening, and Felton as rarely. But enough of this Jeremiad, for last night, we were really intensely interested in the conversation of Dr. Hayes, the Arctic explorer and one of Dr. Kane's
companions. He is gentle and modest and pleasing, and talks so
well of all he had seen, of the wonders of icebergs with lakes of
crystal water in their tops and cascades flowing down their sides, of
the beautiful contrasts of a soft Italian sky and this grim nature,
of long avenues, of bergs of every shade of color, of the sudden blow
of an axe splitting one from top to bottom (a small one), and of a
crack in the ice running along a mile with the roar of greatly prolonged cannon. Then of the strange Esquimaux and their odd religious ideas, making their evil spirit a *woman* and the wife of the
good spirit! (I told him he could hardly be a *happy* spirit) and of
the awful, soundless silence of those regions nearly driving one mad,
etc. etc. etc. I could fancy how Desdemona devoured Othello's nar-
rations, for it is very fascinating, this getting adventures from the
hero of them instead of from a book. He is going off now to find that
strange unfrozen sea Morton discovered and says his health has been
far better for all his sufferings there, and for delicate lungs there is
no place like Greenland!

To Samuel Longfellow

May 7, 1860

. . . Henry has, this morning, a letter from abroad, enclosing a
German translation of "Excelsior." The gentleman who sends it
says, "The day it appeared in the *Boten für Tirol* the students of
Innsbruck meeting Thurold, the translator, in the street, rushed
towards him, embraced and kissed him with such joy and transport
that he looks upon that moment as the brightest and happiest of his
life."

That is pleasant, is it not? When would our students manifest such
enthusiasm to the poet himself? All the real nourishment of sympathy he has had nearly, has come over the sea, which is about as

comforting as having to purchase your drinking water instead of having it freshly flowing by your door. . . .

Letters from Mrs. Longfellow to her husband are very rare, for the two were seldom separated. It is all the more of an event, therefore, that the summer of 1860—the last full summer of Fanny's life— should have left us two letters written on the same day.

To HENRY WADSWORTH LONGFELLOW

Nahant, July 24, 1860

Best beloved,

I have just received your letter, which was welcomed with shouts of joy by all the house, that is by the most precious portion of it. Annie hugged it, and all eyes brightened over it. It seemed to bring you near us again.

After you had gone I wished I had given you many more kisses, and vainly sent them after the *Nelly* as she ploughed her way through the blue water.

I was thankful it cleared with such a lovely afternoon, sunny and warm, with a very soft, south wind. I thought you would find it hot inland.

Tom drove later than usual, and as I feared the night air for my cough, I took a walk instead to the Willow Beach, with Edie and Annie. They wanted to go as far as Bailie's Hill, but the sun was too powerful and supper waiting. So Edie would not return with me, but lingered behind with very valiant intentions of an independent promenade—soon put to flight by wandering cows. . . .

I am very glad there is such a splendid day for the Regatta, here quite autumnal, with a cool northwest wind, and probably not too warm with you.

Little Annie slept with me, and it was very sweet to have her, but her restlessness and my cough gave me very little sleep. . . .

Tell Charley if he is with you that Trap was very mournful yesterday, and whined and looked about very piteously, but was good and obedient to Erny, and slept in his room very quietly.

Today Charley Lovering begged to take Erny with him in the *Dolphin* for an excursion to Salem to see the Zouaves, so they have departed, leaving Trap to solitary meditations on the lower veranda, and will return, as they can, by rail or by sea. Tom goes over to dine at papa's, so I shall have a very quiet dinner with the three graces, or furies, whichever they prove themselves. . . .

Miss Susie Amory came over fair and bonnetless, under an umbrella, to ask, this morning, if you would be back by Saturday, so the dinner may be for that day. But do not hurry away from Berkshire— let the warm sun and air exorcise all the demons bronchial before you leave it. It is hard to think this sparkling splendor of sapphire is only the serpent's eye above his cruel fang, nor will I yet.

I hope Charley is with you. If so, give him my love and kiss. Remember me to all the Sedgwicks.

Ever and ever thine,

Fanny

July 24, 1860

Best beloved,

I think I can venture upon another letter, to thank you for your two last, which reached me this morning.

I am sorry you had such a noisy night at Worcester, and am thinking you are now, perhaps, arrived at Stockbridge, to escape more student enthusiasm.

A fine triumph for Harvard to carry off all the honors! The chimes must ring out, "See the conquering Hero comes" with all their din, and to the despair of all the old ladies in the neighborhood.

Erny has just written you doubtless of his yesterday's and today's exploits. Tom might as well be in Worcester as here for the benefit his society gives me. He dined with papa yesterday, and passed the night in town to see the Zouaves at the theater and has not yet appeared (6 o'clock P.M.) but will by the late boat. . . .

Poor James, yesterday, met with a sad accident, which will disable him for some days. The pump at the stable, in some way, tore dreadfully the top of his right thumb to below the joint.

The women were horrified at its appearance, so I ordered him at once to Dr. Mifflin, who sewed it up, and said last night it was doing well.

No drives therefore this week.

I did walk by the Willows with you last evening, and the waves were dashing with fine freshness—"with might with might"—but it looked very solitary and sad. Last night I had better rest, but my cough is like yours and voice nearly gone—Annie's is however nearly well, so I think we may be encouraged.

The Cadets deliciously playing . . . have just gone through the village to their chill camp, and papa has brought over a tall Western Appleton who regrets not seeing you. The little girls send many kisses. They are pretty good. I write on this paper to remind you of the sea. Get better, dearest, and be careful of Berkshire night-dews. I wished you had not been so timid of tender words—keep me in your thoughts as thou art ever in mine. I got your photograph today and showed it to Annie. She put it at my lips and then at her own. She has a rapport with me—my love child, or child of love.

Ever and forever

thy

Fanny

Here, again, is a very important letter, written on the day Abraham Lincoln was elected President of the United States. In addition to its references to American politics, the letter reflects Fanny's interest in European (specifically, Italian) affairs, and in the situation which, ten years later, made an end of the temporal powers of the Papacy. More than these matters of great import, however, many readers will enjoy its account of the current American tour of the Prince of Wales, later King Edward VII.

John Bell, of Tennessee, and Edward Everett, of Massachusetts, were Constitutional Unionist candidates for president and vice-president. William Appleton, with whose views Fanny did not sympathize, was running for Congress as a Whig. "Uncle" was a courtesy title; he was the son of Nathan Appleton's brother Joseph. He served as congressman in the special session from July 4 to August 6, 1861, then resigned.

TO SAMUEL LONGFELLOW

November 6, 1860

This is the eventful day of the Election, and I am sure your sympathies are with us, and you feel, as we do, the awful import of this day's decision—the blight or the blessing it will bring to the vast territories, and to all our future policy. It is painfully sublime, but we have very few fears for the result, although the capitalists in New York are making immense efforts, and even got up a business panic . . . to counteract Pennsylvania's noble vote in our favor. Traitors at the South as usual talk of secession, but others there besiege Lincoln for offices, and the country will probably resign itself to its own will with the quiet its free action gives, after even the unequalled emotion of the contest. It has been raining all the morning but now the sun comes out, a good omen! These torchlight processions the Republicans set going, and the Bell and Everetts imitated, have been illuming all the towns nightly, making the streets rivers of fire with the many colored lanterns, and very lively with rockets, transparencies, bands of music, and songs. The Republican ones especially, in which were more Americans, have been like the marching of armies for order, discipline, and great masses, to imitate the rail, roaring like fiery serpents through the streets, while their opponents ring many little *bells*, very like the clanking of chains in my ears. Beacon Street was brilliantly illuminated last night for my Uncle William and the show pretty but sad. We, of course, hope he will be defeated, and I think he is quite resigned to it himself. It is strange a man of such genuine piety, such tender heart should be so indifferent to the sorrows of slavery. One of those strange contradictions in human nature.

The Prince, as you have heard doubtless, was most warmly welcomed throughout the country, and an intense interest, in spite of the absorbing politics, was felt to see him and to make every thing pleasant to him. Nothing disagreeable happily occurred, though the breakdown of the ballroom floor at New York was rather humiliating after all their boasting and efforts to be very grand. Our ball went off very agreeably, though the Governor was thought slighted by his wife's being given as partner after the Mayoress, and through some confusion at supper, caused by the Prince rushing thither before he was expected. He charmed us all by his graceful, modest manners, his perfect self-possession on all occasions, having said or done nothing amiss in his whole tour, and by his intelligence and gentleness. He promises well for the future. We all felt deeply the historical significance of such a visit to a revolted province, and the touching scene of his visit to Washington's tomb, reverently uncovering as the dirge sounded from behind the trees.

My sister Hatty had the honor to be chosen by him as partner. The theater was too gaudily decorated, but it was a very handsome ball. The singing of the school children, in the Music Halls, Dr. Holmes's fine new version of "God Save the Queen" and other good music impressed his party especially. When the twelve hundred waved their kerchiefs at his entrance the effect was beautiful also. I was presented to the Duke of Newcastle and some others of the party, and they all spoke of Henry in the most ardent manner. The Prince wished to come here when he visited Cambridge (he also complimented H.) but had not time. The array of students to receive him at the great gates, through their ranks, was very fine. Felton received him in the Library, and showed him, at his request, a student's room (where he found a pretty damsel whom he admired) and the other buildings. But the breakfast in Gore Hall became a lunch by the delay, and offering the Prince tea he asked for wine, which was not there, neither ale, to his evident amazement, and which has made fun in the papers. Felton had to explain awkwardly the College did not give wine, but sent to his own house for some which was refused by his wife, thinking the servants wished it for themselves!!

The prettiest sight I had of H.R.H. was going statelily down Beacon Street in his red military coat on a black horse, with a brilliant staff, to review the troops on the Common. It was a perfect Indian summer day, and the trees were as golden as his saddle, and he lifted his hat and showed his bashful downcast face to the ladies on our balcony very charmingly. In Europe where you can see a Prince every day, this must sound extravagant to you, all this enthusiasm, but here it was not so, and has bridged over all ill-feeling forever, I trust. I never saw such eager nor such good-natured crowds as followed him everywhere.

How nobly Garibaldi goes on, like a great hero, as he is. If the Pope will only be content with his "potager," the Vatican garden, as L. N. told Lord Brougham he ought, then all will go as the world desires. I hope you are enjoying every moment. I know not when this will find you, but wherever it is may joy and peace be yours. Mr. Peabody I liked better last Sunday on the Communion with the text, "It is I, be not afraid," inviting all, especially those who thought themselves unworthy, and rejecting every obstacle to their approach. He said well, "Christ does not receive you at his table with censorious criticism like a worldly host, but with true love and welcome. . . ."

From here nearly to the end Mrs. Longfellow's letters are concerned almost entirely with the rapidly approaching war. "It seems like a dream to be living in such days"—so she expresses it in one of her letters to Emmeline Wadsworth, who was in Europe—"and must seem stranger to you who do not get the general crescendo of events and feeling as we do. . . ."

We who were not alive in those days missed that crescendo also, and it is most illuminating and enlightening to look upon the great crisis, through Fanny's eyes, in prospect as it were, and not, as we customarily do, in retrospect. How the proportions and emphases change with the shift of vantage point, and how much of the human capacity for self-deception—so painfully familiar to us in connection with our own wars—was similarly manifested by the men and women of 1861!

TO MARY APPLETON MACKINTOSH

December 16, 1860

. . . Our political horizon is not much clearer, though many think there are signs of coming peace, as many others of war. We hope the South will be cured of its madness by the sufferings it brings on itself, which will be more effectual than extorting concessions from the North to be perpetually renewed if successful. Wendell Phillips, of course, favors disunion, but the patriotic feeling at the North has bound us all more strongly together, which is a good thing, and the states are all ready to support the government. . . .

To Thomas G. Appleton

December 19, 1860

. . . The Convention has met at Charleston, but we do not yet hear of secession as a *fait accompli*. There seems rather, the last few days, less zeal for it everywhere, and the great fear is now of unworthy compromises being extorted from the North—far worse than losing those few troublesome states. I trust, however, the Republicans will stand firm, after such encouragement from the people to do so, and such a struggle and victory. The decided expression of non-sympathy with the South from England and France has somewhat sobered the mad traitors apparently. *Vanity Fair* has a capital caricature of Buchanan's vacillating policy, Dogberry's (B) charge to Seacoal [18] (Lincoln) in making him captain of the watch, "to arrest all 'vagrom men.'" "But if they will not stand?" "Then let them go, in God's name." . . .

Henry has bought the Nahant cottage, conjointly with you, for $5,000. This was as cheap as he could get it, as some one else wanted it. So that is secure and will always be of value. . . .

Henry has a poem in the January *Atlantic*—"Paul Revere's Ride." Poor Alice comes in frozen in her skates.

To Emmeline Austin Wadsworth

December 24, 1860

. . . I suppose you are anxious to know if we are all falling apart because South Carolina has been crazy enough to vote herself out of our company, but I imagine it will prove the North is the *pot de fer* in this instance, and we fear her fate will be piteous if she does not

[18] The comic constables in Shakespeare's *Much Ado About Nothing*.

speedily come back again, while we are not likely to miss her except, as the Senator of Ohio says, by the unwonted quiet we enjoy without her. She seems, however, in spite of always having had her own way, and now "owning the President," so that he [19] surrenders Fort Moultrie at her wish, thus violating his oath to preserve the Government property (for which it is generally hoped he will be impeached), to have nourished such a hate of us that it will be difficult for her ever to be friends again. We hope the North will stand firm and stand together, and these refractory states comes to their senses before long. They hope we are in great distress (through this whole trouble showing a most blood-thirsty spirit), but we are not, and are not likely to be with such resources behind us. Mrs. Field was telling me how firmly Fisher resolved to stay in the Union, and his wife hated it like a foreign enemy, and of course there will be this difficulty in other families. We pity their folly and madness, and it is wonderful the forebearance of the people with their constant murdering of unoffending northern travellers. . . .

To Thomas G. Appleton

December 25, 1860

A merry Christmas to you! We hope to have one at papa's with the children and the young ladies. Last night I got up a tree at home, and not being able to secure the right kind in time, we illuminated the old lemon tree and it was very pretty with its light foliage, sparkling tapers, and pendant gifts. Your boxes had the place of honor and were much admired, and we played the game of one of them the rest of the evening.

The opening of the great box was delightful, and we all enjoyed it much.

The packing was such a work of art that it seemed a pity to disturb it, and I called Rachel down to admire. As Henry sent the invoice in, it was as perfect as when it left the packer's hands.

I am charmed with all my things. The ball-dress is beautiful in color and decoration, and the bonnet is exquisite, ditto headdress.

[19] Buchanan.

The street dress too very elegant. Alice was charmed with Emmeline's dainty present, and it was really like being in Paris for half an hour, a glimpse into a world of refinement we are far from attaining, if we get more solid comforts.

The country is as unsettled as ever, though the other States seem to pause before joining South Carolina's mad career. Her arrogance and dictation they do not relish, and her wish to be the ruling power, though so small a state. She has nourished so intense a hatred for us, while we have only pity for her sin and folly, that she is hoping we are suffering great distress from her misconduct, but as yet there has been but very little trouble financially. The mills have cotton for six months and are going on as usual. . . .

January 7, 1861

. . . The departure of the Palmetto Kingdom made very little stir, but the spirited act of Major Anderson in leaving Fort Moultrie, which the President refused to strengthen, and saving his devoted band by removing to Fort Sumter, which is impregnable, sent a thrill through all the country, and he is the hero of the hour. Such an act of patriotism was so refreshing amidst the treachery of the Cabinet and the President. This has so roused the people that the latter tries now to be a little firmer and truer to his duty, but hardly Arnold has been thought of with such indignation. His Fast-day, intended for us to confess our sins for daring to elect Lincoln, gave occasion to the clergymen to "speak out in meetin'" and they did it here patriotically but bravely. . . .

I think it a pity they cannot be allowed to go, but if it is allowed as possible in our Constitution all the States are held but by a rope of sand, and we cannot give up to them all the forts and the mouth of the Mississippi. They have helped themselves in South Carolina to the Arsenal, etc. (thought treason when John Brown did it) and seem surprised we are so indignant. It is to be hoped bloodshed may be saved, but it looks very squally. Field thinks a little will do us good! on the Tennysonian principle. The papers are as exciting as possible, but the people keep calm and patient waiting the result. . . .

To Mary Appleton Mackintosh

February 4, 1861

. . . Everything is as unsettled as ever. The southern states go on seceding and helping themselves to all the forts and navy yards they can, and the government, for fear of bloodshed, does little or nothing to stop them. The Border states we hoped to save (though if there must be separation it would be better perhaps to have all the slavery ones together) but, though some are very unwilling to desert the Union, they will probably go. Lincoln's election is but an excuse for all this treason—it is a plot of many years growth, and has its root in the intense greed of the South for undivided power—"to rule or ruin" is their motto. But so to push it on without money or credit, and with so few white men that one of our smallest states is equal to all theirs, is an insanity without parallel. It would seem as if they had not one sensible man among them, but the truth is they are over-powered by the threats of the mob, led on by their worst politicians, and many of the better feeling, attached to the Union, groan over their disunion.

I am sorry the London *Times* speaks of them as the true United States if successful, for they are so inferior to us in numbers, in everything that makes civilization that it would be as wise to call Ireland Great Britain if standing alone. All the compromises offered thus far are atrocious, and the North cannot accept them. That of Mr. Crittenden [20] the Border States are trying to make us swallow, is to put slavery as a perpetual fact in the Constitution, and fasten it forever in all territories, disfranchise our black citizens and other such mild demands. You know the Constitution has not a word about slavery in it, only a vague phrase by which fugitives are claimed, so imagine what an outrage it would be, in this age, to make it protect it forever.

Sumner is among the firmest of the Republicans, and we regret that Mr. [Charles Francis] Adams offers such a compromise as would make New Mexico, with the worst of slave codes, a slave state at once. He thinks slavery can never flourish there, but it is not

[20] Senator John Jordan Crittenden of Kentucky.

for us to make terms with rebels. We must keep firm and quiet, and let them weary of their bad bargain. Kansas is in happily, which is some comfort.

General Scott is very anxious about the safety of Washington, and if Virginia secedes before the fourth of March, there is great danger, but he has now troops there and all our states offer him more at a moment's notice. I fear Lincoln may be attacked at some unguarded moment, though he will be well watched, but, even if killed, Hamlin must be President, whom the South has declared, before its Negroes, to be a mulatto, because he has a dark complexion!

The poor Negroes, from their masters' talk, think Lincoln is to free them, and will be sadly disappointed, but the South boasts will fight for them if necessary. I do not think we shall have a war—all parties shrink from that or the revolution would not have reached such a head, but if Fort Sumter is attacked, as they now threaten, there may be some bloodshed, for Anderson has will and power to defend himself. . . .

To EMMELINE AUSTIN WADSWORTH

February 12, 1861

. . . My father is very feeble this winter, and I cannot but feel that his useful and beloved life will not "be stretched out on the rack of this rough world" much longer. . . . He is naturally depressed by the state of the country, which, as yet, shows but little blue sky, but we hope that after the fourth of March a firmer hand will guide us to calmer waters.

If the rebellion at the South had been checked, at the outset, by sufficient federal force off Charleston, I believe it would not have spread so far. Is it not inconceivable that these traitors, who have always had their own way, and have wrung from the reluctant North so much, should now sacrilegiously try to destroy the government because it cannot be ruled by them for the next four years? But it is, evidently, a long-laid plan, which accounts for the incredible loss of loyalty on their part, in so apparently short a time. Conceive the

horror which thrilled us when we heard they had fired on the national flag, and trampled on it with joy—the flag which has protected
them in all their barbarian exactions from the civilized North, and
shielded them from the execrations of the world. It is this dreadful
doctrine of state sovereignty, carried too far, which, if allowed, will
soon leave us no longer a nation. The Border States seem reluctant
to leave the Union, but still maintain this demoralizing doctrine,
which makes it difficult for the loyal States to come to any understanding with them. But for this loosening idea I cannot but wish
all the slaves states might leave us to form a nation worthy of respect
and fame, with this troublesome and painful question forever set at
rest, but they would be very quarrelsome neighbors. Would we had
the man for the hour, who could firmly set us right, and keep us so.
I have great hopes in Lincoln; he has shown such dignified reticence
through all this excitement, and is thought very fearless and firm in
not compromising with traitors. The Republicans have kept true to
their principles for the most part, but some Boston people have
been willing to grant any atrocity the South might demand to keep
peace for the present.

Think of Southern mobs singing the "Marseillaise" within hearing
of their slaves and then murdering any Northern traveler for fear he
should arouse them! But their folly and their recklessness have been
beyond bounds, and the better among them know it and dare not
speak. How it will all end God alone can know, but it looks like a
great crisis He is bringing about for his own purposes, and as it must
come some day, it is better to have it over before our children are
men.

February 17. . . . My children have been well all winter, always
excepting colds, and I have great pleasure in teaching my little
girls. They are so good and ready to learn. Annie is a droll little
thing, and has just been having church for her dolls, and preaching
at a great rate about the Lamb and the seven candles (which I hope
is not thought irreverent from her innocent mouth), and the angels
singing and dancing. She and Edie live over every phase of married
life with their dolls, and get as excited as if it were all real, I only
fear sometimes too much so for their little brains. Alice is a very
good child too, and so wise she is quite a companion for me. The

boys study at home, and I read them Shakespeare and Scott to illustrate their history lessons—*Kenilworth* we all found most freshly interesting. . . .

Motley's History [21] is at last out, having been kept back by the Harpers on account of the evil times, and will read, from extracts I have seen, most picturesquely and richly, no doubt. His loyal love of liberty gives a peculiar soul-intensity to his subject lacking in many historians. . . . Such a charming sketch I saw the other day at [Hamilton] Wild's (the painter's) of the [William Wetmore] Storys and Brownings and old Savage Landor reading and serving al fresco at Siena, with the little Browning boy with his long curls driving, in the background, the two little Story boys as his ponies. Think of a summer palace at Siena for one *hundred* dollars a year! They retreat there from the heat of Rome. . . .

To Thomas G. Appleton

February 19, 1861

. . . The President-elect is on his way, making speeches in a hearty Western manner, taking all the enthusiasm as proofs of devotion to the Union, not to him, and carrying the hearts of the people with him. I think he will prove just the man for the hour. . . .

February 25, 1861

. . . Mr. Lincoln has reached Washington safely, and we hope soon to feel his firm hand on the helm. It will be a relief if the inauguration gets over without any accident, which we trust it will, thanks to General Scott's wise foresight in having a strong force at the Capitol. A New Jersey member has been brutally attacked, on the steps of the Capitol, for praising the North in a speech, and there are no doubt wretches there who would glory in an assassination. . . .

March 7, 1861

. . . The fourth was a most interesting day to us, so full of anxious fear lest anything should happen to mar the Inauguration and also

[21] *The History of the United Netherlands.*

of intense desire to know what the new President would say. His Inaugural is strong and sensible, and very conciliatory—it could not be more so without giving up the government and perjuring himself, and yet the Southern states talk of it as a declaration of war—so they will anything that will not recognize their treason. All went off quietly, thanks to General Scott.

The foreign appointments are not known yet, but the Cabinet is a good one, with two from those states in it which may retain the Border States.

It has been an awful crisis, a well-planned plot—but apparently its back is now broken, though we can never recover our prestige among the nations. . . .

To Emmeline Austin Wadsworth

April 19, 1861

You will be pained to hear that war is upon us.

After every attempt at conciliation had failed, the South has taken his awful responsibility, and the spirit of rebellion is fast seizing the Border States, so long apparently loyal. Virginia has seceded, and I suppose the rest will follow, which will make the contest a very serious one. But the people North and West are roused to a state of patriotism which fuses all parties in the one resolve to protect the government, seriously threatened at Washington, and volunteers are pouring south like a spring tide, with all the enthusiasm of '76—men leaving their business and families at an hour's notice—and the poor women (who always have the hardest lot on these occasions), burying their sad thoughts in busy labors—in making shirts for the soldiers, and possibly later will have the sadder duty of preparing for the wounded.

The South had so alienated itself from us by its atrocious acts, by its vile ambition, and utter disregard of all the claims of the past, that this cruel necessity of war (for ours will be only in self-defence) is not as terrible as it would once have been, and I, for one, should feel more one with England. I have no sympathy with the thoughts, desires, civilization (if it can be called such) of the South, and they seem more alien to me than English people.

I have, fortunately, no private friendships to disturb this feeling, but still I abhor war wherever and whenever produced, and trust this will be a short one.

If the President had the right to cut them off from us peaceably forever, I should be rejoiced (for we can never make one nation), but as he has not and the people would not give it to him, he must do his duty. He has been almost too long patient and forbearing, and the fall of Sumter (where seventy starved men had to yield to seven thousand and most powerful batteries) has stirred all our hearts with horror and indignation. Boston has been full of the departing soldiers, and the Massachusetts regiments will be the first to arrive to the country's aid. It seems like a dream to be living in such days, and must seem stranger to you who do not get the gradual crescendo of events and feeling as we do. . . .

April 29, 1861

. . . Well may you sigh over such a state of things, but painful as it is, it is better than our past apathy, when we yielded principle and power to these corrupt men until they believed they could make us obey their behests like their own slaves. Now the North is roused with a glorious heart-beat for liberty, such as has never been in our time, and the South is amazed and chagrined at the unanimous feeling of loyalty. It hoped we were too divided in opinion to stand against them, and cannot comprehend the intense love of country, and not of state only all classes here display. I am proud to live at such a time, and sublime as was the spectacle this summer of such a prosperous people risking all for an idea of right, it is even more thrilling to see it aroused like one man, and making every self-sacrifice to sustain its flag from further outrage. It was worth some loss of life and property to behold the heroic virtues so alive after our long dream of self-indulgence.

It is not against the people of the South we wage war, but against these rebels and traitors who have silenced their loyalty and tried to overthrow ours. . . .

I hope we shall have a peaceful old age, dear, to talk over all this, though I do not despair yet of renewing my impressions with my children. . . .

Many ladies are offering themselves for nurses, and some are studying in the hospitals—all the rest of the sex are working in some way for the soldiers. . . .

Sewing machines are going like a factory in many houses, and Papanti gave the Boston girls the use of his hall for a week, winding up with a ball! I think if we can blockade the Southern ports soon enough the rebels will be brought to terms without bloodshed. We need much a young leader. . . . In New York they are getting ferocious and like not the defensive policy only. Baltimore has been in a fearful state, a reign of terror from the mob, the Union men silenced and fleeing for their lives. Those little, gay, chattering women must be as silent as birds in a storm. But our resolve to have free access to the Capitol has apparently roused them to better loyalty. . . .

I am trying to read Motley and find it most interesting, but with history acting before our eyes it is hard to read anything but newspapers. The nineteenth of April has a new association, one we shall be as proud of.

Pray for us that God will shield the right, if that needs praying for. . . .

CHAPTER VIII

Chariot of Fire

Though people are fond of saying that writers and other artists are too much given to exaggeration, no artist's imagination has ever been able to come within hailing distance of the monstrous exaggeration which is life itself. Fate rarely prepares us for her tragic climaxes as the tragic poet is required to do. That a woman of such charm and goodness as Fanny Appleton Longfellow should have met such a terrible death is a circumstance which even the lapse of nearly a century has not sufficed to rob of its horror. But dreadful as the story is, it cannot be left out.

To Mary Appleton Mackintosh

July 5, 1861

. . . Yesterday was the *fourth*, and as usual a very hot, noisy day, but tranquil enough here. Robert [1] dined with us and did not go to town to see the crowd until the afternoon, when he beheld the balloons go up and the fireworks in the evening, coming out with us after. We took Alice in to see them, for the first time, and she enjoyed them much, as they were remarkably pretty. The immense, well-behaved crowd is a fine part of the show, but when the patriotic emblems appeared there was more enthusiasm than usual, of course. It seemed a pity to waste all that powder on mere display, but as it employs many workmen, I suppose the Governor did not like to give it up. The city economized to the extent of giving up the annual dinner, I believe. It is a day of as solemn import to us as the first we kept, and it was sad to think it had no longer any interest or enthusiasm over any portion of the country. England, though more friendly, does not yet seem to appreciate this struggle for national

[1] Robert Mackintosh, Mary's husband, who was visiting in Boston.

existence on our part, and the impossibility of our allowing a military despotism on our southern border, controlling all the Gulf and such an inland frontier, extending into Mexico, and, if necessary, invoking foreign protection, which we should have too much pride ever to do. If this war is now stopped, without success on our part, the South would form a navy, and, in a few years, there would be a worse one. It could not be escaped, and must be settled now forever. You and all Americans abroad should aid public opinion on the right side, the side of civilization against barbarism. General Patterson has crossed the Potomac and entered the north of Virginia, defeating several thousand rebels, with no loss on his side, and this advance of one wing of our army will be followed at once, probaby, by that near Washington and the Western force, possibly driving the rebels south without much of a battle.

July 7. We go to Nahant next Thursday—the weather is so hot and the children beginning to droop. It is only a little farther away, and I can get up by the boat, in a hour, to see dear papa. . . .

The President's Message is a quiet, sober document, rather too timid and too polite to the rebels, I think, but he wishes to convince them he has no angry feeling, only obeys his duty to the laws. We hope Congress will be short and sensible. . . .

The following is Fanny Longfellow's last letter in the collection at Longfellow House.

To Ernest W. Longfellow

July 7, 1861

Dear Erny,

I hope you are enjoying yourself to your heart's content, although you have not Charley Lovering all the time, but have to take your boat for a playfellow.

You are lucky in such hot weather, and we are all sighing for the good sea breeze instead of this stifling land one filled with dust. If I could have known the heat would last so long, I should have tried to get down a week sooner, but, from Charley's account, the house is none too ready for us. I hope you have been careful not to be out too long in the hot sun. I am making a stavelock for your cap, but, with a straw hat it would not do.

Alice wrote you a letter about her enjoyment of the fireworks, which you will find at the Post Office.

I hope Mrs. Lovering was not alarmed at the sight of your big box, but we thought it must pass for a trunk, as you would find it inconvenient to run to the house for everything, and I am sure you will do nothing to annoy her and make her regret keeping you so long. I shall send you a few socks as I think you must be in want.

Dear Grandpapa is very feeble, but much the same as when you left. We wish he could get down to Lynn, thinking the sea air might strengthen him a little, but as it is three weeks since he drove out we fear to attempt it.

Poor Annie is very droopy with the heat, and Edie has to get her hair in a net to free her neck from its weight.

Uncle Robert will probably come down with us, and get a room in the village.

I miss you much today, dear boy. It seems strange to have you away on Sunday, but I am glad you are getting the good of the change. At night your room seems very lonely.

I took Alice yesterday to see the whale, and it quite refreshed us to see it swashing about in its great tub. She went in for the dentist, who disappointed her, so she must try again.

The Gordon regiment goes tomorrow, and the young ladies are full of interest, and will come to Aunt Hatty's balcony to give God-speed to their heroes.

Remember me kindly to Mrs. Lovering. I am sorry she should be troubled with Master Trap, and hope he has behaved himself. Love to Charley L. The girls and papa send love and kisses.

Affectionately your mother

The fullest contemporary account of the circumstances of Mrs. Longfellow's death [1] *is in four letters in the Houghton Library,* [2] *from Harvard's President Felton to Longfellow's friend, Charles Summer.*

[1] *See,* further, Chapter XVII of my *Longfellow, A Full-Length Portrait.*
[2] Quoted by kind permission of the Harvard College Library.

CORNELIUS C. FELTON TO CHARLES SUMNER

Cambridge, July 10, 1861

An hour since, I saw the lifeless body of Fanny Longfellow! My God! that such a tragedy should have ended such happiness. Yesterday afternoon, she was sealing a small paper package, containing a lock of one of her children's hair. The light sleeve took fire: in an instant she was wrapped in a sheet of flame, flying from the library to the front room where Longfellow was sitting. He sprang up, threw a rug round her, but it was not large enough. She broke away, flew towards the entry; then turned and rushed towards him. He received her in his arms, and so protected her face, and part of her person: but she was dreadfully burned: her dress was entirely consumed. It was all light and gauzy: no woollen on any part of her person. She was carried to her room: physician sent for. She bore the agony like a martyr dying at the stake. The first efforts were to quiet the suffering by ether or other appliances. She sank into quiet: was conscious through the night: asked for coffee in the morning: became insensible: breathing till 10 minutes past 10: died. Her face was pale and calm and sweet, as ever in life. Poor Longfellow: he was dreadfully but not fatally burned. His hands and face suffered most severely. He has been under ether and laudanum ever since: wanders: thinks he is growing idiotic, begs not to be sent to an asylum: could not see Fanny when she was dying.

Was there ever such a woeful scene—such an awful and inexplicable overthrow. God help our dear friend in his unparalleled bereavement. God help us all in this weary world.

July 14, 1861

Yesterday was poor Fanny's funeral—the eighteenth anniversary of her wedding day. The day was the loveliest of this summer: the sky soft and blue, with a few silver clouds here and there moving on the warm breeze. We assembled at 12 o'clock in the library—the scene of so many pleasures, and of one awful tragedy. The coffin was placed on a table in the center of the room, covered with wreaths and bouquets of the sweetest flowers. The head, in its magnificent and tender beauty, was adorned with a wreath of orange-blossoms in allusion to the anniversary: a cross of white roses lay upon her breast: and flowers in profusion were placed beside her. All was still—hushed—in the presence of death—such a death, and such a victim! The sad and solemn scene filled all eyes with tears: and half suppressed sobs showed the emotion that even men could not wholly control. Dr. Peabody performed the service. Poor Longfellow was still in bed—too ill to attend. . . . After the service they still lingered, as if reluctant to take the last look: but after a time, the procession started for Mt. Auburn. Arrived there we surrounded the tomb and listened to a short and fervent prayer from Dr. Gannett. I cannot express to you the beauty of the hour and the place. The tomb is surrounded by tall trees, now in full leaf. The sunlight stole in through the overarching foliage, and fell in bright spots upon the green earth where still lay the open coffin, and we still looked upon the placid countenance, more lovely, at the very last moment, than ever. As I stood with indescribable feelings, scarcely able to turn away, I took a white rose from a cluster at her side, a leaf of which I enclose in this letter. The coffin was at length closed, and I slowly walked away, oppressed by a weight of sorrow that no words can tell: yet filled with a sense of the soothing power of nature, the harmony of the scene with the character of Fanny, and the surpassing sweetness of every memory connected with her beautiful and happy life.

I have not seen Longfellow. He has seen no one yet, out of his immediate family. I dread to think of him bereaved of Fanny: she was so perfect a companion of his daily existence, and sharer of his glory. But his children remain, and they must fill in part, her place. God help them all. The world henceforth will be strangely changed for him.

July 19, 1861

You are entirely right not to leave a post of public duty for any private sorrows. I do not, however, wonder at your feeling. You loved our dear friend now gone and she always spoke and thought of you as one singularly near and dear. Longfellow is in a calm state of mind. I sat by him Wednesday evening an hour or two and had a most interesting conversation. His sweet and lovely nature never showed itself so beautifully as in this great affliction. As the plant secluded from the open air, turns in the direction of the sunbeam that steals through a crevice, so his soul, which has affinity with the light, turns to the consolations that belong to even this tragedy. He recalls all the happiness of eighteen years, over which scarcely a cloud flitted. He speaks of Fanny—her life and death—with natural freedom—though with the deepest emotion. He dwells upon the thought that she has perhaps been spared a long and lingering decay: that sad as the bereavement is, she will be present to him always in the perfection of her beauty. . . . You will readily see how much I was relieved and consoled by this conversation. It will be long long before he will recover perfectly from his wounds. His hands are badly burned, and give him much pain: but he says he sleeps better when he suffers the most physical pain. I told him of your letter to me. He said he had also received one; and begged me to thank you for both. He is, of course, unable to answer at present; indeed he is unable to read the numerous letters that already pour in upon him from every quarter. Yours and Hillard's [?] and one or two others he has read. They soothe and tranquillize him.

I omitted the customary reception of Commencement evening: no less on account of the general feeling in society here than from the utter repugnance my family and myself have to anything of a festive nature in my house. Part of the evening I was with Longfellow: the rest we sat quietly looking out upon the exquisite beauty of the evening. The college premises were perfectly still: scarcely a sound broke the deep repose: so strange for Commencement night. . . .

July 21, 1861

. . . I passed the forenoon today with Longfellow, instead of going to church. He looks much better than he did two days ago. His face is still swollen, and he cannot yet shave: but the burns on his nose and his left cheek are already healed. He talks readily and with interest upon the topics of the day. I have read to him Mr. Everett's recent speeches: and he will soon be in a condition to listen to much more. But he dreads his recovery from the physical pain of his wounds: "then," he says, "then I shall have to take up the great burden, and I do not know how I shall bear it." Pain has really been a blessing to him: as the pain lessens his sense of bereavement increases. This is natural: but the consolations will come too, in good time: and many years of quiet happiness, in the society of his children and friends, and in literature, are still in store for him. . . .

But, even here, the last word must go not to mortal woe but to the immortal art which, like the soul of goodness in things evil, can be brought out of it.

THE CROSS OF SNOW

In the long, sleepless watches of the night,
    A gentle face—the face of one long dead—
    Looks at me from the wall, where round its head
The night-lamp casts a halo of pale light.
Here in this room she died; and soul more white
    Never through martyrdom of fire was led
    To its repose; nor can in books be read
The legend of a life more benedight.
There is a mountain in the distant West
    That, sun-defying, in its deep ravines
    Displays a cross of snow upon its side.
Such is the cross I wear upon my breast
    These eighteen years, through all the changing scenes
    And seasons, changeless since the day she died.

Henry Wadsworth Longfellow, 1879

On My New Year's Candlestick

by James Russell Lowell [1]

To make fit candle for the stand
Which Fannia gave, the bees shall seek
The choicest blooms of every land
On pearl-day's culled from June's best week.

From scarceblown lilies they shall glean
Ere dew hath fled, gold-dusted wax;
The shy forgetmenot halfseen,
Sunloving heartsease they shall tax.

Hands rosysoft as Edith's own
Shall then to form the treasure mould,
Her hair shall give the hue its tone
Of holy thistle's tenderest gold.

The wick of cotton shall be twined
That gathered snowiness in lands
Labored by sun & rain & wind,
With no forced help of slavish hands.

And, kindling it, I will not muse
Of Fannia's beauty, wit, & grace,
But of that light which still renews
With nobler womanhood her face;

The light from fireside fountains caught
Of duties graces through cultured years,
Of household charities, of thought
Not truant to the school of tears;

---

[1] This poem was written for Mrs. Longfellow; see p. 207. The manuscript is in the Longfellow House. It is printed here by permission of the Harvard College Library and the Longfellow Trustees.

The light that makes the matron's heart
The dearest lustre of the home,
And guides the muse's feet to art
Than Greece less stern, more warm than Rome.

Nor shall the poet be forgot
Whose lyre hath made our Cambridge known
And honored, far as any spot
Where seeds of culture have been blown.

And, when I quench it, I will think
How deep the gloom, how dense the night
Of lives forlorn that cannot drink
Of womanhood's more perfect light.

And I will pray that many a year
Earth may through happy seasons swim,
Ere God shall need his candle clear
To shine on altars nearer him.

With many Happy New Years to F.A.L.

                        from the friend
                        of her & hers
Jany. 1st. 1857.   J.R.L.
                        who asks pardon for the blots
                        not having time to make a fair copy.

Index